THE

APPORTIONMENT

CASES

THE

APPORTIONMENT

CASES

BY RICHARD C. CORTNER

THE UNIVERSITY OF TENNESSEE PRESS : KNOXVILLE

LIBRARY OF CONGRESS CATALOG CARD NUMBER 75–100408

STANDARD BOOK NUMBER 87049–107–5

COPYRIGHT © 1970 BY THE UNIVERSITY OF TENNESSEE PRESS, KNOXVILLE

MANUFACTURED IN THE UNITED STATES OF AMERICA

FIRST EDITION

I do not find anything in the law of God, that a Lord shall choose 20 Burgesses, and a Gentleman but two, or a poor man shall choose none. I find no such thing in the law of nature, nor in the law of nations. But I do find, that all Englishmen must be subject to English laws, and I do verily believe, that there is no man but will say, that the foundation of all law lies in the people. . . . Therefore I do [think] and am still of the same opinion; that every man born in England cannot, ought not, neither by the law of God nor the law of nature, to be exempted from the choice of those who are to make laws, for him to live under, and for him, for aught I know, to lose his life under.

From the *Debates on the Putney Project*, 1647

IN THE 1960's the United States Supreme Court initiated one of the most far-reaching policies in the recent history of the Court. Its decisions in the Tennessee and Alabama apportionment cases, *Baker* v. *Carr* and *Reynolds* v. *Sims*, first opened the federal courts to challenges of state legislative apportionments and finally established the doctrine of "one man, one vote." The effect of these decisions has been dramatic, as a massive shift of political power to the urban areas of the nation occurred with reapportionment in almost all of the states. And the impact of the decisions on the political process in the United States will be felt for years to come.

My interest in the apportionment cases began in the fall of 1961 when the Tennessee case, *Baker* v. *Carr*, was pending reargument before the Supreme Court. It seemed likely then that the Court was finally going to open the federal courts to suits challenging legislative apportionments. And when this proved the case, the result was an unprecedented use of federal judicial power in supervising reapportionment in state after state. In my research on the apportionment cases, I was interested in analyzing the cases as examples of the use of judicial power to enunciate and implement political policy. In the chapters which follow, I have therefore presented my thoughts on the strengths and weaknesses of judicial power as an instrument of political policy as revealed in the apportionment cases. On this point, I have especially compared the apportionment cases with the desegregation cases of the previous decade.

As a student of the Constitution, I have also been attracted to the apportionment cases as manifestations of the emergence of the constitutional guarantee of equality which has been increasingly visible in recent years. From the standpoint of constitutional development, these cases represent the burgeoning of a line of development that began at least as early as the white primary cases and led to the desegregation decisions of the 1950's. Until *Baker* v. *Carr* the doctrine of equality developed by the Court in cases involving racial discrimination was of course insulated from the issue of unequal apportionment of legislatures by the doctrine of political questions. And I have in this study traced the doctrinal breakthrough which has resulted in the application of the constitutional right of equality not only in the field of racial discrimination but in the field of geographic discrimination as well.

Since I was aware that many cases before the Supreme Court are the products of organized, group litigation, I was also keenly interested in the kinds of individuals and groups involved in sponsoring the litigation in the apportionment cases. I was fortunate in my work on both the Tennessee and Alabama cases to receive very full cooperation from the principal individuals involved in the litigation in those cases. I discovered that in both cases, unlike many Supreme Court cases, no formal, organized interest groups were primarily responsible for sponsoring the litigation. Rather, in both Tennessee and Alabama, I found *ad hoc* alliances of individuals and groups, which I call "litigating coalitions," to be the sponsors of the apportionment litigation.

These coalitions were more like electoral or temporary lobbying coalitions than the permanent, organized interest groups so often encountered in constitutional litigation. While organized in a similar fashion, the Tennessee and Alabama litigating coalitions also differed significantly in terms of the kinds of political forces they represented. The Tennessee coalition was a bipartisan coalition representing established, and on the whole somewhat conservative, political forces in that state. The Alabama coalition, on the other hand, was composed of relatively young, liberal loyalist or "national" Democrats. Both were of course composed of elements disadvantaged by the prevailing apportionment systems in their states and therefore struck at the status quo through the judicial process. I have recorded their success in litigation in the pages that follow—a success that is also now recorded in legislative chambers across the nation.

I am indebted to the many individuals active on both sides of the apportionment litigation in Tennessee and Alabama who took time

viii

to answer my questions both in personal interviews and by correspondence. I am indebted particularly to the late Walter Chandler of Memphis, the late Hobart Atkins of Knoxville, Z. T. Osborn of Nashville, and Tennessee Attorney General George McCanless, not only for answering my questions on *Baker* v. *Carr* but also for allowing me access to their files on that case. To Robert Vance, David Vann, and Jerome Cooper, all of Birmingham, John McConnell of Mobile, and McLean Pitts of Selma, Alabama, I express equal appreciation for cooperation in my research on *Reynolds* v. *Sims*.

Professors David Fellman, Department of Political Science, University of Wisconsin; William Buchanan, Department of Political Science, Washington and Lee University; T. McNider Simpson, Department of Political Science, University of Tennessee; and Clifford M. Lytle, Department of Government, University of Arizona, read all or part of the manuscript at various stages of completion, and I am deeply grateful for their comments and criticisms. I confer upon them, however, the traditional absolution for any sins of commission or omission which follow.

R. C. C.

Tucson
Summer, 1969

CONTENTS

Preface   vii
   I Courts, Politics, and Apportionment   3
  II Apportionment Litigation in Tennessee: The First Round   28
 III The Genesis of *Baker* v. *Carr*   51
  IV The Appeal   74
   V *Baker* v. *Carr* Before the Court   95
  VI Breakthrough: The Court Decides   133
 VII *Reynolds* v. *Sims*: The Revolt of the Loyalists   160
VIII Equal Protection and Representation:
         The Clash of Argument   192
  IX One Man, One Vote   222
   X Apportionment, the Court, and the Judicial Process   253
Appendixes   267
Index   277

THE
APPORTIONMENT
CASES

CHAPTER I

COURTS, POLITICS, AND APPORTIONMENT

THE APPORTIONMENT OF SEATS in a legislature is the apportionment of power within the community. Any scheme of legislative apportionment represents choices regarding how much power shall be allocated to the diverse interests within the society. No men were ever more conscious of the power-allocating nature of legislative apportionment than were the delegates to the constitutional convention at Philadelphia in 1787. The proper basis of representation in the new Congress they were creating caused a fundamental conflict among the delegates, and came close to causing a dissolution of the convention, and thus the Union. This result was of course averted when one of the great compromises of the convention produced a House of Representatives apportioned primarily on a population basis and a Senate apportioned on the basis of state equality.

The compromise on legislative apportionment in the Philadelphia convention demonstrated that while the theory of equal population apportionment was supported widely in the United States, its implementation in apportionment systems was subject to being tempered by consideration of other factors as legitimate, and competing, bases of representation—such as representation of political subdivisions and economic interests. Indeed, during the first half of the twentieth century, the number of American state legislatures apportioned on a population basis decreased steadily. With the rise of the city, legislatures became more and more reluctant to accord representation to these new concentrations of population commensurate with their numbers. While failure to reapportion contributed greatly to the decline of equal population representation in state legislatures, further barriers to such equality were imposed in many states by constitutional provisions that recognized factors other than population in determining the bases of representation. A survey of the apportionment provisions of state constitutions in 1955 found that population, without qualification, was the basis of representation in the upper houses of the legislatures of only twenty-two states and the lower houses of only twelve. Most legislative houses were apportioned upon a basis composed of mixed area and population factors.[1]

The theory of equal population apportionment, therefore, obviously competed with other theories that rejected population as the only legitimate basis of representation. When the state constitutional provisions deviating from or disregarding population as the basis of apportionment are coupled with the disinclination of legislators to alter the distribution of their seats, it is apparent that most state legislatures, during most of the twentieth century, were apportioned on the basis of factors other than population alone. As a result, the potential state legislative power of urban areas was contained, and contained effectively. A survey of state legislative representation by Paul David and Ralph Eisenberg in 1961 revealed that "the progressive disenfranchisement of the urban voter has been going on in the country at large for at least fifty years on a scale that suggests that only some decisive change in the system could bring a general reversal."[2]

The prospects for such a "decisive change in the system" were rather bleak for those who were adversely affected by the steady decline in apportionment by population. The legislatures had proven themselves unmovable on the question of reapportionment. Constitutional conventions in most states required legislative authorization, and the delegates to conventions, if authorized, were usually allocated on the basis of legislative districts, thus reflecting an apportionment as unrepresentative of population as the legislatures themselves.[3] The initiative and referendum could be used to bypass the legislatures on apportionment questions in some states, but experience had shown that only initiated constitutional amendments were entirely effective,

[1] Malcolm E. Jewell, "Constitutional Provisions for State Legislative Apportionment," *Western Political Quarterly*, Vol. 8 (1955), pp. 271, 272.

[2] *Devaluation of the Urban and Suburban Vote* (Charlottesville: Bureau of Public Administration, University of Virginia, 1961), I, 10.

[3] John B. Wheeler, Jr. (ed.), *Salient Issues of Constitutional Revision* (New York: The National Municipal League, 1961), pp. 49–62; see also, William L. Hindman, "Roadblocks to Conventions," *National Municipal Review*, Vol. 37 (March, 1948), p. 129. Hereinafter the *National Municipal Review* will be cited as *NMR*.

because they were unamendable by the legislatures.[4] In addition, with the initiative and referendum process there was no assurance that the population standard could gain a popular majority within the states.[5]

Because of the minimal chances of success either through the legislatures or in the electoral process, those seeking changes in apportionment sought relief in the judicial process. But again relief was not forthcoming until the 1960's.

Between 1890 and 1910 a flurry of litigation on the apportionment question occurred in the state courts. The courts were willing to adjudicate challenges of legislative apportionment acts without raising questions about their jurisdiction or competence to do so.[6] Although it was asserted that apportionment was a political question and therefore beyond judicial cognizance, in a typical reaction the Illinois Supreme Court stated in an 1895 case that its jurisdiction was "not affected, when the question is properly raised in a suit at law, by the fact that only political rights of the parties are involved, nor by the contention that the statute in question is the mere product of the exercise of that political power residing in the legislature, wherein its decision is final."[7] Typical also was the statement of the Wisconsin

[4] Washington voters, for example, adopted an initiative proposal for reapportionment promoted by the League of Women Voters in 1956, only to have the legislature amend the proposal after its adoption, with the result that the apportionment situation was not substantially altered by application of the initiative and referendum process. See Gordon E. Baker, *The Politics of Reapportionment in Washington State*, Eagleton Institute Cases in Practical Politics, Case 3 (New York: McGraw-Hill, 1960); see also, Julia D. Stewart, "Women Carry the Day," *NMR*, Vol. 46 (Feb., 1957), p. 66; *NMR*, Vol. 47 (Feb., 1958), pp. 56, 74.

[5] The attempt to change the non-population basis of the California Senate apportionment in 1948, for example, found the Los Angeles and San Francisco areas voting overwhelmingly against the proposal, even though these areas were the areas most underrepresented under the existing apportionment. See Thomas S. Barclay, "The Reapportionment Struggle in California in 1948," *Western Political Quarterly*, Vol. 4 (1951), p. 313. Michigan voters in 1952 and Colorado voters in 1962 similarly rejected substantially population-based apportionment plans. See Karl A. Lamb, William J. Pierce, and John P. White, *Apportionment and Representative Institutions: The Michigan Experience* (Washington, D. C.: The Institute for Social Science Research, 1963), pp. 134–35; *Lucas v. Colorado General Assembly*, 377 U.S. 713, 717–18 (1964).

[6] Anthony Lewis, "Legislative Apportionment and the Federal Courts," 71 *Harvard Law Review* 1057, 1066–70 (1958); Charles W. Shull, "Legislative Apportionment and the Law," 18 *Temple University Law Quarterly* 338 (1944); David O. Walter, "Reapportionment of State Legislative Districts," 37 *Illinois Law Review* 20 (1942); Lamb, Pierce, and White, pp. 14–27.

[7] *People v. Thompson*, 155 Ill. 451, at 461–62 (1895).

5

Supreme Court in 1892 that if "the remedy for these great public wrongs cannot be found in this court it exists nowhere. It would be idle to recommit such an apportionment to the voluntary action of the body that made it."[8]

The state courts, however, universally failed to fashion any positive relief for malapportionment beyond invalidating apportionment acts that violated state constitutional provisions. For instance, in 1907 the Kentucky Supreme Court rose to oratorical heights in denouncing an apportionment act. Holding that equality of representation "is a vital principle of democracy," the court declared that where equality of representation was denied, "the government becomes oligarchical or monarchical. Without equality Republican institutions are impossible. Inequality of representation is a tyranny to which no people worthy of freedom will tamely submit."[9] Yet the remedy the Kentucky court produced for the situation, denounced in such wrathful language, was simply to invalidate the act under review, passed in 1906, and to order elections for the next legislature to be held on the basis of the apportionment act of 1893. Reapportionment was left to the legislature, the court trusting that its members, "impelled by their sense of duty, the obligations of their oath of office, together with that spirit of justice which is the heritage of the race, will redistrict the State as the Constitution requires."[10]

Despite the "heritage of the race," the Kentucky legislature declined to enact a reapportionment act until 1918, based on the 1910 census, and thereafter no further reapportionment occurred until 1930.[11] The 1930 apportionment act, however, was in turn invalidated by the court, which again in ringing terms denounced unrepresentative government. Equality of representation "in the lawmaking tax-levying bodies is a fundamental requisite of a free government," the court said, and no "unbiased, fair, or just man has any right to claim a greater share of the voting power of the people than is granted to every other man similarly situated." The court went on to proclaim,

---

[8] *State* v. *Cunningham*, 81 Wis. 440, at 481–84 (1892).

[9] *Ragland* v. *Anderson*, 125 Ky. 141, at 160 (1907).

[10] *Ibid.*, at 161.

[11] See *Stiglitz* v. *Schardien*, 239 Ky. 799, at 802–803 (1931); the court in a 1907 case, *Adams* v. *Bosworth*, 126 Ky. 611, upheld the validity of the 1893 apportionment act on the grounds that the Republicans challenging the act had slept on their rights and passively consented to the act.

"From the ruins of all ancient states along the bloody trail of the tyranny that has terrorized humanity on its onward struggle for freedom and right blazes forth the living truth that nothing founded upon injustice can permanently endure. The security of the people depends on strict adherence to the admonition found in Proverbs: 'Remove not the ancient landmark which thy fathers have set.' "[12] The court, having denounced and invalidated the act of 1930, revived an ancient landmark of its own, the apportionment act of 1918, upon which the next election to the legislature was to be based.

The Kentucky experience illustrated the ineffectiveness of judicial relief for malapportionment in other states as well.[13] While the state courts did not generally regard apportionment as a political question and were usually willing to invalidate apportionments patently contrary to state constitutional provisions, they were unwilling to afford

[12] *Stiglitz* v. *Schardien*, 239 Ky. 799, at 812 (1931).

[13] Indiana: In *Parker* v. *State*, 133 Ind. 178 (1892), the Indiana Supreme Court invalidated the apportionment acts of 1891 and 1879, throwing the election of legislators back on the act of 1885; in *Denny* v. *State*, 144 Ind. 503 (1895), the court invalidated the acts of 1893 and 1895, again putting the basis of the legislative elections on the act of 1885; but in *Fesler* v. *Brayton*, 145 Ind. 71 (1896), the court refused to invalidate the 1885 act on the grounds that such action would "start the people of this state on a voyage that may lead them into the troubled sea of anarchy . . ." because the "government of the State would be at an end" (at 77). Again, in 1904 the court invalidated the act of 1901 in *Brooks* v. *State*, 162 Ind. 568, reviving in the process the act of 1897. Michigan: The Michigan Supreme Court, in *Bd. of Supervisors* v. *Blacker*, 92 Mich. 638 (1892), invalidated the house apportionment act of 1891, returning the house to the basis of the act of 1881; in *Giddings* v. *Blacker*, 93 Mich. 1 (1892), the court invalidated the senate apportionment of 1891, returning that body to the act of 1881; after the *Giddings* case, the legislature reapportioned in 1892, and in 1895 re-enacted the 1892 act; there was reapportionment in 1901 and 1905; the 1905 senate act was invalidated in *Williams* v. *Sec. of State*, 145 Mich. 447 (1906), and the 1895 act revived as a result; in 1913 another reapportionment occurred, but was invalidated in *Stevens* v. *Sec. of State*, 181 Mich. 199 (1914), which resulted in the revival of the 1905 act for the house. Nevada: In *State* v. *Stoddard*, 25 Nev. 452 (1900), the Nevada Supreme Court admitted the invalidity of the apportionment act of 1899, but pointed out that all previous ones were equally invalid and refused to intervene because to do so might "deprive the state of all legislative action at the time fixed by the constitution." Oklahoma: The Oklahoma Supreme Court, confronted with a similar problem in *Jones* v. *Freeman*, 193 Okla. 554 (1943), also declined to act, saying that it would "refuse to exercise the powers given us when to do so would merely increase the wrongs sought to be prevented. We decline to further diminish the representation of an already underrepresented group or to increase that of an already overrepresented group, under the guise of affording relief" (at 563).

positive relief, such as effective reapportionment by judicial decree. Reapportionment was considered a duty which legislatures could not be compelled to perform by the judiciary.[14]

The state courts regarded some apportionment system as a necessary basis for the legislature. Therefore, when invalidating an apportionment act, the courts often revived the most recent preceding apportionment act that had not been invalidated. This very often turned out to be a rather ancient statute, as in the Kentucky cases. A judicial challenge of a legislative apportionment statute was thus not only futile, but in many instances folly, since the statute revived by a court might very well be more damaging to the interests of those initiating such a challenge than the statute under attack. Probably for these reasons, state court apportionment litigation declined significantly following the 1890–1910 period, a period that embraced the rise of the urban areas and the increasing reluctance of state legislators to reapportion. Surveying the results of the litigation of this period, V. O. Key, Jr., remarked that interested parties "are hesitant to inaugurate proceedings which may result in making their lot worse without prospect of immediate rectification of the difficulty," and he concluded that "judicial review of legislative action on apportionment has proved an inadequate remedy against unfairness."[15]

Having found little possibility of relief through state court litigation, those dissatisfied with state apportionment systems turned to the federal courts but found them also indisposed to grant relief. However, the federal courts declined to act because, in contrast to the state courts, they held that apportionment cases involved "political questions" that the federal courts should not decide. A classic statement of the doctrine of political questions by the United States Supreme Court resulted from the conflict over suffrage and representation in Rhode Island during the 1840's.

Rhode Island had retained its colonial charter as its constitution after the Revolution. As population shifted within the state and the

[14] On this point, see *Fergus v. Marks*, 321 Ill. 510 (1926); *Fergus v. Kinney*, 333 Ill. 437 (1929); *People v. Blackwell*, 342 Ill. 223 (1930); *Parker v. State*, 133 Ind. 178 (1892); *Denny v. State*, 144 Ind. 503 (1895); *Brooks v. State*, 162 Ind. 568 (1904); *Bd. of Supervisors v. Blacker*, 92 Mich. 638 (1892); *Williams v. Sec. of State*, 145 Mich. 447 (1906); *Smith v. Holm*, 220 Minn. 486 (1943); *Burns v. Flynn*, 268 N.Y. 601 (1935); *State v. Howell*, 92 Wash. 540 (1916); *State v. Zimmerman*, 249 Wis. 101 (1946).

[15] "Procedures in State Legislative Apportionment," *American Political Science Review*, Vol. 26 (1932), pp. 1050, 1053.

state became more industrialized, the number of persons qualified to vote under the old charter's freehold requirements decreased, and the newer urbanized centers of the state, notably Providence, were considerably underrepresented in the legislature on the basis of population. Forces led by Thomas W. Dorr drafted a new constitution to deal with these problems and ratified it in a referendum. Dorr was elected governor, and members of a legislature were also elected under the new constitution. The charter government, however, refused to abdicate in favor of the Dorr government, and Rhode Island as a result possessed for a time two competing governments. The charter government declared martial law, and on June 27, 1842, John T. Child, a quartermaster in the first brigade of the Rhode Island militia, was ordered to arrest anyone in Warren who was "in the least degree suspicious, or who expressed the least willingness to assist the insurgents." Child thereupon ordered Luther Borden and other members of the militia to arrest Martin Luther, apparently because of Luther's involvement with the Dorr forces, which, it was feared, were about to attack the town. The militiamen broke into Luther's home in the attempt to ferret him out, and subsequently, in October, 1842, Luther, a citizen of Massachusetts, brought suit against the militiamen for trespass in the Circuit Court of the United States for the District of Rhode Island.[16]

In the circuit court, Luther's counsel argued that the people of Rhode Island had acted upon the principles enunciated in the Declaration of Independence and had adopted a new form of government that supplanted the charter government; the acts of the militiamen, therefore, had no valid legal sanction because of their authorization by a government without legal existence. The case thus came to turn upon a determination of which of the two competing governments was the legitimate government of Rhode Island. If the charter government were legitimate, then the acts of the defendants were sanctioned by the legally constituted authority of the state. The circuit court refused to allow Luther to offer proof that the Dorr government was the legitimate government of the state and also refused to instruct the jury in a manner favorable to Luther's theory. Upon the jury's verdict favorable to the defendants, an appeal was taken to the United States Supreme Court.[17]

[16] 7 Howard, at 2–10.
[17] *Ibid.*, at 11–21.

Luther v. *Borden*[18] was pending before the Supreme Court from 1845 to 1848, and Chief Justice Roger B. Taney did not announce the Court's opinion in the case until January, 1849. Taney pointed out in his opinion for the Court that if the Court should undertake to decide the question as urged by Luther, the effect would be to invalidate all the laws passed, taxes collected, or judicial decisions made under the authority of the charter government. "When the decision of this court might lead to such results," he said, "it becomes its duty to examine very carefully its own powers before it undertakes to exercise jurisdiction."[19] The Rhode Island courts, Taney said, had uniformly adhered to the position that the charter government was the legitimate government within the state, and the federal courts were without power to revise a determination by state courts of a question relating to constitutions and laws of the states. Also, even if the federal court could have decided the question, it would have had to determine which government had been supported by a majority of those qualified to vote in Rhode Island—a question almost impossible to answer through the judicial process.[20]

Finally, and most importantly, Taney felt that "the Constitution of the United States, as far as it has provided for an emergency of this kind, and authorized the general government to interfere in the domestic concerns of a State, has treated the subject as political in its nature, and placed the power in the hands of that department."[21] Article IV, section 4, of the Constitution, which guarantees each state a republican form of government and provides for federal protection of the states from invasion or from domestic insurrection, was therefore to be enforced by the Congress and the President and not by the federal judiciary. Congress, in deciding to admit the representatives of the various states, Taney continued, recognizes the legitimacy of the state governments, and this decision is binding on the other branches of the federal government. Additionally, Taney said, the Congress had authorized the President to come to the aid of a state government threatened by insurrection upon the application of the legislature or of the governor when the legislature could not be convened. Acting in accordance with this authorization, the

[18] 7 Howard 1 (1849).
[19] *Ibid.*, at 39.
[20] *Ibid.*, at 41–42.
[21] *Ibid.*, at 42.

President must determine which government within a state is legitimate, and again the courts may not question this determination. While the President had not intervened in the Dorr War, Taney pointed out that he had assured the charter government that he would do so if necessary, and "no court of the United States, with a knowledge of this decision, would have been justified in recognizing the opposing party as the lawful government; or in treating as wrongdoers or insurgents the officers of the government which the President had recognized, and was prepared to support by armed force."[22]

The Court proceeded to sustain the decision of the circuit court, holding that the search of Luther's home was a lawful proceeding authorized by the legitimate government of Rhode Island acting under martial law necessitated by the insurrection. Taney concluded for the Court by expressing no doubt that "the sovereignty in every State resides in the people of the State, and that they may alter and change their form of government at their own pleasure." But, he added, "whether they have changed it or not by abolishing an old government, and establishing a new one in its place, is a question to be settled by the political power. And when that power has decided, the courts are bound to take notice of its decision and to follow it."[23]

The Court thus consigned the enforcement of the guaranty clause of the Constitution to the elective branches of the government, where it has since remained.[24] Challenges of institutional features of state governments as well as apportionment systems could not, under the political questions doctrine of the *Luther* case, be successfully pursued in the federal courts as deviations from the "Republican Form of Government." However, with the adoption of the Fourteenth Amendment in 1868, which prohibited the states from denying persons the "equal protection of the laws," it became possible to argue that state apportionment systems not based upon population discriminated against persons on a geographic basis and thus denied the equal protection of the laws.

The doctrine of political questions, however, came to be regarded

[22] *Ibid.*, at 44.
[23] *Ibid.*, at 47.
[24] See *Pacific Telephone Co.* v. *Oregon,* 223 U.S. 118 (1912); *Kiernan* v. *Portland, Ore.,* 223 U.S. 151 (1912); *Davis* v. *Ohio,* 241 U.S. 565 (1916); *Ohio* v. *Akron Park District,* 281 U.S. 74 (1930); *O'Neill* v. *Leamer,* 239 U.S. 244 (1915); *Highland Farms Dairy* v. *Agnew,* 300 U.S. 608 (1937); *Forsyth* v. *Hammond,* 166 U.S. 506 (1897).

as preventing the federal courts from hearing challenges of state apportionment systems on equal protection grounds also. The application of the doctrine of political questions to cases asserting equal protection arguments was substantially affected by the conflict over both congressional and state legislative apportionment in Illinois, a conflict that continued sporadically throughout the first half of the twentieth century.

The legislature of Illinois was not reapportioned between 1901 and 1955. A constitutional convention in 1920, which sought to revise the constitution of 1870, almost broke up over the issue of apportionment. The efforts of down-state delegates, backed by the Anti-Saloon League, to limit Chicago's representation in the legislature caused some Chicago delegates to withdraw from the convention. A compromise was finally reached which allowed full representation to Chicago in the lower house of the legislature, but limited its representation to not more than one-third of the membership of the upper house. The revised constitution containing these provisions, however, was defeated in a referendum in 1922, and the first major effort to break the legislative apportionment deadlock in Illinois failed.[25]

The conflict flared again in 1925, when the legislature again failed to reapportion. On the basis of the 1920 census, Cook County (Chicago) was entitled to an increase of five representatives in the senate and fifteen representatives in the lower house of the legislature, and Cook County and Chicago officials attempted a variety of countermeasures in the face of the legislature's refusal to reapportion. On June 1, 1925, the Cook County Board of Commissioners directed the county treasurer to withhold state taxes collected within the county until reapportionment was accomplished; on June 17 the Chicago City Council ordered the corporation counsel to bring court proceedings to compel the legislature to reapportion; and on June 30 the city council adopted a resolution calling for a two-year campaign for legislative reapportionment organized by a citizens committee, to

---

[25] *NMR*, Vol. 9 (July, 1920), p. 457; Vol. 10 (Feb., 1921), p. 104; Vol. 11 (Sept., 1922), p. 297; Vol. 11 (Dec., 1922), p. 422; Vol. 12 (Feb., 1923), p. 100; although the revised constitution was defeated by a majority of about 700,000, and Chicago contributed about 500,000 of this majority, it appears that the apportionment factor was not decisive in the defeat of the proposed constitution; see Gilbert Y. Steiner and Samuel K. Gove, *Legislative Politics in Illinois* (Urbana: University of Illinois Press, 1960), p. 88, note 4.

be followed by a request to be allowed to secede from the state if the campaign proved a failure.[26]

Nothing came of these efforts, and efforts to force reapportionment through the courts proved similarly fruitless. John B. Fergus, an eighty-four-year-old representative from Chicago, led the fight for reapportionment in the 1925 legislature, and, failing there, turned to the courts seeking judicial enforcement of the state constitution's apportionment provisions. He first sought a writ of mandamus to compel the legislature to reapportion. The Illinois Supreme Court, however, pointed out that the "duty to reapportion the State is a specific legislative duty imposed by the constitution solely upon the legislative department of the State, and it, alone, is responsible to the people for a failure to perform that duty."[27] In 1929 an attempt by Fergus to enjoin the state treasurer from paying the salaries of the state legislators was similarly rebuffed by the court, and the United States Supreme Court refused to review the case.[28] Finally, in 1930 the Illinois Supreme Court dismissed quo warranto proceedings initiated by Fergus against the members of the legislature, again pointing out that the "matters complained of are solely within the province of the General Assembly and the courts have no power to coerce or direct its action."[29]

After the failure of these efforts by Fergus, the drive to obtain judicial relief for Illinois' apportionment problem was continued by John W. Koegh, a well-to-do Chicagoan who had apparently become obsessed with the apportionment question. In 1930, Koegh refused to pay his federal income tax because he alleged the federal government had forfeited its power to collect income taxes in Illinois by its failure to enforce Article IV of the Constitution, which guaranteed to each state a republican form of government. The Illinois legislature's failure

[26] C. M. Kneifer, "Chicago Threatens to Revolt," *NMR*, Vol. 14 (Oct., 1925), pp. 600–603; Detroit also was threatening to secede during this period, and the Detroit Bureau of Governmental Research published a memorandum by Professor Thomas H. Reed in May, 1925, on "Methods of State Separation," *NMR*, Vol. 14 (Oct., 1925), p. 603, note 1.

[27] *Fergus* v. *Marks*, 321 Ill. 510, at 517 (1926).

[28] *Fergus* v. *Kinney*, 333 Ill. 437 (1929); cert. den., 279 U.S. 854 (1929); the Illinois Supreme Court in the same year also rejected an attack on the validity of a conviction under the Illinois Deadly Weapons Act of 1925 based on the failure of the legislature to reapportion; see *People* v. *Clardy*, 334 Ill. 160 (1929).

[29] *Fergus* v. *Blackwell*, 342 Ill. 223, at 226 (1930).

to reapportion since 1901 had deprived the state of a republican form of government, Koegh argued, and the federal government's failure to remedy the situation had absolved Illinois citizens of their duty to pay federal taxes. A federal district court in Illinois dismissed Koegh's suit for an injunction against the collection of federal income taxes on the grounds that the complaint failed to state a cause of action. On appeal, the court of appeals said that the courts had "no power to stay the hand of the federal government in the collection of constitutionally authorized taxes, upon the ground alone that the government had itself been derelict in its observance of other provisions of the federal Constitution, and particularly not when such other provisions in no manner affect the taxes at issue." Koegh was equally unsuccessful in the U. S. Supreme Court, which dismissed his suit in November, 1931.[30]

Koegh's efforts to obtain legislative reapportionment in Illinois came to a tragic conclusion. In January, 1936, in a foreclosure proceeding against one of his buildings, Koegh's argument that the action should be dismissed because the failure of the legislature to reapportion had made the Illinois Supreme Court an illegal body was overruled by the judge, whereupon Koegh shot and killed the opposing counsel and fired two shots at the judge, who, fortunately, had taken refuge behind the bench. Koegh was reported to have said that he had no personal animosity toward either the opposing counsel or the judge, but that the death of the attorney was "a sacrifice to the cause" and necessary to bring the reapportionment problem to the public's attention.[31]

The legal attack on Illinois' apportionment problems turned for a time to the question of congressional districting within the state. The congressional districting act passed by the legislature in 1931, containing districts varying in population from 158,738 to 541,785, was invalidated by the Illinois Supreme Court in 1932 as violating the 1911 congressional act, which required that districts be of approximately equal population, and also as violating the Illinois con-

[30] *Koegh* v. *Neeley*, 50 F.2d 685, at 687 (7th Cir. 1931); dismissed, 285 U.S. 526; cert. den., 286 U.S. 529; petition for a writ of mandamus dismissed, 286 U.S. 534 (1932).
[31] *The New York Times*, Jan. 14, 1936, p. 3; see also David O. Walter, "Representation of Metropolitan Districts," *NMR*, Vol. 27 (March, 1938), pp. 131–32; Lewis, "Legislative Apportionment," p. 1070, note 77.

stitution's requirement of free and equal elections.[32] The result of this decision, however, was to reinstitute the only previous act providing for congressional districts in the state—the act of 1901, in which the districts varied in population from 112,116 to 914,053. An attack on the 1901 act subsequently failed before the Illinois Supreme Court in 1941. Since the U.S. Supreme Court had ruled in an intervening case[33] that the 1911 congressional act requiring districts of approximately equal population had been repealed by the 1929 congressional apportionment act, the Illinois court ruled that the congressional districts were unassailable under the federal statutes. The court in addition ruled that the Illinois constitutional requirement of free and equal elections did not require that every vote cast in one district must be equal to every vote cast in every other district, this being a "millennium which cannot be reached." The court concluded, "This suit is, obviously, an attempt to ask the court to do indirectly what it cannot do directly,—*i.e.*, pass on a purely political question."[34]

In 1945 the legislature of Illinois refused to authorize a referendum on the question of holding a constitutional convention, despite support for the referendum by Governor Dwight H. Green. One observer reported that the overshadowing reason the measure was defeated was that many legislators feared reapportionment. The legislature also ignored Governor Green's appeal "to correct the inequities of our congressional apportionment under which Illinois now has both the largest and smallest congressional districts in the United States, one nine times the size of the other."[35]

Since a legislative remedy for both the state legislative and congressional apportionment problem again failed to materialize, Kenneth W. Colegrove, a member of the political science department at Northwestern University, Kenneth C. Sears, a professor of law at the University of Chicago Law School, and Peter Chamales, an attorney of Barrington, Illinois, brought suit in federal district court against Governor Green, Secretary of State Edward J. Barrett, and State Au-

---

[32] *Moran v. Bowley*, 347 Ill. 148 (1932). The requirement of equality of population among congressional districts was originally passed by Congress in 1872 and was continued as a part of congressional regulations governing state districting for the election of congressmen until 1929.

[33] *Wood v. Broom*, 287 U.S. 1, at 370 (1932).

[34] *Daley v. County of Madison*, 378 Ill. 357, at 370 (1941).

[35] *NMR*, Vol. 34 (April, 1945), p. 186; Vol. 34 (June, 1945), p. 290.

ditor Arthur C. Lueder, in their capacities as members *ex officio* of the state primary certifying board. They asked the court to enjoin the board from certifying candidates for Congress under the 1901 apportionment act and to declare an election of congressmen at large. The suit alleged that the 1901 act was invalid because of its conflict with federal requirements that congressional districts be compact, contiguous, and as nearly as practical of equal populations. In addition, the suit alleged that the 1901 act denied the equal protection of the laws guaranteed by the Fourteenth Amendment because it discriminated against the voters residing in the more populous districts. The plaintiffs also contended that the Illinois act abridged their right to vote for congressmen—a privilege of U. S. citizenship which the Fourteenth Amendment protected against abridgement by the states—and that the act violated Article I of the Constitution, which provided that representatives be apportioned "among the several States according to their respective numbers" and that they be chosen "by the people of the several States."

Colegrove, who resided in a congressional district with a population of 914,053, explained why he had sought judicial relief for the situation. As a teacher he had attempted to teach his students respect for the law, but for "35 years the legislature of Illinois has violated the federal law" regarding the reapportionment of congressional districts. "I could not look my students in the face," he said, "if I did not exert myself to correct this brazen breach of the law in Illinois." In addition, Colegrove continued, "if a state lacks the courage to take the leadership in fulfilling the constitutional responsibilities of the state legislature, the private citizens are compelled to resort to judicial means to correct such abuse."[36]

Colegrove's case was favored by several Supreme Court decisions that related either directly or indirectly to elections and the right to vote. On the equal protection issue, the Court in two of the white primary cases, *Nixon* v. *Herndon*[37] and *Nixon* v. *Condon*,[38] had held that state legislation that prohibited participation by Negroes in primary elections was a denial of the equal protection of the laws under the Fourteenth Amendment. From these cases, it could be argued that

[36] The description of the complaint as well as the quote from Colegrove is drawn from *NMR*, Vol. 36 (March, 1946), p. 130.
[37] 273 U.S. 536 (1927).
[38] 286 U.S. 73 (1932).

state legislation which, while not prohibiting the participation of a given class of voters in an election, did through a system of districting give relatively greater weight to the votes of some persons and less weight to the votes of others was also a denial of the equal protection of the laws. The white primary cases culminated in *Smith v. Allwright*,[39] in which the Court held that primaries were an integral part of the electoral process and that the prohibition of Negro voting in primaries was a denial of the right to vote on the grounds of race or color in violation of the Fifteenth Amendment. And while the Fifteenth Amendment was not involved in the *Colegrove* case, the white primary cases could be cited as illustrations of the Court's willingness to intervene in electoral matters to protect constitutional rights, despite arguments that electoral questions were necessarily "political questions." Indeed, in answer to the argument that the suit in *Nixon v. Herndon* involved a political question, Justice Holmes had said for the Court that such an argument was "little more than a play upon words." Of course, he said, "the petition concerns political action, but it alleges and seeks to recover for private damage. That private damage may be caused by such political action, and may be recovered for in a suit at law, hardly has been doubted for over two hundred years...."[40]

Colegrove's case was further strengthened, insofar as it rested on Article I grounds, by the Court's decision in *United States* v. *Classic* in 1941.[41] In that case the Court had held that Article I, section 2, in providing that members of the House of Representatives be chosen by the people of the several states whose qualifications as voters are to be the same as the qualifications of voters for the larger house of the state legislatures, created a "right of qualified voters within a state to cast their ballots and have them counted at congressional elections."[42] It could thus be argued that malapportionment of congressional districts substantially impaired this right to vote in a congressional election by weighting the ballots cast in some districts to

[39] 321 U.S. 649 (1944); reversing *Grovey* v. *Townsend*, 295 U.S. 45 (1935), which had held that the exclusion of Negroes from a party by a state party convention was not state action denying the equal protection of the laws; see also *Rice* v. *Elmore*, 165 F.2d 387 (4th Cir. 1947); cert. den., 333 U.S. 875 (1948); *Terry* v. *Adams*, 345 U.S. 461 (1953).

[40] 273 U.S., at 540.
[41] 313 U.S. 299 (1941).
[42] *Ibid.*, at 315.

count more in terms of representation than those in other districts; and, insofar as districts varied in population, the Article I requirement that representatives be chosen by the people of the several states would be violated, since the provision implied equal participation of the population of a state in the selection of representatives.[43]

The *Nixon* cases, however, were undermined as precedents by the rather unusual circumstances that led the Court to decide them under the Fourteenth rather than the Fifteenth Amendment. Until the *Classic* case in 1941, the Court had not held that the primary election was an election in the constitutional sense, which involved a right to vote. Doubt on this score was evident in *Newberry v. United States*[44] and continued until the *Classic* case in 1941 when the Court decided that primaries were elections and an integral part of the electoral process. As long as this question was in doubt, however, the Court could not logically rely on the Fifteenth Amendment to invalidate denials to Negroes of the right to vote in primaries, since it would have had to rule that the primary was an election in which the right to vote was protected by the Fifteenth Amendment. Doubt about the precise status of the primaries, therefore, apparently led the Court to base its decisions in the early white primary cases on the Fourteenth Amendment, because, whether or not an election or the right to vote was involved, there was state action denying the equal protection of the laws to Negroes. But once the *Classic* case cleared up the status of the primary, the Court turned to the Fifteenth Amendment in *Smith v. Allwright*, with no longer any doubt that in such cases the right to vote was being denied on the grounds of race or color in violation of the Fifteenth Amendment.[45] The unusual factors conditioning the Court's choice of the Fourteenth rather than the Fifteenth Amendment in the early white primary cases, therefore, might undermine their usefulness as equal protection precedents in *Colegrove* and future apportionment cases.[46]

[43] This was of course the argument ultimately in *Wesberry v. Sanders*, 376 U.S. 1 (1964), in which the Court held that congressional districts must be as nearly as practicable equal in population.

[44] 256 U.S. 232 (1921).

[45] See Justice Reed's comments on this in *Smith v. Allwright*, 321 U.S., at 658–61; and Justice Harlan's comments in *Reynolds v. Sims*, 377 U.S. 533, at 614, note 72 (1964).

[46] This of course ultimately turned out not to be the case. See the Court's use of the white primary cases in *Reynolds v. Sims*, 377 U.S., at 555.

The remedy sought in the *Colegrove* case—an injunction against an election held under the existing districts and an order for an election of congressmen at large—was also not unprecedented. In *Smiley* v. *Holm*[47] the Court had ruled that Article I, section 4, of the Constitution, which conferred power upon the states to provide for congressional elections through their legislatures, meant that state regulations of congressional elections were to be passed by the regular legislative processes of the states as provided for by the states' constitutions. A congressional districting statute, passed by the legislature of Minnesota but vetoed by the governor, was therefore not valid, since the Minnesota constitution provided for the governor's participation in the legislative process by the use of the veto power. As a result of this decision, an injunction was issued against the election of Minnesota's congressmen under the districting created by the legislature, and the election was ordered to be held at large.[48]

The contention in the *Colegrove* case, however, that the provisions of the 1911 congressional apportionment act required compactness, contiguity, and equality of population in districts was completely undermined by *Wood* v. *Broom*,[49] decided by the Court in 1932. In this case, the Court ruled that the Congress had not re-enacted the compactness, contiguity, and equal population requirements when it passed the apportionment act of 1929. It should also be noted that the Court reserved the question of whether the subject matter of the suit in *Wood* v. *Broom* involved a political or nonjusticiable question. Chief Justice Hughes, who wrote the opinion of the Court, stated that it was "unnecessary to consider the questions raised as to the right of the complainant to relief in equity upon the allegations of the bill of complaint, or as to the justiciability of the controversy. . . . Upon these questions the Court expresses no opinion." Justices Brandeis, Stone, Cardozo, and Roberts were of the opinion that the Court should not have expressed an opinion on the apportionment act in question, but should have dismissed the bill for want of equity.[50] On both the substantive apportionment act issue and the political

[47] 285 U.S. 355 (1932).

[48] The same result was also reached in a companion case, *Carroll* v. *Becker*, 285 U.S. 380 (1932); see Lewis, "Legislative Apportionment," pp. 1087–90, who points out other lower court decisions that resulted in elections at large.

[49] 287 U.S. 1 (1932).

[50] *Ibid.*, at 8.

question issue, therefore, the *Wood* case did not bode well for the *Colegrove* case.

Colegrove v. *Green*[51] was argued before the Supreme Court in March, 1946, and the decision of the Court dismissing the case was announced on June 10. Chief Justice Stone died on April 22, and Justice Jackson was absent from the Court, pursuing his duties as prosecutor at the Nuremberg trials. It was, as Justice Clark later said, a "bob-tailed" Court which decided the *Colegrove* case, with only seven justices participating. Justice Frankfurter, in an opinion in which he was joined by Justices Burton and Reed, first held that the legal merits of the case were settled by the decision in *Wood* v. *Broom* that the provisions of the 1911 apportionment act had not been re-enacted by Congress in 1929. Frankfurter stated also, however, that "we agree with the four Justices . . . who were of the opinion that the bill in *Wood* v. *Broom* . . . should be 'dismissed for want of equity.' " The Court's opinion, Frankfurter continued, was "that the petitioners ask of this Court what is beyond its competence to grant. This is one of those demands on judicial power which cannot be met by verbal fencing about 'jurisdiction.' It must be resolved by considerations on the basis of which this Court, from time to time, has refused to intervene in controversies. It has refused to do so because due regard for the effective working of our government revealed this issue to be of a peculiarly political nature and therefore not meet for judicial determination."[52]

The Court, the Justice continued, was being asked to redress not a private wrong, but "a wrong suffered by Illinois as a polity." The remedy for this would require the federal courts to "reconstruct the electoral process of Illinois in order that it may be adequately represented in the councils of the Nation." All the courts could do, he said, would be to invalidate the then existing districting system in Illinois, and, assuming the Illinois legislature failed to act, the result would be the election of the Illinois congressmen at large. Not only would such a decision destroy the districting principle as provided for by Congress, but, assuming acceptance of the decision by Illinois officials, Congress might not accept it and might instead, exercising its power to judge the qualifications of its members, deny seats to congressmen elected in such a manner. "Nothing is clearer," Frankfurter

[51] 328 U.S. 549 (1946).
[52] 328 U.S., at 552.

said, "than that this controversy concerns matters that bring courts into immediate and active relations with party contests. From the determination of such issues this Court has traditionally held aloof. It is hostile to a democratic system to involve the judiciary in the politics of the people. And it is not less pernicious if such judicial intervention in an essentially political contest be dressed up in the abstract phrases of the law."[53] Article I of the Constitution, Frankfurter concluded, in giving Congress the power to alter state regulations respecting congressional elections, had "conferred upon Congress exclusive authority to secure fair representation by the States in the popular House and left to that House determination whether States have fulfilled their responsibility." The subject of congressional districting had always been embroiled in politics, he said, and courts "ought not to enter this political thicket. The remedy for unfairness in districting is to secure State legislatures that will apportion properly, or to invoke the ample powers of Congress."[54]

Justice Rutledge, concurring in the dismissal of the case, expressed the view that, were it not for the precedent of *Smiley* v. *Holm*, he would have thought the issues in *Colegrove* nonjusticiable. Admitting that the *Smiley* case made the issues justiciable, and thus disagreeing with the views of Frankfurter, Burton, and Reed on this point, Rutledge nevertheless felt that the case should be dismissed for want of equity. "Assuming that the controversy is justiciable," he said, "I think the cause is of so delicate a character . . . that the jurisdiction should be exercised only in the most compelling circumstances." In addition, Rutledge felt that the case should be dismissed because of the shortness of the time before congressional elections, making the implementation of any remedy before the elections doubtful. Also, he doubted the propriety of an election at large as a remedy, since it would deprive the people of Illinois of the districting system provided for by Congress, a cure that "may be worse than the disease." Rutledge therefore cast the deciding vote for dismissal of the case.[55]

Justice Black, with whom Justices Douglas and Murphy concurred, dissented. Pointing out the failure of the state legislature in Illinois to reapportion both the state legislative and congressional districts since 1901 and the failure of the state courts to grant relief, Black found it

[53] *Ibid.*, at 553–54.
[54] *Ibid.*, at 554–55.
[55] *Ibid.*, at 565–66.

difficult "to see why the 1901 State Apportionment Act does not deny petitioners equal protection of the laws." Relying on the white primary cases, Black viewed the equal protection clause of the Fourteenth Amendment as not allowing states "to pick out certain qualified citizens and deny them the right to vote at all. . . . No one would deny that the equal protection clause would also prohibit a law that would expressly give certain citizens a half-vote and others a full vote." Black pointed out that the probable effect of the 1901 apportionment act in the coming election would be that "certain citizens, and among them the petitioners, will in some instances have votes only one-ninth as effective in choosing representatives to Congress as the votes of other citizens. Such discriminatory legislation seems to me exactly the kind that the equal protection clause was intended to prohibit."[56]

Black also agreed with the plaintiff's arguments that the Illinois apportionment act violated Article I of the Constitution by abridging the right of the people of the state to participate equally in the election of congressmen. And he felt this guarantee of Article I was bolstered by section 2 of the Fourteenth Amendment, which provided for the apportionment of representatives among the states "according to their respective numbers." This provision, he said, was meant to prohibit "Congressional 'rotten boroughs' within the States, such as the ones here involved." Thus, a state legislature, he said, "cannot deny eligible voters the right to vote for Congressmen and the right to have their vote counted. It can no more destroy the effectiveness of their vote in part and no more accomplish this in the name of 'apportionment' than under any other name."[57]

Black also disagreed with the contention that the issues involved in the case were political questions or that the issues, if justiciable, were ones over which the federal courts should decline to exercise their equitable jurisdiction. The Court was simply being asked, he felt, to do what it had done in *Smiley* v. *Holm*—that is, to declare the apportionment act involved invalid and enjoin state officials from enforcing it—and this would involve no greater difficulties than those involved in the *Smiley* case.[58]

Although only three justices—Frankfurter, Burton, and Reed—had felt that the federal courts should not take jurisdiction because of the

[56] *Ibid.*, at 569.
[57] *Ibid.*, at 570–71.
[58] *Ibid.*, at 572–74.

political nature of the issues in this kind of case, *Colegrove* v. *Green*
soon developed as a barrier to suits challenging either congressional
districting or state legislative apportionments. This transformation of
the minority views in *Colegrove* came through a series of *per curiam*
opinions issued by the Court during the late 1940's and the 1950's in
which the Court declined to hear such cases. In 1946, the same year as
the *Colegrove* case, for example, the Court dismissed *Turman* v.
Duckworth and *Cook* v. *Fortson*,[59] which were appeals from the lower
federal court in Georgia involving challenges to the Georgia county
unit system.

The Georgia county unit system had begun in 1876 as a system of
apportioning county delegates to the Democratic state convention.
When the primary election was substituted for the state convention
as the method of nominating candidates of the Democratic party in
1898, the unit system was retained as a method of weighting the voting
power of the counties in such primaries. Except for the period of
1906–1908, the unit system continued to govern Georgia Democratic
primaries, and was enacted into law in 1917.[60] Under this system, the
8 most populous counties received six unit votes each, 30 other counties received four unit votes each, and the 121 remaining counties
received two unit votes each.[61] In order to be nominated in the Democratic primary, candidates were required to carry a majority of the
county unit vote, and because the unit vote did not correspond to the
population of the counties, the system made it possible for a minority
of the population to control the nomination of Democratic candidates.
The ultimate result of the unit system was that Fulton County (Atlanta) averaged more than ninety-two thousand residents per unit
vote—nine times greater than the state average.[62]

The *Cook* case challenged this system as it applied to candidates for
Congress, and the *Turman* case applied to nominations for governor.
In the 1946 primary, Eugene Talmadge had defeated James V. Car-
michael for the Democratic nomination for governor with a majority

[59] 329 U.S. 675.
[60] Emmet J. Bondurant, "A Stream Polluted at its Source: The Georgia County Unit System," *Journal of Public Law*, Vol. 12, No. 1 (1963), pp. 86, 88–89.
[61] It should be noted that this system was revised in April, 1962, to make the
assignment of unit votes somewhat more in accordance with population; this
latter revision was invalidated by the Supreme Court in *Gray* v. *Sanders*, 372
U.S. 368 (1963).
[62] Bondurant, "A Stream Polluted at its Source," p. 89.

of the county unit votes but about fifteen thousand fewer popular votes. Cullen G. Gosnell and Mrs. Robert Lee Turman brought the *Turman* case as a direct response.[63] Talmadge denounced the suit as a plan to "destroy our traditional Democratic White Primary and our County Unit System of voting. Destruction of one they know will make the death of the other an easy matter for them."[64]

The Supreme Court, as noted above, dismissed the cases, with Justices Black, Douglas, and Rutledge dissenting.[65] In *South* v. *Peters*[66] in 1950 the Court again refused to hear a case challenging the county unit system. "The federal courts," the Court said *per curiam*, "consistently refuse to exercise their equity powers in cases posing political issues arising from a state's geographical distribution of electoral strength among its political subdivisions." Justices Douglas and Black again dissented, saying that the "creation by law of favored groups of citizens and the grant to them of preferred political rights is the worst of all discriminations under a democratic system of government."[67] Two years later, in *Cox* v. *Peters*,[68] the Court again dismissed another challenge to the unit system, with Justices Black and Douglas voting to note probable jurisdiction.

After the *Colegrove* case, suits challenging state legislative apportionment systems met the same fate at the hands of the Court as the county unit cases. The Illinois residents involved in *Colegrove* v. *Green*, having lost that suit, decided to attack the state legislative apportionment system, which had also not been altered since 1901, on the grounds that the system discriminated against some voters while favoring others, thus denying the equal protection of the laws. Their suit, *Colegrove* v. *Barrett*, was dismissed in the federal district court, however, in January, 1947, although the court said that were it not for the earlier *Colegrove* case, "we would have thought the law to be as

---

63 *Ibid.*, p. 88; see also Cullen B. Gosnell, "Sue to Discard County Unit System," *NMR*, Vol. 47 (May, 1958), p. 226, for a brief description of Gosnell's role in the *Turman* case.

64 *Ibid.*, p. 97, note 40.

65 The Court did not, however, rely upon the *Colegrove* case in its dismissal of the cases, but instead cited *U.S.* v. *Anchor Coal Co.*, 279 U.S. 812 (1929), a case in which appeals were dismissed because the issues were moot. Black and Douglas would have noted probable jurisdiction. Rutledge would have reserved the question of jurisdiction until argument.

66 339 U.S. 276.

67 339 U.S. at 279.

68 342 U.S. 936 (1952).

stated by Mr. Justice Black in his dissenting opinion." The case was appealed to the Supreme Court because the appointment of Chief Justice Vinson and Justice Jackson's return to the Court had added two votes that could change the views of the Court as expressed in the first *Colegrove* case.[69] But the Court dismissed the suit "for a want of a substantial federal question" without citation of precedent, while Justice Rutledge concurred because of the Court's previous disposition of the *Colegrove*, *Cook*, and *Turman* cases; Justices Black and Douglas would have noted probable jurisdiction.[70] In 1952 the Court similarly disposed of challenges of the Pennsylvania and California state legislative apportionment systems in *Remmy* v. *Smith*[71] and *Anderson* v. *Jordan*.[72]

By the mid-1950's, therefore, it appeared that the *Colegrove* case had become an insuperable barrier to suits challenging both congressional districting and state legislative apportionment systems. The *Colegrove* case appeared to prevent challenges of state apportionment systems under the equal protection clause of the Fourteenth Amendment, just as *Luther* v. *Borden* prevented challenges to features of state governments under the guaranty clause. In addition, the position of those seeking population-based apportionment systems was further weakened by the Court's opinion in *MacDougall* v. *Green*[73] decided by the Court in 1948. In *MacDougall* the Court sustained the requirement under Illinois election law that a party nominating candidates by petition must secure 25,000 signatures, of which 200 must be from 50 of the state's 102 counties. The Progressive party, whose nominees had been refused a place on the ballot because of its failure to comply with this requirement, challenged the requirement as violating due process and equal protection of the laws since it prevented a majority of the state's population, residing in Cook County, from forming a

[69] Franklin L. Burdette, "Illinois Legislative Districts Attacked in Federal Courts," *NMR*, Vol. 36 (March, 1947), p. 152.

[70] 330 U.S. 804 (1947). While attempts to gain federal judicial relief for both the state legislative and congressional apportionment problems in Illinois thus failed, it should be noted that the state's congressional districts were redrawn in 1947 "amid yells, cat-calls, boos and pounding of desks" and after a filibuster by down-state Republicans. The redistricting gave Cook and Lake counties three additional seats; *NMR*, Vol. 36 (July, 1947), p. 391; fear of future federal judicial intervention was apparently a factor in the passage of the bill; see Lewis, "Legislative Apportionment," p. 1088, note 179.

[71] 342 U.S. 916.

[72] 343 U.S. 913.

[73] 335 U.S. 281.

political party and placing the names of the party's candidates on the ballot. Affirming the dismissal of a suit for an injunction against the enforcement of the Illinois statute, the Court said *per curiam* that it would be "strange indeed, and doctrinaire, for this Court, applying such broad constitutional concepts as due process and equal protection of the laws, to deny a State the power to assure a proper diffusion of political initiative as between its thinly populated counties and those having concentrated masses, in view of the fact that the latter have practical opportunities for exerting their political weight at the polls not available to the former."[74]

As in the *Colegrove* case, Justice Rutledge concurred on the grounds that federal judicial intervention would disrupt the election process in Illinois, and Justice Douglas, joined by Black and Murphy, dissented, condemning the "notion that one group can be granted greater voting strength than another" as being "hostile to our standards for popular representative government."[75] But the majority's language in the *MacDougall* case seemed to portend that, even if those seeking equal population apportionment could break through *Colegrove v. Green* and obtain federal court hearings of apportionment challenges, they could not expect the federal courts to apply an equal population standard under the equal protection clause. If a state could constitutionally provide for a "diffusion of political initiative" among its more and less populated areas in the electoral process, the same diffusion, it could be argued, was allowable in the apportionment of its legislature.

The judicial process, like all the avenues through which the apportionment systems in most states could be attacked, thus seemed to lead to a dead end. The position of those who sought change in apportionment through the courts before the 1960's was in many ways similar to the position occupied by Negroes before the 1950's. Both were unable to secure their policy objectives through the electoral process and thus persisted in seeking relief through the judicial process. In the judicial process, however, both were faced with a formidable array of precedents which seemed to deny the validity of their objectives, and both were therefore forced by circumstances to play a creative role in their litigation activities, seeking to convince the courts to change existing legal or constitutional doctrine.[76]

[74] *Ibid.*, at 284.
[75] *Ibid.*, at 290.
[76] Both the Negroes and reapportionment forces were thus heavily dependent

A state whose constitution required substantially equal population apportionment and whose legislature had ignored this requirement over a long period of time would provide the ideal springboard for new assaults on the Court's precedents. Such a state would be preferable strategically to a state whose constitution allowed considerable deviation from population as the standard of apportionment, because the alleged wrong resulting from malapportionment and the case for federal judicial intervention could be more graphically presented.

With regard to legal strategy, Tennessee met those ideal conditions both in relation to constitutional requirements and legislative inaction. And it was Tennessee that produced the litigation that, after almost eight years of struggle, opened the federal courts to challenges of state legislative apportionment systems. The result of the Supreme Court's decision in *Baker* v. *Carr*[77] in 1962 was a revolution in state legislative representation and a reversal of the decline of urban representation at the state level.

---

upon nonprecedential materials to persuade the courts to change existing doctrines. For example, the NAACP in the Restrictive Covenant Cases, *Shelley* v. *Kraemer*, 334 U.S. 1 (1948), and *Hurd* v. *Hodge*, 334 U.S. 24 (1948), relied heavily on Professor Dudley O. McGovney's articles in the *California Law Review* to bolster their attack on the restrictive covenant; see Clement E. Vose, *Caucasians Only* (Berkeley: University of California Press, 1959), pp. 68–70, 133, 135, 139. Similarly, the attack on state apportionment systems in the federal courts was bolstered by Lewis' article, "Legislative Apportionment."

[77] 369 U.S. 186.

CHAPTER II

APPORTIONMENT LITIGATION IN TENNESSEE:

THE FIRST ROUND

THE THREE GRAND DIVISIONS of the state of Tennessee are as dissimilar as three separate states, and their unique qualities, even eccentricities, are recognized even in law. The eastern division, with its urban centers of Chattanooga and Knoxville, is a mountainous area that was generally Unionist during the Civil War, and "murdered by the rebels" may be found as an epitaph in the older churchyards of the area. It continues to be Republican oriented in its politics. The middle division, centering on Nashville, extends from the Cumberland Plateau in the east to the Tennessee River in the west. It is generally Democratic in its politics. The western division extends from the Tennessee River to the Mississippi River, where its principal city, Memphis, is located. Politics in West Tennessee have traditionally been solidly Democratic, with more of a Deep South flavor than is found in the rest of the state, and Confederate memorials populate the courthouse lawns of the area.[1]

Unlike the other seceding states after the Civil War, Tennessee did not experience military reconstruction, but instead was readmitted to the Union upon its ratification of the Fourteenth Amendment and its abolition of slavery. Following a brief Unionist rule led by Governor William G. Brownlow, during which Confederate sympathizers had been disenfranchised, the state reverted to the control of conservative Democrats who directed the drafting of the constitution of 1870, which remains the fundamental law of Tennessee.[2]

The apportionment provisions of the Tennessee Constitution, unlike

[1] For a more detailed description of the state, see Lee S. Greene and Robert S. Avery, *Government in Tennessee*, Second Edition (Knoxville: University of Tennessee Press, 1966), chap. 1; and V. O. Key, Jr., *Southern Politics* (New York: Vintage Books, 1949), chap. 4.

[2] Greene and Avery, *Government in Tennessee*, pp. 21–23.

those of many other state constitutions, base both houses of the legislature substantially on population. It provides that the ninety-nine members of the house of representatives shall "be apportioned among the several counties or districts, according to the number of qualified voters in each," but also provides that if a county possesses two-thirds of the number of qualified voters required for a representative, it should be granted a representative. The senate is also to be "apportioned among the several counties or districts according to the number of qualified electors in each," and in the apportioning of senators "the fraction that may be lost by any county or counties, in the apportionment of the members of the House of Representatives, shall be made up to such county or counties in the Senate, as near as may be practicable." In addition, the constitution provides that elections "shall be free and equal."

There was immediate conflict over the apportionment of the legislature under these provisions. When the apportionment act of 1871 was adopted by the legislature, it was denounced as a "system of representation as correct in principle as that in the days of George the Third," and two members of the legislature recorded their "eternal aversion to unfair representation in a free government."[3] Reapportionment occurred in 1881 and again in 1891. Then, in 1901, the legislature reapportioned the state for the last time until 1962.[4] The Knoxville *Journal and Tribune*, a leading Republican newspaper, denounced the 1901 act as an "inequitous redistricting bill" produced by a "despotic oligarchy that calls itself the Democratic Party." Two East Tennessee Republicans condemned the bill and asserted that Republicans had been kept off the reapportionment committees and that the legislature did not know the number of qualified voters in the state. The bill passed the house on April 2 by a vote of 66 to 23, and passed the senate on March 29 by a vote of 29 to 3.[5]

The 1901 apportionment act did not accurately reflect the population of the state even at the time it was passed. For example, thirteen of the senatorial districts in 1901 were 20 percent or more either above

---

[3] Dr. Robert H. White, "A Documented Survey of Legislative Apportionment in Tennessee, 1870–1959," reprinted in the Record, *Baker* v. *Carr*, p. 128. The pagination is that of the Record; the White document and the Record will hereinafter be referred to as B. v. C., Record.

[4] There were some minor changes during this period, but they affected the apportionment of the state under the act of 1901 only slightly.

[5] B. v. C., Record, pp. 142–43.

or below the proper population standard. Hamilton (Chattanooga) and Shelby (Memphis) counties were particularly discriminated against by the act.[6] There were sporadic attempts in the legislature to change the 1901 apportionment, but all were unsuccessful. Gubernatorial urging was equally unavailing. In 1913, Governor Ben W. Hooper devoted twenty-four pages of a special message to the legislature to the apportionment problem, pointing out the "gross injustice and inequality of the present apportionment" and urging legislative action, but without effect. And in 1955 and 1957, Governor Frank G. Clement pointed out the "glaring inequalities" and urged legislative action, but the legislators were again unmoved.[7]

The result of this inaction was an ever wider disparity among the populations of the legislative districts. Based on the 1950 census, there were twenty-three counties electing a total of twenty-five representatives under the act of 1901, although the populations of only two of these counties justified the assignment of a representative. There were ten counties whose populations justified the assignment of a total of forty-five representatives, yet under the 1901 act they elected only twenty representatives. The senatorial districts ranged in population from a low of 26,204 to a high of more than 131,000 (see Appendix A).

Although the apportionment of the Tennessee legislature thus continued to become less representative of the population as the decades passed, a move to impose upon the state a variation of the county unit system, which would have further weakened the more populous counties politically, was defeated in 1938. The county unit system arose out of a dispute between Governor Gordon Browning and "Boss" Ed Crump of Memphis. Shelby County had been threatened previously in 1929, because of Crump's involvement in state politics. Governor Henry Horton, whom Crump had opposed, had attempted to deprive Shelby County of one senator and two representatives in the legislature. But Horton's reapportionment plan was defeated in the legislature.[8]

In 1934, Gordon Browning had campaigned for the United States Senate without Crump's support and received only 5,444 votes in Shelby County. In 1936, Browning, in alliance with Crump, success-

[6] Harry N. Williams, "Legislative Apportionment in Tennessee," 20 *Tennessee Law Review* 235, 238 (1948).

[7] B. v. C., Record, pp. 146–57.

[8] William D. Miller, *Mr. Crump of Memphis* (Baton Rouge: Louisiana State University Press, 1964), pp. 152–53.

30

fully ran for governor and received 59,874 votes in Shelby County.[9] The alliance between Crump and Browning was short-lived, however, and in 1937, Browning called a special session of the legislature and in an address to the legislators pointed out that Crump had already registered 117,000 people to vote in the next primary and was threatening to register more. Browning proposed a primary system "whereby a definite influence in determining the results of a primary would be assigned and guaranteed to each county" so that "the peculiar advantage enjoyed now by one county where votes are habitually counted as a unit would not any longer be unique, and if the stench of ballot box debauchery anywhere arose, its influence would be confined to the county of its locality."[10]

At the request of the governor, the legislature enacted a county unit system that accorded each county, in primary elections for governor, U. S. senator, and railroad and public utilities commissioners, a unit vote equal to the number of votes cast in each county for the party nominee for governor in the last general election, divided by one hundred. The maximum unit vote per county was not to exceed, however, one-eighth of one percent of the county's population.[11] This system allowed Shelby County approximately 380 unit votes, whereas without the maximum upper limit it would have been entitled to approximately 600 unit votes.[12] The governor further requested and received legislation enlarging the State Board of Elections, allowing gubernatorial control of the county election commissions,[13] and legislation providing for the purging of registration lists,[14] creating a crime commission to investigate criminal activities in the state,[15] and revising the ouster laws, allowing ouster suits without jury trials.[16] Crump pronounced the unit system the act of a "crazy man," and declared that "Huey Long in his desperation didn't dare try a thing that is now proposed for Tennessee."[17] And the Chattanooga *Times* asserted that the legislature had made Governor Browning "the

[9] Key, *Southern Politics*, p. 62.

[10] See *Gates* v. *Long*, 172 Tenn. 471, at 500 (1938).

[11] Chap. 2, Public and Private Acts of Tennessee, Extraordinary Sessions, 1937, p. 45.

[12] *NMR*, Vol. 26 (Dec., 1937), pp. 604–605.

[13] Public and Private Acts of Tennessee, p. 324.

[14] *Ibid*., p. 85.

[15] *Ibid*., p. 343.

[16] *Ibid*., p. 329. See also *NMR*, Vol. 27 (March, 1938), p. 168.

[17] Miller, *Crump*, p. 243.

political dictator of the state; it has given him absolute control of the election machinery and a primary system under which he can use the election machinery to play off against the large, urban counties the great majority of small rural counties."[18]

The county unit system was declared unconstitutional by the state supreme court early in 1938.[19] The court, citing the white primary cases, relied on the equal protection clause of the Fourteenth Amendment and similar provisions of the Tennessee Constitution.[20] The legislature could not abridge the right to vote "in one class of voters," the court said, "and leave the right whole in another class of voters. The one-eighth of one per cent limitation in those counties which it reaches amounts to excluding some of the voters from their party's primary or of debasing the ballots of all the voters."[21]

Crump had by the summer of 1938 allegedly registered 125,000 persons in Shelby County in anticipation of the Democratic primary. Governor Browning announced he would set aside many of these registrations, and the Shelby County Election Commission, controlled by the governor, announced rules that set aside more of the registrations. In addition, the crime commission set about demanding the registration certificates of voters, particularly Negroes, in Shelby County, whereupon the certificates were punched with a ticket punch and the voter was advised that his registration was thus invalidated. Rumors persisted also that the governor intended to use troops to keep the Crump organization's supporters from the polls on election day.[22]

Prentice Cooper, the Crump-endorsed candidate for governor, and other candidates filed suit for an injunction against Browning to prevent his interference with the election in Shelby County. Federal Judge John D. Martin, a second cousin of Crump who had been elevated to the federal bench in 1920 with the support of Crump and Senator Kenneth D. McKellar, announced that he could not issue "a more just writ, placing the judicial power of the United States by court order at the disposal of the citizens of this county to defend them from the unjustified, tyrannical, unconstitutional, despotic invasion by a swashbuckling governor."[23] In the opinion filed in the case,

---

[18] Quoted in *NMR*, Vol. 26 (Dec., 1937), p. 605.
[19] *Gates* v. *Long*, 172 Tenn. 471 (1938).
[20] Art. I, § 8, and Art. 11, § 8.
[21] 172 Tenn., at 477.
[22] See *Joyner* v. *Browning*, 30 F. Supp. 512 (W.D. Tenn. 1939).
[23] Miller, *Crump*, p. 258.

Martin found that it was the purpose of "Gordon Browning, the then dictatorial and tyrannical Governor of Tennessee," to prevent "thousands of persons from voting who, in fact, were lawfully entitled to vote, with the probable result of the prevention of any election at all in Shelby County." For this proposed action, Martin said, "there was no redress except the injunctive processes of this court."[24] Judge Martin's injunction was read to Governor Browning in Memphis by a U. S. marshal, who interrupted the governor during a speech that had already been made difficult by a switch engine puffing "up and down noisily nearby."[25] In the election that followed, Browning received only 9,315 votes in Shelby County, in contrast to the 59,784 votes he had received two years earlier.[26]

Browning's defeat in 1938 ended the political crisis in which the county unit system was a major factor, and the threat of reducing the electoral influence of the urban counties in state-wide elections was not renewed. The Crump organization and its allies had been exceedingly successful in checking Governor Browning by resort to the state and federal judiciaries. At the same time, however, the influence of the urban counties in the legislature continued to be steadily, and less spectacularly, reduced as decade after decade passed with no change in the apportionment of 1901, and until the 1950's there were no challenges of the apportionment system in the courts.

Tennessee's Constitution, unlike the constitutions of some other states, does not provide for the initiative and referendum. Without this means of bypassing the legislature, those disadvantaged by the apportionment system in Tennessee did not possess any remedy that was not conditioned by legislative approval, except resort to the courts. The Tennessee Constitution does provide that the people of the state "have at all times, an unalienable and indefeasible right to alter, reform or abolish the government in such manner as they may think proper." It denounces the doctrine of nonresistance to arbitrary power as "absurd, slavish, and destructive of the good and happiness of mankind," thus seeming to imply a right of revolution, but no resort to the revolutionary process seemed in the offing in Tennessee. The governor in Tennessee has historically possessed political control of

---

[24] *Joyner* v. *Browning*, 30 F. Supp., at 519.

[25] Key, *Southern Politics*, p. 68, note 15. This was the last speech Browning made in Memphis for ten years.

[26] *Ibid.*, p. 62.

the legislature, but, while governors occasionally called upon the legislature to remedy the apportionment situation, no governor saw fit to make reapportionment a high priority item on his legislative agenda. Constitutional amendment in Tennessee also depends on legislative action and, until 1953, proved impossible on any subject including apportionment, leaving Tennessee until that year with the oldest unamended state constitution in the nation.

Constitutional amendments until 1953 had to be passed in one legislative session by a majority vote in both houses, pass both houses of the next legislature by a two-thirds vote, and be approved by a majority of the voters in the next election of representatives. The question of calling a constitutional convention could also be put to the voters by a majority of both houses of the legislature; this was done twelve times up to 1952, and on each occasion a convention was rejected by the voters.[27] In 1945, however, Governor Jim McCord appointed a commission to study the possibility of constitutional revision. The commission recommended a limited constitutional convention to consider revision of specified provisions of the constitution, including those relating to legislative apportionment. The legislature in 1949 submitted the proposal of a limited convention to the voters and it was narrowly defeated. Had it been approved, the convention would have been authorized to decide whether or not to "alter, reform or abolish" the apportionment provisions of the constitution. But, of course, the convention would have been composed of delegates elected on the basis of the 1901 apportionment act, thus reflecting the unequal population apportionment of the legislature.[28]

In 1951 the legislature again proposed a limited convention, and the voters approved in August, 1952. The apportionment of the legislature, however, was not among the items to which the convention's deliberations were limited. The amendments proposed by the 1953 convention, and subsequently approved by the voters, modified somewhat the amending process, raised legislative pay, granted the governor the item vote and increased his term to four years, eliminated the poll tax, restricted special legislation and granted extensive home-

[27] Greene and Avery, *Government in Tennessee*, pp. 29–30.
[28] Chap. 49, Public Acts of Tennessee, 1949, pp. 179–81; Greene and Avery, *Government in Tennessee*, p. 33; *NMR*, Vol. 34 (Nov., 1945), pp. 503–504; Vol. 35 (Dec., 1946), p. 601.

rule to municipalities, and provided for city-county consolidation procedures.[29]

The success of the movement for constitutional change in 1953 resulted to a great extent from the efforts of almost every major group in the state, including business, labor, farm, and civic groups, in addition to the organized bar, the press, and the Tennessee Municipal League.[30] Such unity of purpose was lacking on the question of legislative apportionment. The Tennessee Municipal League, which might have been expected to be concerned with the apportionment problem, showed little interest in it.[31] The League concentrated during the 1950's upon securing home-rule provisions and prohibitions against special legislation in the constitution, and was successful when such provisions were adopted in the limited constitutional convention. The League was also successful in securing gubernatorial support for a return to municipalities of one cent per gallon of the state gasoline tax, a proposal the legislature ultimately enacted.[32]

Among the leaders of the TML, however, Ben West, mayor of Nashville, was vociferous in denouncing the apportionment system in Tennessee. West, a graduate of Vanderbilt University and Vanderbilt Law School, served as assistant district attorney general from 1934 to 1943, was elected state senator in 1949, and served as vice-mayor of Nashville from 1947 to 1951, when he was elected mayor. West was president of the Tennessee Municipal League in 1955–56 and served as president of the American Municipal Association during 1957–58.[33] He hammered at the need for reapportionment before every available forum, and ultimately lent significant support to the attack on the existing apportionment system in the federal courts. But the TML as a group, representing the large cities disadvantaged by the existing system, as well as the smaller towns and cities, many of

[29] Greene and Avery, *Government in Tennessee*, pp. 33–36.

[30] For a list of the groups endorsing the convention, see *Tennessee Town & City*, Vol. 3 (May, 1952) pp. 4–5.

[31] This statement is based on a review of the League's publication, *Tennessee Town & City*, and conversations with individuals familiar with the League's work.

[32] *Tennessee Town & City*, Vol. 7 (Jan., 1956), pp. 5–6; the League was also able to secure a form of bureaucratic representation with the creation of the Municipal Technical Advisory Service at the University of Tennessee in 1949; see *Tennessee Town & City*, Vol. 2 (Sept., 1951), p. 15.

[33] *Ibid.*, p. 6.

which were favored by the existing apportionment, was not to be active in the apportionment struggle in Tennessee.

Organized labor, which in some other states had taken an active role in attempts to secure reapportionment, was also quiescent on the issue in Tennessee. As a political force, labor has been relatively weak in Tennessee politics, as shown by the existence of a right-to-work law, passed in 1947.[34] In addition, groups such as labor which must work with a legislature have tended to avoid the issue of apportionment, which strikes at the heart of many legislators' political security, and at least one Tennessee labor leader expressed a preference for dealing with rural rather than urban legislators.[35] The League of Women Voters in Tennessee, as in many other states, was perhaps the most active group in the state on the issue of apportionment, but had no demonstrable impact on the legislature.[36]

This lack of any existing group willing and able to devote sufficient time, effort, and money to an all-out attack upon the apportionment system indicated that such an attack would necessarily come from an *ad hoc* group organized for the purpose. Also, the lack of any effective alternative remedies indicated litigation as the best line of attack. This, in turn, meant that the recruitment of legal talent and the securing of adequate finances would be crucial and that the attack upon the apportionment system would be largely directed by lawyers. Therefore, the *ad hoc* group ultimately would be a "litigating coalition," bound together by a common interest in changing the apportionment status quo, directed largely by attorneys, and devoted to a challenge of the existing system in the judicial process.

Such a coalition was begun in November, 1954, when a small group of conservative Republicans and Democrats met in Johnson City to discuss the problem of legislative apportionment. Although not grossly underrepresented in the lower house of the legislature according to its population, Washington County (Johnson City), along with Carter, Greene, Johnson, and Unicoi counties, formed the first senatorial district. At over ninety-nine thousand in population according to the 1950 census, it was the fifth largest senatorial district in the

---

34 Key, *Southern Politics*, p. 73.

35 Malcolm Jewell, *The Politics of Reapportionment* (New York: Atherton Press, 1962), p. 32.

36 Wilder Crane, Jr., "Tennessee: Inertia and the Courts," in *ibid.*, p. 317; see also *Inventory of Work on Reapportionment by State Leagues of Women Voters* (Washington, D.C.: League of Women Voters of the U.S., 1960), p. 14.

state and the most underrepresented according to population after the large metropolitan counties, Hamilton (Chattanooga), Shelby (Memphis), Davidson (Nashville), and Knox (Knoxville). The small group concluded that any effort to persuade the legislature to reapportion would be useless. "It's just not human nature for a majority of Tennessee's legislators to hold that they are not fairly entitled to their own seats," Haynes Miller, a Johnson City attorney in the group, said later. "After reaching that negative but reasonable conclusion," he said, "we embraced the positive conclusion that our route to equal rights was through the courts."[37] The group also decided to attempt to finance the litigation by forming a Tennessee Committee for Constitutional Reapportionment, which would solicit memberships from interested citizens at ten dollars each. Chapters of the organization were soon formed in Carter and Washington counties in East Tennessee. Clarence Bralley, a Johnson City attorney, and Mrs. May Ross McDowell were the officers of the Washington County chapter. A chapter was also subsequently organized in Nashville.[38] The Tennessee Committee for Constitutional Reapportionment, headed by Frank Bryant, another Johnson City attorney, was able to raise approximately half of the four-thousand-dollar cost of the challenge of the apportionment system in the Tennessee courts, but the attorneys involved were forced to pay part of the costs themselves.[39]

The attorneys who initially joined in the planning of the litigation were a Johnson City group, brothers Haynes and Mayne Miller, Clarence Bralley and Kent Herrin, and Peter Hampton of Elizabethton, Tennessee. Subsequently, Z. T. Osborn, Jr., and state Representative Maclin P. Davis of Nashville joined this group of East Tennesseans in the case. The addition of Osborn to the group was to prove significant; he furnished brilliant aid not only in the challenge of the apportionment system in the Tennessee courts, but also in the later successful challenge in the federal courts. A graduate of the YMCA Law School in Nashville, he had been an assistant United States attorney and served as city attorney of Nashville under Mayor Ben West from 1951 to 1953, and in 1955 was rapidly emerging as one of the most astute attorneys at the Nashville bar.[40]

---

[37] Nashville *Tennessean*, March 6, 1955, p. 18A.
[38] *Ibid.*
[39] Nashville *Tennessean*, April 7, 1956, p. 1.
[40] Nashville *Tennessean*, Nov. 21, 1963, p. 3. In a tragic series of events,

A complaint was drafted seeking an injunction against Attorney General George McCanless, the secretary of state, the State Board of Elections, the Democratic and Republican state primary election commissioners, and the county election commissions in Washington, Carter, and Davidson counties, to prevent the holding of an election under the 1901 apportionment statute, which the complaint asked to be declared unconstitutional. The complaint was filed in the chancery court of Davidson County on behalf of Gates Kidd and four other residents of Washington County, six residents of Carter County and Mrs. James M. Todd, a leader of the LWV, and Jack W. Lee, a realtor, of Davidson County. The chancery court was asked in addition either to declare a mathematical reapportionment of the state in accordance with the provisions of the state constitution or to declare that the next legislative election be held at large.[41]

The complaint was filed before the chancery court on March 8, 1955. Z. T. Osborn announced to the press that the suit was "the first step in what may be a years long effort to bring equal rights in state government to all the people of Tennessee."[42] Both Osborn and Haynes Miller agreed that the issue would ultimately be appealed to the United States Supreme Court. "If we should win in the state court, it is practically certain that our opponents seeking to protect a stacked deck in state government will take the issue on up through the federal courts," Miller said. "If we should lose, we certainly do not intend to stop short of the highest court in the land." The attorneys admitted that both state and federal court apportionment suits had been unsuccessful in other states in the past, but they were convinced that the Tennessee Constitution's provision for equal voting rights differentiated their case, and pointed specifically to the state supreme court's decision invalidating the county unit system and the later federal court decision supporting voting rights in 1937–38.[43]

Haynes Miller also believed that "the professional politicians of both parties will line up against reapportionment efforts as they always have before," but in this he was at least partially mistaken. On

Osborn was disbarred in November, 1963, for jury tampering in a case involving the Teamsters' Union. See *Osborn* v. *United States*, 385 U.S. 323 (1966), in which his federal conviction for jury tampering was affirmed by the Supreme Court.

[41] A good review of the issues in the case may be found in Note on *Kidd* v. *McCanless*, 24 *Tennessee Law Review* 1042 (1957).

[42] Nashville *Tennessean*, March 9, 1955, p. 1.

[43] Nashville *Tennessean*, March 6, 1955, p. 18A.

April 18, Guy L. Smith, chairman of the state Republican Executive Committee and editor of the conservative Republican Knoxville *Journal*, announced that the Republican primary election commission would not oppose the suit, but instead would intervene on the side of the plaintiffs. The coalition favoring reapportionment was thus considerably strengthened by official Republican party support. The strength of the party was traditionally in East Tennessee, and East Tennessee was the most underrepresented grand division in the state. Eight of the ten counties possessing less than their proper share of representation in the lower house of the legislature were located in East Tennessee. (See Appendix A, Table II.) The attorney for the Republican primary election commissioners, Hobart Atkins of Knoxville, also added considerable legal and political ability to the apportionment drive. Atkins had long been active in Republican politics, and in 1956 would be elected to the state senate from Knoxville. Also, like Z. T. Osborn, he would be a permanent addition to the reapportionment cause in Tennessee and would later play a significant role in the successful litigation in the federal courts.[44]

The filing of the chancery court suit presented Attorney General George McCanless with a somewhat embarrassing problem. It was clear that the legislature had consistently violated the state constitution for over fifty years, a constitution the attorney general is pledged to support. On the other hand, the attorney general's duty is also to defend state statutes against challenges in court. In a state in which the attorney general is elected, making the office a position from which an incumbent often can move to higher political office, this situation would have perhaps been even more embarrassing to a politically ambitious attorney general. In Tennessee, however, the attorney general is not elected, but is selected by the state supreme court and serves a term of eight years. The Tennessee attorney general is traditionally from East Tennessee; the supreme court is composed of five justices, two each from West and Middle Tennessee, but only one from the eastern grand division, and the position of attorney general is regarded as making up the geographic underrepresentation of East Tennessee on the court.[45]

On April 5, Attorney General McCanless announced his decision

---

[44] Nashville *Tennessean*, April 19, 1955, p. 1; Knoxville *Journal*, Dec. 4, 1956, p. 1.

[45] Greene and Avery, *Government in Tennessee*, p. 170.

to fight the suit. "Reapportionment of Tennessee's legislative seats," he said, "is the responsibility of the legislature, not the judiciary." From the legal standpoint, of course, the attorney general's position was supported by the overwhelming weight of legal authority. McCanless stated, however, that the suit would be a "friendly suit," in that the defendants would only file a demurrer to the bill and ask for a ruling from the court without disputing the facts. "As attorney general," he said, "it is my duty to support the constitution. The suit is a matter of interpreting the constitution, and I do not agree with complainants' interpretation."[46]

The legislature was in session in Nashville when the suit was filed, and Governor Frank Clement called upon the legislators to appoint a committee to study the apportionment problem and make recommendations to the next legislature. The governor's proposal as well as a proposal to authorize the Legislative Council to study the problem was rejected by the legislature. A bill providing for reapportionment was defeated in the house by a vote of 66 to 33.[47] The Nashville *Tennessean* editorially denounced the legislature's failure to act, asserting that the "minority looks with suspicion on anything that would upset the *status quo*. It is not enough they retain the seats they now have; they are also determined to maintain their unconstitutional dominance." The Committee for Constitutional Reapportionment, the *Tennessean* said, thus understandably concluded that reapportionment was impossible through the legislature. "And it is natural that in the face of such a conclusion they propose to seek relief—and the rights which they and the majority of their fellow Tennesseans are now denied—through the courts." The newspaper concluded, "In that direction now lies the greatest hope for a restoration of democratic government in this state."[48]

Chancellor Thomas Wardlaw Steele, a graduate of Vanderbilt University and the University of Virginia Law School, announced his decision in *Kidd* v. *McCanless* in November, 1955. The chancellor refused to order an election at large or to reapportion mathematically himself, as requested by the plaintiffs, and he also refused to issue an order requiring the governor and legislature to reapportion, as requested by the Republican primary board in its cross bill. Steele re-

[46] Nashville *Tennessean*, April 6, 1955, p. 1.
[47] B. v. C., Record, pp. 155–56.
[48] Nashville *Tennessean*, March 7, 1955, p. 1.

jected, however, the attorney general's argument that apportionment was a political question within the exclusive discretion of the legislature. "This Court cannot accede to," he said, "but must respectfully demur to the proposition that when citizens and voters, as in this case, seek its relief against alleged infringements upon their constitutional rights, the Court must decline to hear them on the delicate grounds that it must approach an act or power of a coordinate branch of government with such awe and hesitation that a sense of propriety dictates that it must if possible refrain from considering the question." The courts, Steele declared, represent "the sovereign will of the people just as much as does the Legislature."[49]

The attorney general had argued in addition that, if the court declared the apportionment act of 1901 unconstitutional, chaos and confusion would result. Steele ruled, however, that the court would presume that once it "exercised its constitutional duty in this proceeding to declare that there is no authority for the holding of an election for the members of the General Assembly of 1956," the governor and legislature would likewise perform their duties by providing for a valid basis for such an election in a special session. "That the present General Assembly," he said, "may thus act as a *de facto* body, the Court entertains not the slightest doubt. . . . The *de facto* doctrine is well established in Tennessee, particularly in matters involving public policy and necessity." For the legislature not to act, the chancellor said, "is inconceivable to this Court."[50] Steele proceeded to issue a declaratory judgment holding the apportionment act of 1901 invalid.

Kidd v. McCanless was immediately appealed by the attorney general to the Tennessee Supreme Court, which rendered its decision reversing the chancellor on April 5, 1956. Justice Swepston, in a unanimous opinion for the court, held that the courts "have no power to compel either the legislative or executive department to perform the duties committed exclusively to their respective domains by the fundamental law."[51] The court ruled that the chancellor had incorrectly interpreted the *de facto* doctrine in Tennessee, and held that a *de facto* office or officer could exist in Tennessee only until a judicial determination of the invalidity of the same. It followed, then, that if

[49] 24 *Tennessee Law Review* 1042, 1043–44. Steele relied particularly on *State* v. *Cunningham*, 81 Wis. 440 (1892).
[50] 200 Tenn. 273, at 278–79.
[51] *Kidd* v. *McCanless*, 200 Tenn. 273, at 279 (1956).

the 1901 act were invalid, there would be no legislature legally in existence to enact a valid apportionment statute. "If the Chancellor is correct in holding that this statute has expired by the passage of the decade following its enactment," Justice Swepston said, "then for the same reason all prior apportionment acts have expired by a like lapse of time and are non-existent. Therefore we would not only not have any existing members of the General Assembly, but we would have no apportionment act whatever under which a new election could be held for the election of members of the General Assembly."[52]

The court held that there was "no provision of law for election of our General Assembly by an election at large over the State," and because there was no prior apportionment act to fall back upon, "a holding invalidating the 1901 act would deprive us of the present Legislature and the means of electing a new one and ultimately bring about the destruction of the State itself."[53] Relying on decisions in similar cases in Indiana, Nevada, and Wyoming, the court thus reversed the decision of the chancery court.[54]

After the announcement of the supreme court's opinion, Justice Swepston stated in an interview with the press that the urban areas in Tennessee could win adequate representation if candidates from those areas would make reapportionment the main issue in their campaigns.[55] Justice Hamilton Burnett of Knoxville, in a later interview with a reporter for the Knoxville *News-Sentinel* which amounted to a concurring opinion, stated that the 1901 apportionment act "unquestionably is unconstitutional" because "it is entirely out of line with the requirements of the state constitution, and is unfair and unjust." The

[52] *Ibid.*, at 280–81.

[53] *Ibid.*, at 282.

[54] The Indiana case was *Fesler* v. *Brayton*, 145 Ind. 71 (1896); in this case the Indiana Supreme Court, having previously declared invalid the apportionment acts of 1891 and 1879, *Parker* v. *State*, 133 Ind. 178 (1892), and the apportionment acts of 1893 and 1895 invalid, *Denny* v. *State*, 144 Ind. 503 (1895), reinstating each time the act of 1885, refused to invalidate the act of 1885 because there was no other valid act in existence. The Nevada case was *State* v. *Stoddard*, 25 Nev. 452 (1900), where the Nevada Supreme Court refused to declare the apportionment act of 1899 invalid and return the election of the legislature to the act of 1891, since the latter act was subject to the same infirmities as the 1899 act, as were all previous acts. The Wyoming case was *State* v. *Schnitzer*, 16 Wyo. 479 (1908), in which the Wyoming Supreme Court refused to invalidate the apportionment acts of 1893, 1901, and 1907 and throw the apportionment back to provisions of the constitution, which did not afford representation to counties created after its adoption.

[55] Memphis *Commercial Appeal*, April 6, 1956, p. 1.

justice said that the act as passed in 1901 was a "gerrymander" and "rigged in creation of legislative districts to the great advantage of one political party and greatly to the disadvantage of the other." The act, he said, "ignored the clear right of the people to an equitable basis of representation in their law-making body." The justice defended the court's decision, however, on the grounds that there was no prior apportionment act to fall back upon if the 1901 act were invalidated and there were no provisions for election of the legislature at large. Justice Burnett declared that the solution of the problem was with the people. "I hope that reapportionment will be made the paramount issue in every legislative race in the state this year," he said. Every candidate for the legislature should be "pressured into coming clean" and forced to take a position on the issue. "In that way," the justice concluded his unusual concurring opinion, "we can get a legislature that will enact a fair and just reapportionment law."[56]

A number of potential candidates for the legislature who had withheld announcing their candidacies until the state supreme court acted in the case now began their campaigns. Legislators from the overrepresented areas generally expressed satisfaction with the court's decision. Representative James Bomar of Shelbyville, speaker of the house in 1955, announced support for whatever method of apportionment would protect both rural and urban areas, but emphasized that there must be "plenty of safeguards" for the less populous areas of the state. Representative James Cummings of Woodbury also announced that he would propose to the 1957 legislature a constitutional amendment that would allow one house of the legislature to be based on population and the other house to be composed of one representative for each county. Representative Maclin Davis, Jr., of Nashville, a leader of the reapportionment forces, called upon Governor Clement to summon a special session of the legislature to reapportion.[57]

Z. T. Osborn opposed Representative Cummings' proposed constitutional amendment on the grounds that it "accomplishes nothing at all, and would kill the voice of the majority forever." Osborn, calling the state supreme court's decision absurd, proposed that the plaintiffs petition for a rehearing. "Instead of deciding our case, the justices set themselves up a case and decided it," he said. "They overlooked the nature of the complaint made and the relief requested." Both

[56] Nashville *Tennessean*, June 24, 1956, p. 18A.
[57] Nashville *Tennessean*, April 6, 1956, p. 1.

Osborn and Haynes Miller announced that they were contemplating the possibility of an appeal to the United States Supreme Court, since a denial of the equal protection of the laws under the Fourteenth Amendment had been alleged in the suit. "It is the same grounds," Osborn said, "on which Negroes have successfully challenged segregation in schools and parks."[58]

Members of the Committee for Constitutional Reapportionment also expressed disappointment over the loss in the state supreme court, but indicated that they did not consider the matter closed. "It's a specious argument," Frank Bryant, chairman of the group, said, "that a thing once bad has got to remain bad forever." Miss Ella V. Ross, dean of students at East Tennessee State University and a leader in the reapportionment effort, declared that since the court had "seen fit to turn down the request of the citizens committee, we must find a new method of requiring constitutional government for Tennessee." Hobart Atkins, attorney for the Republican primary commission, also criticized the court's decision. "When the constitutional limitation placed upon the discretion of the legislature has been wholly ignored and completely disregarded," he said, "it is hard to understand how the court can justify such a wide and bold departure from the constitution."[59]

As Osborn suggested, the plaintiffs filed a petition for a rehearing before the state supreme court, but they were again disappointed when the petition was denied on June 8. The group now seriously considered an appeal to the United States Supreme Court, but found themselves being handicapped by lack of finances. The case had already cost three thousand dollars, and the attorneys involved had been required to bear over a thousand dollars of this expense. An appeal would cost an estimated thousand dollars more.[60] The problem of finances was surmounted, however, and a notice of appeal to the Supreme Court was filed on July 19.

The Tennessee group could draw some encouragement about the possible success of their appeal from the renewed application of the equal protection clause of the Fourteenth Amendment in recent Supreme Court decisions. Mr. Justice Holmes had once characterized the equal protection clause as "the last resort of constitutional law-

58 Nashville *Tennessean*, April 6 and 7, 1956, p. 1.
59 Knoxville *Journal*, April 6, 1956, p. 1.
60 Nashville *Tennessean*, April 7, 1956, p. 1.

yers," but two scholars, writing in 1949, had pointed out that "after eighty years of relative desuetude, the equal protection clause is now coming into its own." These scholars, after analyzing the Court's recent interpretations of the clause, concluded that the Court's decisions "unmistakably indicate its growing importance."[61] Subsequent decisions demonstrated their prescience, as the Court continued to invigorate equal protection as a vital constitutional provision.[62] Most notably, in 1954, the same year the Tennesseans had decided to resort to the courts, the Court used the equal protection clause as the constitutional basis of its decision in *Brown* v. *Board of Education*,[63] in which it declared the segregation of public schools on the basis of race to be unconstitutional. The equal protection clause, by the time the Tennesseans appealed *Kidd* v. *McCanless*, had thus formed the basis of the most far-reaching use of judicial power in the Court's history, and the Court's ruling was being extended to prohibit racial segregation in an ever broadening range of public facilities.[64]

If the Court should perceive that geographic discrimination, in which areas of equal population were unequally represented, was analogous to the racial discrimination that it had condemned under the equal protection clause, then the Tennesseans could hope to win a favorable decision. Encouraging in this respect was the case *Dyer* v. *Kazuhisa Abe*,[65] decided in February, 1956, by the federal district court in Hawaii. After the initial apportionment of the territorial legislature of Hawaii, there had been no further apportionments for fifty-five years, with the result that the island of Oahu was particularly underrepresented. The court, in sustaining allegations against the constitutionality of the apportionment act in the *Dyer* case, said it was "merely an easy way out" for courts to be reluctant to interfere in legislative apportionment matters. "To say something is delicate," the court declared, "does not make it immune from the principles of justice. . . . To allow 'rotten boroughs' to continue in open contravention

---

[61] Joseph Tussman and Jacobus tenBroek, "The Equal Protection of the Laws," 37 *California Law Review* 341 (1949).

[62] For an analysis of the restrictive covenant cases, which were an important part of this trend, see Clement E. Vose, *Caucasians Only* (Berkeley: University of California Press, 1959).

[63] 347 U.S. 483 (1954).

[64] For a good review of the desegregation cases, see Albert B. Blaustein and Clarence Clyde Ferguson, *Desegregation and the Law* (New York: Vintage Books, 2d rev. ed., 1962).

[65] 138 F. Supp. 220 (D. Hawaii 1956).

of constitutional law, is a direct contravention of the principles of justice."[66]

The court proceeded to hold the apportionment act invalid under the Organic Act of Hawaii and the due process clause of the Fifth Amendment, which embraces a concept of equal protection. The court distinguished the *Colegrove* case and other cases in which the Supreme Court had refused to act upon apportionment questions, pointing out that the Supreme Court had recently ordered the desegregation of schools in a decision in which the "assumed delicacy of federal-state relations bowed to the principles of the Constitution." The court went on to hold that a "classification which discriminates geographically" had the same result as a racial classification. Therefore, the court said, reasons of "delicacy should no longer stay the judicial hand. The people of Hawaii need no court intervention to insure a democratic school system. They do need judicial aid in achieving a democratic legislature. Any distinction between racial and geographic discrimination is artificial and unrealistic. Both should be abolished."[67]

Although the Hawaii court did not base its decision in the *Dyer* case on the equal protection clause of the Fourteenth Amendment,[68] it did base its decision partially upon the concept of equal protection embodied in the due process clause of the Fifth Amendment.[69] The *Dyer* case was therefore useful as a precedent, even though not based on the Fourteenth Amendment, and the Tennessee group cited it, along with the white primary cases, to bolster their equal protection arguments in the jurisdictional statement filed with the Supreme Court urging a hearing in the *Kidd* case.[70] An indication that the *Dyer* case was not altogether persuasive, however, was given in October when a federal district court in Alabama dismissed a suit challenging the Alabama legislative apportionment system—a suit based to a great extent on the *Dyer* case.[71]

The Tennessee attorney general argued that the appeal of the *Kidd*

[66] *Ibid.*, at 224.
[67] *Ibid.*, at 236.
[68] *Ibid.*, at 225.
[69] See *Bolling* v. *Sharpe*, 347 U.S. 497 (1954), where the Court held that racial segregation in the public schools of the District of Columbia was prohibited by the due process clause of the Fifth Amendment.
[70] Jurisdictional Statement of Appellants, *Kidd* v. *McCanless*, U. S. Supreme Court, Oct. 1956 Term, No. 469.
[71] *Perry* v. *Folsom*, 144 F. Supp. 874 (N.D. Ala. 1956).

case should be dismissed by the Supreme Court on the grounds that the Tennessee Supreme Court's decision rested on adequate, nonfederal grounds, that there was a lack of a substantial federal question, and that apportionment was a political question. The decision by the state supreme court that Tennessee legislators could not act as *de facto* officers, the attorney general argued, was an independent, nonfederal ground upon which the decision below rested, precluding therefore review by the Supreme Court. In addition, he pointed out that the appellants could point to no previous case in which the Court had held that the apportionment of state legislatures raised a federal question under the Fourteenth Amendment. Finally, the attorney general argued that the "Colegrove decision clearly supports the appellees' position in this case, and the question of reapportioning congressional districts is patently stronger than one involving the reapportionment of the general assembly of a state." Citing the similar cases arising since *Colegrove* in which the Court had refused to act, the attorney general argued that "the decisions of this Court declare the problem of reapportionment to be a political question which should be addressed to the people of Tennessee and their General Assembly. . . . They are capable of determining political and governmental issues arising in connection with their state government. They should be permitted to resolve the question of reapportionment in their own way."[72]

The Supreme Court on December 3, 1956, granted the motion to dismiss the *Kidd* case,[73] citing *Colegrove v. Green*[74] and *Anderson v. Jordan*.[75] After more than two years of planning, fund-raising, and litigation, the Tennessee group was legally back where it had started. Hobart Atkins promptly announced that a bill providing for reapportionment would be introduced in the 1957 state legislature, but legislative action, in view of the history of apportionment in Tennessee, could not be expected.[76] Indeed, any chances of legislative action may have been diminished further, if possible, by the outcome of the *Kidd* litigation.

[72] Statement in Opposition to Appellants' Statement of Jurisdiction and Motion to Dismiss, *Kidd* v. *McCanless*, U. S. Supreme Court, Oct. 1956 Term, No. 469.
[73] 352 U.S. 920.
[74] 328 U.S. 549 (1946).
[75] 343 U.S. 912 (1952).
[76] Knoxville *Journal*, Dec. 4, 1956, p. 1.

From a broader perspective, prospects for a judicial remedy for the apportionment situation were hardly encouraging. Although the Supreme Court had revitalized the equal protection clause in the desegregation cases and had accepted the necessity of an extensive use of federal judicial power to enforce the equal protection policy of desegregation, the Court in the late 1950's was finding it increasingly difficult to implement its desegregation decree. Enforcement depended upon acceptance by state and federal officials, as well as courts, and such acceptance was lacking in many important instances. In many southern states the Court's decision met with massive resistance, Negro litigants were harassed, and many southern judges were reluctant to act. As a result, desegregation had slowed to a snail's pace.[77]

Presidential endorsement for the Court's decision on either legal or moral grounds was not forthcoming; President Eisenhower was driven to support it only after an absolute defiance of federal law by Governor Orval Faubus of Arkansas in 1957, and Eisenhower never did endorse the Court's decision during his administration as President.[78] In the Congress, although support for the decision was sufficient to prevent any direct attack on the Court, segregationists did join with other congressmen disaffected by the Court's decisions in the areas of subversion, congressional investigations, and federal-state relations to mount an almost successful attack on the Court's appellate jurisdiction in 1957–58.[79] And finally, from the bar itself, the Court was drawing increasing fire, especially from the Conference of State Supreme Court Chief Justices and the American Bar Association.[80]

In light of these circumstances, the Court might well hestitate before committing federal judicial power to the reapportionment of state legislatures. Reapportionment by federal judicial decree would require the use of judicial power to an extent as great, or greater, than that demanded by desegregation. And the disaffection that would result

[77] See Jack Peltason, *Fifty-Eight Lonely Men* (New York: Harcourt, Brace and World, 1961); R. B. McKay, "With All Deliberate Speed: Legislative Reaction and Judicial Developments, 1956–57," 43 *Virginia Law Review* 1 (1957); W. F. Murphy, "The South Counterattacks: The Anti-NAACP Laws," *Western Political Quarterly*, Vol. 12 (1959), p. 371.

[78] See Corine Silverman, "The Little Rock Story," The Inter-University Case Program, Case No. 41 (1959 rev.).

[79] See Walter F. Murphy, *Congress and the Court* (Chicago: University of Chicago Press, 1962).

[80] See John R. Schmidhauser, *The Supreme Court* (New York: Holt, Rinehart and Winston, 1960), chap. 4.

would not be concentrated in one section of the nation, as with desegregation, but would be found across the nation among the groups and officials who would be disadvantaged by the reapportionment of state legislatures.

Whatever the reason, the Court continued to stay out of the apportionment arena after the *Kidd* case; in 1957 it affirmed a decision of a federal district court in Oklahoma rejecting a suit that challenged the legislative apportionment system in that state. The Oklahoma federal court, in *Radford* v. *Gary*,[81] acknowledged the Oklahoma attorney general's concession that the legislature had failed to reapportion since 1910, but held nevertheless that there was "nothing in the so-called civil rights cases indicating a disposition to reverse, modify or repudiate the rule so firmly established in the former cases, and it is not the function of this court to psycho-analyze the justices of the Supreme Court in order to divine the trend of decisions. It is sufficient that the Supreme Court has authoritatively spoken in the question before us, and we are bound until it speaks again."[82] The Supreme Court affirmed this decision, rather than merely dismissing it, marking the first time it had affirmed such a decision in the long line of *per curiam* refusals to hear such cases issued since the *Colegrove* case.[83]

The following year the Court dismissed *Hartsfield* v. *Sloan*,[84] which was another attempt, this time by Atlanta Mayor Hartsfield, to overturn the Georgia county unit system; the mayor's suit was also supported by the U. S. Conference of Mayors as *amicus curiae*.[85] The suit, which involved a motion for leave to file a petition for a writ of mandamus to compel a hearing in the district court, was encouraging to advocates of reapportionment, however, because Chief Justice Warren and Justice Black, Douglas, and Brennan voted to issue a rule to show cause why a writ of mandamus should not be granted. Assuming that these votes indicated a desire to grant a hearing in such cases, they were sufficient to bring a case up on appeal or on certiorari, which requires only four votes.[86]

[81] 145 F. Supp. 541 (W.D. Okla. 1956).
[82] *Ibid.*, at 544.
[83] 352 U.S. 991 (1957).
[84] 357 U.S. 916 (1958).
[85] For comments on the case, see *NMR*, Vol. 47 (July, 1958), p. 336; (May, 1958), pp. 226–27.
[86] The *Hartsfield* case was also interesting because it was based on the Civil Rights Act of 1957; see *NMR*, Vol. 47 (May, 1958), p. 227.

The factors governing federal judicial relief in apportionment cases were thus mixed, although generally unfavorable.[87] The Tennessee group had only succeeded in contributing another in the growing line of *per curiam* refusals by the Court to enter the apportionment arena. The group had, however, aroused more interest in reapportionment in Tennessee than had been evident for some time, and had demonstrated that the diverse interests of the grand divisions of the state could be overcome for the purpose of attacking the apportionment system through the judicial process. The coalition which litigated *Kidd* v. *McCanless* was an East Tennessee–Middle Tennessee alliance of Republicans and Democrats which had proven reasonably effective. Most important, the litigation in the *Kidd* case drew into the apportionment fight individuals who would continue to furnish leadership for the cause in Tennessee. First, Hobart Atkins of Knoxville and Z. T. Osborn of Nashville had gained experience in apportionment litigation and would continue to provide leadership when the attack on the apportionment system was made in the federal courts. In addition, Atkins and Guy Smith of Knoxville would lend considerable Republican support to the reapportionment movement. Smith, as editor of the Knoxville *Journal*, would also give press support for the cause in East Tennessee, augmenting the Nashville *Tennessean*, the leading Democratic newspaper in Middle Tennessee.

But the Kidd coalition still lacked overt support in West Tennessee, particularly Shelby County, and it lacked money. Statewide unity and coordination among the large metropolitan counties would broaden the base of support for the coalition, and it would also help to insure adequate finances. These defects had to be remedied before a new attack on the Tennessee apportionment system could be launched in the federal courts.

[87] *Matthews* v. *Handley*, 361 U.S. 127 (1959).

CHAPTER III

THE GENESIS OF *BAKER* v. *CARR*

AFTER THE DISMISSAL OF *Kidd* v. *McCanless*,[1] there appeared for a time to be a lack of interest in any further apportionment litigation in Tennessee, and the General Assembly in its 1957 session maintained a tradition by handily defeating reapportionment bills and refusing to authorize a study of the problem.[2] In November, 1957, however, a sequence of events began well to the north, in Minnesota, which would affect the apportionment system in Tennessee profoundly. In Minnesota, Daniel B. McGraw, John O. Erickson, Ruth H. O'Dell, and Arthur R. Swan filed suit in the federal district court challenging the constitutionality of the apportionment act of 1913 and seeking an injunction prohibiting further elections under its provisions.[3]

The apportionment situation in Minnesota in many respects paralleled the one in Tennessee. The legislature had not reapportioned since 1913, and in a suit challenging the 1913 act the Minnesota Supreme Court had sustained its provisions, although there were considerable variations in population among the legislative districts.[4] As the decades passed, the population among the districts of 1913 grew sharply disproportionate, with the Minneapolis-St. Paul area particularly disadvantaged in proportion to its population. Finally, in 1945, Jay W. Smith, a candidate for the legislature, challenged the constitutionality of the 1913 act again, pointing out that his district in Minneapolis was equal in population to fifteen other counties in Minnesota, but those counties had five and one-half times as many representatives in the legislature. Smith won his case in the Ramsay County district court,

---

[1] 200 Tenn. 273 (1956).

[2] B. v. C., Record, p. 157.

[3] *McGraw* v. *Donovan*, 163 F. Supp. 184 (D. Minn. 1958); see also *NMR*, Vol. 47 (Jan., 1958), p. 25.

[4] *State* v. *Weatherbill*, 125 Minn. 336 (1914).

but on appeal to the state supreme court the lower court was reversed and any judicial remedy for the situation denied.[5]

"The responsibility to heed the constitutional mandate to redistrict," the Minnesota Supreme Court said, "is laid upon the legislature, and it is, at most, only when as of the time of enactment there appears a clear and palpable violation of the fundamental law that the courts would have the power to upset the law. . . . Absent a violation of the announced rule in the enactment, the mere change in relative population and consequent inequality of representation subsequent to enactment does not render the act void." The court pointed out that it lacked the power to compel the legislature to reapportion and, therefore, the legislature's "judgment and discretion are its own to exercise or not, as its conscience permits."[6]

The resort to the state judicial process in Minnesota, as in Tennessee, thus failed to produce any remedy for the apportionment problem. There appeared to be, as one student of the Minnesota situation said, "no legal method to compel the legislature to carry out its sworn duty under the constitution of Minnesota."[7] In *McGraw* v. *Donovan*,[8] however, the federal district court, after hearing expert testimony on apportionment from Professor Emeritus William Anderson of the University of Minnesota and Professor John A. Bond of North Dakota State Agricultural College, issued an opinion in July, 1958, postponing any decision in order to permit the 1959 session of the Minnesota legislature to consider reapportionment. Pointing out that it was the legislature's "unmistakable duty to reapportion," the federal court said that it was "not to be presumed that the legislature will refuse to take such action as is necessary to comply with its duty under the State Constitution." The court, reserving decision on all issues involved, including its power to grant relief, postponed a decision until it could be shown that the legislature "advisedly and deliberately failed and refused to perform its constitutional duty to redistrict the State."[9]

---

[5] For a brief description of this litigation, see *NMR*, Vol. 34 (Nov., 1945), p. 504; the case in the state supreme court was *Smith* v. *Holm*, 220 Minn. 486 (1945).

[6] *Smith* v. *Holm*, 220 Minn. 486, at 490–91.

[7] Louis C. Dorweiler, Jr., "Minnesota Farmers Rule Cities," *NMR*, Vol. 35 (March, 1946), pp. 115, 120.

[8] 163 F. Supp. 184 (D. Minn. 1958).

[9] *Ibid.*, at 187–88; see also *NMR*, Vol. 47 (July, 1958), p. 336; Vol. 48 (Oct., 1958), p. 457.

The legislature responded to this judicial lecture on its duty and the implicit threat of judicial relief by passing a reapportionment act in 1959. The act increased the representation of the Minneapolis–St. Paul area by ten representatives and five senators.[10] The reapportionment act was not entirely satisfactory in population terms, but the plaintiffs in the *McGraw* case moved for a dismissal, which the court subsequently granted.[11] Although the dismissal precluded adjudication on the merits in the *McGraw* case, the fact that a state legislature had for the first time reapportioned in response to the threat of federal court litigation encouraged those who were concerned with the apportionment systems in other states. The effects of the *McGraw* case were felt especially in Tennessee, where they would ultimately lead to a breakthrough that would open the federal courts completely to those seeking to challenge state apportionment systems.

The Shelby County Commission and the City of Memphis in 1959 retained Walter Chandler of Memphis to represent the interests of the city and county before the legislature in an attempt to obtain a more favorable apportionment.[12] Shelby County and Memphis no longer wielded the political power that they once had under E. H. Crump. Crump had been badly beaten in the 1948 Democratic primaries when Estes Kefauver and Crump's old enemy, Gordon Browning, had captured the senatorial and gubernatorial nominations. The primary broke the classic Crump coalition of Shelby County and parts of West Tennessee with East Tennessee, and Crump's death in 1954 made the decline of Shelby County's former influence permanent.[13] By 1958, both Shelby County and Memphis were experiencing a financial pinch. Local officials claimed the problem was aggravated by the discriminatory allocation of state aid in favor of the less populous counties. This discrimination, they said, resulted from the underrepresentation of the populous counties in the legislature.[14]

Walter Chandler, who was retained to represent the interests of

[10] Lloyd M. Short, "Minnesota Adopts Reapportionment Act," *NMR*, Vol. 48 (Sept., 1959), p. 415.

[11] *McGraw* v. *Donovan*, 177 F. Supp. 803 (D. Minn. 1959); see also, *NMR*, Vol. 49 (Jan., 1960), p. 22.

[12] *Inventory of Work on Reapportionment by State Leagues of Women Voters* (Washington, D. C.: League of Women Voters of the U. S., 1960), p. 14.

[13] The foregoing comments on the political position of Shelby County and Memphis are based on the unpublished research of Leonard G. Ritt, "Changing Patterns in Tennessee Politics, 1948–62."

[14] This statement is based upon comments by Walter Chandler.

Memphis and Shelby County, had been a member of the Crump organization for many years. He had been elected to the legislature in 1920, had served as Memphis city attorney during the 1920's, and had been elected to Congress in 1934, where he served until 1939, when he returned to Memphis to run successfully for mayor. He served as mayor of Memphis from 1940 to 1946, when he resigned, apparently due to differences with Crump over city finances.[15] Shelby County and Memphis added significant force to the interest in reapportionment already demonstrated in East and Middle Tennessee. Memphis and Shelby County would provide valuable financial support to the apportionment fight and make available the considerable legal and political talents of Walter Chandler, a respected figure in state politics.

Chandler was aware of the *McGraw* decision in Minnesota, and he hoped to bring about a similar resolution of the apportionment problem in Tennessee. His original aim was to attempt to bring pressure to bear on the legislature by filing suit in the federal district court during the 1959 legislative session. If the legislature still did not reapportion, the federal court could be apprised of the legislature's failure to act after the filing of the suit, thus putting the plaintiffs in a more favorable tactical position. For this purpose, Chandler succeeded in arousing the interest of Guy Smith and state Senator Hobart Atkins, of Knoxville, who had thrown Republican support to the litigation in *Kidd* v. *McCanless*. Smith agreed that the Republican state committee would finance Hobart Atkins' participation in the challenge of the 1901 apportionment act in federal court. Chandler was aware, as he stated to Atkins, that there were dangers to the metropolitan areas involved and that "we will bring down on our heads the wrath of the rural members of the present legislature, and that, by way of reprisal, a bill to establish proportional representation at the expense of the large counties will be introduced and, possibly, passed by the present legislature, as was done in the Browning administration."[16] Nevertheless, Chandler said, "unless we intend to drop the matter of reapportionment and continue to accept what the parsimony of the rural legislators is willing for us to have, we should fight and take the consequences."[17]

15 William D. Miller, *Mr. Crump of Memphis* (Baton Rouge: Louisiana State University Press, 1964), pp. 134–35, 143, 199, 215–16, 250–51, 271–72, 275, 320–21.
16 See chap. 2.
17 Letter, Chandler to Atkins, Feb. 12, 1959.

Instead of filing suit in federal court during the session of the legislature, however, the attorneys decided to send a letter to every member of the legislature informing them that such a suit would be filed if reapportionment did not come about:

Dear Senator or Representative:

A number of citizens of Tennessee, especially interested in the proper apportionment of the Tennessee Legislature in accordance with the provisions of the State Constitution, have engaged attorneys at law to institute legal proceedings in the Federal Court if the present Tennessee Legislature does not enact legislation in conformity with the constitutional formula for reapportionment, and the undersigned are among the attorneys engaged for the purpose.

We feel that it is proper to notify you, as a member of the 1959 General Assembly, of the contemplated institution of this suit for reapportionment, which will be based, in material part, on the failure of the present Legislature to carry out the mandate of our Constitution. We wish to assure you that there is nothing personal in our approach, as counsel, to the proper solution to this long standing problem, but we feel that you should have knowledge beforehand of the plan referred to in order to take appropriate action before the adjournment of the present Legislature.

With every good wish,

Yours very truly,

Walter Chandler
Hobart Atkins[18]

The Tennessee League of Women Voters also called the legislators' attention to the problem of apportionment by placing on every desk on the opening day of the 1959 session a red sign saying, "STOP—Before you swear to uphold the Tennessee Constitution, see Article II, Sections 3, 4, 5, and 6"—the sections relating to apportionment.[19] Neither the threat of federal court action nor the LWV reminder, however, produced a positive response from the legislature. The senate voted on two apportionment bills, defeating one by a vote of 14 to 18 and the other 13 to 20; the house failed to vote on any reapportionment bill. A joint resolution proposing a Legislative Council study "of steps taken by other states in recent years to reapportion the membership of their legislative bodies" failed of passage in the house by a vote

---

[18] A copy of this letter may be found in B. v. C., Record, p. 14.
[19] *Inventory of Work on Reapportionment by State Leagues of Women Voters* (Washington, D. C.: League of Women Voters of the U. S., 1963), p. 45.

of 37 to 54.[20] The failure of the resolution was not entirely disappointing to Chandler and Atkins, since, as Chandler said, "if the Legislature had adopted the resolution and had kept the matter within its jurisdiction, the three-judge Court might have postponed action until after 1961."[21]

Preparations for litigation began after the rebuff by the legislature, and Chandler and Atkins were joined by Z. T. Osborn, Jr., of Nashville, who had played a leading role in the *Kidd* litigation. Osborn also had been in contact with Mayor Ben West of Nashville in regard to the apportionment situation since the loss in *Kidd*. West's concern for adequate urban representation was well known, and he would ultimately commit the City of Nashville to the litigation in the federal courts, adding financial resources and the technical aid of the Advanced Planning Division of the Nashville Metropolitan Planning Commission to the cause.[22] Therefore, in contrast to the coalition which litigated the *Kidd* case, the litigating coalition in *Baker* v. *Carr* would be state-wide in its scope and adequately financed, with excellent technical aid from the Advanced Planning Division, and would involve a unified effort of all of the largest metropolitan counties, with Memphis, Knoxville, Chattanooga, and Nashville filing complaints in the case.

Before the attorneys filed the complaint in the federal district court in Nashville, they had to recruit willing plaintiffs, since they wished to file a class action in behalf of taxpayers and voters in Memphis, Nashville, Knoxville, and Chattanooga. The Tennessee League of Women Voters gave its aid,[23] and plaintiffs from all four metropolitan counties were recruited; Charles W. Baker, chairman of the Shelby County Court, headed the list.[24] The plaintiffs from the four

[20] B. v. C., Record, p. 15.

[21] Letter, Chandler to Atkins, March 22, 1959.

[22] Letter, Osborn to West, Nov. 22, 1961.

[23] *Inventory of Work on Reapportionment* (1960 ed.), p. 14.

[24] In Tennessee, the county court (of quarterly sessions) is usually the governing body of the county, although in some counties, as in Shelby, a county commission has been grafted onto the older governing body. The other plaintiffs from the metropolitan counties were: David N. Harsh, chairman of the Shelby County Commission; Edmund Orgill, mayor of Memphis; Roy Dixon of Shelby County; Herbert S. Esch of Memphis; Jack W. Lee, a realtor from Davidson County; Mrs. James M. Todd, a leader of the LWV from Davidson County; Guy L. Smith of Knoxville, editor of the Knoxville *Journal*; and John R. McGauley of Hamilton County. Lee, Smith, and Mrs. Todd had also been plaintiffs in the *Kidd* case.

metropolitan counties were joined by W. D. Hudson, judge of the County Court and Criminal Court in Montgomery County. Hudson pointed out that neighboring Stewart County had a population of nine thousand with a full representative in the legislature, whereas Montgomery County had a population of approximately forty-five thousand with only one and one-half representatives in the legislature. "That gives a child in Stewart County five times the representation in the legislature a child in Montgomery County has," he said. "That is not only taxation without representation, but slavery."[25]

Walter Chandler was primarily responsible for the drawing of the complaint, filed on May 18, 1959, which he based to a great extent on the complaint filed in the *McGraw* case in Minnesota. The defendants were Secretary of State Joe C. Carr, Attorney General McCanless, the state co-ordinator of elections, and the members of the State Election Commission. The complaint sought the convening of a three-judge court and a declaratory judgment invalidating the 1901 apportionment act under the Tennessee Constitution and the equal protection clause of the Fourteenth Amendment, plus injunctive relief to assure the plaintiffs "free and equal franchise and equal protection of the laws which are now and have been for many years denied them by the defendants and their predecessors in office." The complaint also requested the court to enjoin further elections under the 1901 act and either to declare that the next legislative election be at large or to re-apportion the state itself on the basis of the formula in the Tennessee Constitution.[26]

The complaint also contained maps setting out the apportionment under the 1901 act and demonstrating the discrimination against the more populous counties. In addition, acts distributing state funds to the counties were appended to demonstrate that the apportionment system under the 1901 act resulted in financial discrimination against the more populous counties.[27] The letter from Chandler and Atkins to the 1959 legislature and excerpts from the legislative journals showing the legislature's rejection of reapportionment bills were also appended to the original complaint.[28]

All defendants filed motions to dismiss in June, arguing that the

---

[25] Letter, Hudson to Chandler, Aug. 17, 1959.
[26] B. v. C., Record, pp. 6, 18–19.
[27] *Ibid.*, pp. 16–18, exhibits A, B, C, D, E, and F.
[28] *Ibid.*, pp. 14–15, and exhibit G.

court lacked jurisdiction, that the complaint failed to state a claim upon which relief could be granted, and that the complaint failed to join indispensable parties.[29] The plaintiffs expected this move, although they had hoped that Hubert Brooks, the Republican member of the State Election Commission, would not adopt the motion to dismiss as he did. There was obviously not complete Republican unity in support of the suit.[30] The defendants supported their contention that the complaint failed to raise a substantial federal question by appending to their motions the papers filed with the United States Supreme Court in the appeal of the *Kidd* case.[31]

The case now entered a crucial stage. If the federal district court dismissed the complaint, an appeal to the Supreme Court would be based on a record that was rather meager and did not contain a full canvassing of the issue in the lower court. The case had been filed before Judge William E. Miller in the Federal District Court for the Middle District of Tennessee in Nashville. Judge Miller is from Johnson City in East Tennessee, where he was born in 1908; he is a graduate of the University of Tennessee and the Yale Law School. A Republican, he was a chancery court judge, an unsuccessful candidate for Congress, a presidential elector in 1940, and a delegate to the Tennessee constitutional convention in 1953. He was appointed to the federal bench by President Eisenhower in 1955. In ordering the successful desegregation of the Nashville school system, Judge Miller had been more forceful than most southern federal judges in enforcing the Supreme Court's desegregation mandate. Indeed, the firmness of Miller in Nashville and of Federal Judge Robert L. Taylor in Knoxville had led the rabid segregationist, John Kasper, to say that "they look like niggers." Kasper also had denounced Miller as being a part of a "Jewish-Communist conspiracy," along with Nashville Mayor Ben West, the Supreme Court, and Nashville newspapers.[32]

Considering Judge Miller's efforts to enforce the desegregation ruling, the plaintiffs could reasonably assume that he would not automatically react negatively to an equal protection argument, as some of the other federal judges in the region might. "It is difficult for me to believe that Judge Miller would grant the motion of the defend-

[29] *Ibid.*, pp. 46–47.
[30] Letter, Chandler to Atkins, June 15, 1959.
[31] B. v. C., Record, pp. 51–87.
[32] See Jack Peltason, *Fifty-Eight Lonely Men* (New York: Harcourt, Brace and World, 1961), pp. 158–61.

ants," Walter Chandler said to his colleagues, "when he is bound to know how grossly unjust is the present apportionment of the legislature. Of course, I expect him to decide the case on the merits, but I certainly think that we are entitled to a trial on the merits, rather than a summary judgment against us."[33]

The plaintiffs hoped that they would have the benefit of a decision in the *McGraw* case in Minnesota before dealing with the motions to dismiss, but the reapportionment of the Minnesota legislature in early 1959 and the subsequent dismissal of the *McGraw* case precluded this. Chandler, Osborn, and Atkins, therefore, had to proceed without a decision from the Minnesota federal court, and, as Chandler said, they had "a heavy burden getting away from the political question." Chandler, at least, continued to be hopeful of a full hearing, believing that if "Judge Miller is the courageous judge that I believe he is, he will not take the easy way out of this case in view of the terrible state of affairs; especially, when he can do so much good by taking the courageous position and giving the people of Tennessee an opportunity to know the type of Legislature under which they must live."[34]

Chandler's faith was rewarded on July 31, when Judge Miller refused to grant the motions to dismiss until a three-judge court could be convened to hear the case.[35] After a careful review of the cases cited and the allegations made by the parties in the suit, Judge Miller said, "The Court has reached the conclusion that the issues presented are of such character that they should be evaluated and considered by a three-judge court as provided by statute and that this Court should not undertake to dismiss the complaint summarily."[36] Judge Miller admitted that in many of the cases bearing on such suits there were expressions "which would indicate that there is no hope of judicial relief in a case of this type," but the federal question raised by the complaint was not "obviously without merit." He discussed the *Colegrove* case,[37] and admitted that it might close "the door to relief in the

---

[33] Letter, Chandler to Atkins and Osborn, June 15, 1959.

[34] Letter, Chandler to Atkins, July 8, 1959.

[35] A suit filed in a federal district court seeking an injunction against a state statute on the grounds of its invalidity under the federal Constitution, if found by the district judge to raise nonfrivolous issues, requires the convening of a three-judge court to decide the issues presented. Appeals from the decisions of three-judge courts are made directly to the Supreme Court, bypassing the courts of appeals.

[36] *Baker* v. *Carr,* 175 F. Supp. 649, at 651 (M.D. Tenn. 1959).

[37] *Colegrove* v. *Green,* 328 U.S. 549 (1946).

present case, but the Court is not prepared to say that this conclusion necessarily follows or that it follows so clearly and distinctly that it is not even debatable."[38]

On August 10, Acting Chief Judge Shackelford Miller, Jr., of the Sixth Circuit Court of Appeals designated court of appeals Judge John D. Martin, Judge Marion S. Boyd of the Federal District Court for the Western District of Tennessee, and Judge William E. Miller to constitute the court to hear the case. Judge Martin was a Tennessean, a graduate of the University of Virginia Law School, and a second cousin of E. H. Crump of Memphis, and had served on the District Court for the Western District of Tennessee from 1920 to 1940, during which time he had issued the injunction against Governor Gordon Browning's attempt to interfere with the 1938 election in Shelby County.[39] Judge Martin had been elevated to the Sixth Circuit Court of Appeals in 1940.

Judge Marion Speed Boyd had also been a member of the Crump organization in Memphis, had served as Shelby County attorney general, and was appointed to the District Court for the Western District of Tennessee with the Crump organization's support in 1940.[40] He is a native Tennessean and a graduate of the University of Tennessee Law School. Judge Boyd, in contrast to Judge Miller, had been slow to enforce the Supreme Court's desegregation decision in Memphis. The desegregation of Memphis State University, for example, was long delayed in Judge Boyd's court, even after the Sixth Circuit Court of Appeals ordered it in 1958, after three years of litigation.[41]

In a sense, then, the federal court which heard *Baker* v. *Carr* was representative of the state, being composed of a Republican from East Tennessee and two Democrats from West Tennessee. Indeed, Judge Martin later pointed out that the chief judge had "designated these three judges, being Tennesseans, to hear this Tennessee case. That very probably was his reason for selecting these three trial judges." Martin pointed out, "He could have sent one from Ohio or one from Michigan if he had wanted to, but he has given you a Court comprised of Tennesseans."[42]

---

[38] 175 F. Supp., at 651.
[39] See chap. 2; see also, Miller, *Crump*, pp. 136, 258.
[40] Miller, *Crump*, pp. 280, 288.
[41] Peltason, *Fifty-Eight Lonely Men*, pp. 20–21.
[42] Transcript of Arguments, Three-Judge Federal Court, Middle District of

After clearing the first hurdle when Judge Miller refused to grant the motions to dismiss, Chandler and Osborn received assurances from Shelby County, Memphis, and Nashville that the case, now that it would be heard, would receive adequate financial support. The City of Chattanooga petitioned to intervene in the case, and was joined by Ben West, who intervened as mayor of Nashville, and ultimately by the City of Knoxville. Mayor West's complaint contained as an exhibit a documented history of apportionment in Tennessee, prepared by Dr. Robert White, the state historian, demonstrating the failure of all apportionment efforts since 1901.[43]

Chandler, Atkins, and Osborn met in late September to map out their strategy for the hearing before the three-judge court and, they hoped, the forthcoming trial on the merits. They decided that Atkins would search the Tennessee statutes to find examples of discrimination against the urban counties by the legislature, Chandler would consolidate and rewrite the briefs, and Osborn would work on proof of discrimination should they win a trial on the merits. The three attorneys also agreed to divide the time in oral argument to allow Walter Chandler to argue principally on the unconstitutionality of the 1901 act, Hobart Atkins to deal with the refutation of cases that denied jurisdiction, and Osborn to devote his attention to the alternative forms of relief which the court might grant.[44]

On November 23 the three-judge court heard oral arguments in the case, and the attitudes the judges revealed during the arguments were anything but encouraging to the attorneys for the plaintiffs. State Solicitor General Allison B. Humphreys opened for the defendants and reiterated the motion to dismiss on the grounds of lack of jurisdiction, failure to state a cause of action, and failure to join indispensable parties. "We assume for the purposes of our discussion," he said, "that all the facts which are well pleaded in the complaint are true."[45] Humphreys argued that the complaint was based on the Minnesota case, but the officials sued in the complaint were not responsible for elections in Tennessee, and therefore indispensable parties had not been joined. He argued that the county election commissioners and

---

Tennessee, Nashville, Tennessee, Nov. 23, 1959, p. 103. The Transcript of Arguments will hereinafter be cited as Arguments.

[43] B. v. C., Record, pp. 221–23, 128.

[44] Letter, Osborn to Atkins and Chandler, Oct. 5, 1959.

[45] Arguments, p. 7.

some members of the legislature should have been made parties to the suit.[46]

Humphreys then argued that the Fourteenth Amendment did not protect any rights upon which the plaintiffs could base their complaint and that "the Supreme Court has held and has never departed from the proposition that the Fourteenth Amendment in and of itself does not make any guarantees with respect to suffrage."[47] In effect, the solicitor general said, the case involved a claim that the apportionment of the Tennessee legislature was contrary to the guaranty clause of the Constitution, and cases arising under this clause had always been considered to raise political questions that the courts would not decide. Humphreys also added that the *Colegrove* and other apportionment cases were conclusive that the claims asserted in the case would not be heard by the federal courts. At this point, Judge Martin interrupted to discuss the *Colegrove* case.[48]

> JUDGE MARTIN: Although that was a three, three and one decision, it has been adhered to in other cases since. There has been no recent doctrine of the Colegrove case applied—
>
> GENERAL HUMPHREYS (interrupting): Absolutely none. If your Honors please, in the Colegrove v. Green case . . . the three-judge District Court in that case followed Wood v. Broom, and said that on the authority of Wood v. Broom, a Federal District Court has no jurisdiction with respect to apportionment of the vote; that is, with respect to the districts in a congressional election matter.
>
> JUDGE MARTIN: Pardon me. It is even more a fortiori, stronger, where the relief sought is to have the United States District Court require conformity by officials of the State to the State law affecting election to the Legislature, a number of people. You would have mostly a federal question, it would seem off hand, in the selection of congressmen who are representing states for the office in the National Assembly or Congress as against localized representation in the government of a sovereign state.

Humphreys agreed with Judge Martin, and added that the *Colegrove* case had been followed in all subsequent cases, with the exception of the *Dyer* case in Hawaii and the *McGraw* case in Minnesota. The *Dyer* case was distinguishable because conditioned by the Or-

[46] *Ibid.*, pp. 4–14.
[47] *Ibid.*, p. 16.
[48] *Ibid.*, pp. 23–24.

ganic Act of Hawaii, Humphreys said, and the *McGraw* case never came to trial on the merits.[49]

Walter Chandler then opened for the plaintiffs and soon discovered, as did Atkins and Osborn, that interruptions from the bench would prevent the delivery of a well-ordered argument. Chandler answered the indispensable parties issue by pointing out that the General Assembly was a transitory body, therefore making it difficult to sue its members, and that the parties sued in *Baker* v. *Carr* were the same parties who had been sued in the *Kidd* case. Judge Martin interrupted to inquire if an election at large would not violate the Tennessee Constitution. Chandler answered no, but Martin said that such an election "seems to me just about as strong an invasion of states' rights, if there are any left, as anything could be if we were to set out the method of choosing the members of the Legislature by a statewide vote rather than by districts as has been the provision of the Constitution always." Chandler answered by pointing out that the Supreme Court had ordered an election at large for Congress in *Smiley* v. *Holm*[50] and that what "is happening here is interference with the rights of the people of the state, not the state. It is the rights of the people that are involved here, and it is those rights which the Fourteenth Amendment is designed to protect. And that is the basis upon which this suit is brought."[51]

Judge Martin and Chandler then engaged in an extended colloquy that revealed deep differences between the two former political allies on the proper role of the federal judiciary in apportionment litigation.[52]

> JUDGE MARTIN: There are still some of us left who think that the dual system of government established by the Constitution should be preserved and that federalism should not run riot to the deprivation of the fundamental rights of the states . . . . Within its constitutional power, the federal government is paramount, but only where it acts according to the Constitution itself . . . because we still have the Tenth Amendment, although it has not been alluded to as much as the Fourteenth and the Fifteenth in recent years. It is still there in the Constitution unchanged.

[49] *Ibid.*, p. 24.
[50] 285 U.S. 355 (1932).
[51] Arguments, pp. 28–29.
[52] *Ibid.*, pp. 46–47.

MR. CHANDLER: I do not disagree with Your Honor's feelings with reference to the states' rights and things of that kind because we stem from the same community and the same section of the country, but I do say that while the federal courts are reluctant to enter the field which we seek that they enter here now, it is their duty to enter because no relief can be gotten anywhere else.

* * * * * * *

JUDGE MARTIN: Brother Chandler, I agree with you, of course, that this may be, you might say, your last chance—

MR. CHANDLER: Last chance, yes, sir.

JUDGE MARTIN:—to enforce the rights that you represent ultimately, but that would not give us jurisdiction if we do not have it. In other words, the extremity of the case would not confer on us the jurisdiction of the United States Courts unless we actually have it.

MR. CHANDLER: That is the very point of difference between Your Honor and ourselves. The extremity of this case does require the intervention of the Federal Court. That is the crowning basis of this case here, that over a period of 60 years, no relief has been gotten to conform to the Tennessee Constitution on reapportionment which provides a mandatory method of setting up the General Assembly of the State.

And when you try the state procedure and fail, and with the Fourteenth Amendment saying that no state shall pass any law which abridges the rights of citizens, then we say that the State has passed this law which abridges the rights of these citizens and, therefore, we invoke that constitutional provision to see that this is corrected and in the method which we contend is one that takes the case back to the people who, after all, created the Constitution of this state and on whom the Legislature is dependent; and there is nothing more equal and fair than an election which will give an election over the whole state. It will then have the effect of majority rule, which, of course, is what we are entitled to.

JUDGE MARTIN: I am not challenging in this little colloquy the merits of the proposition that you urge as to the morality of the case or the fairness of carrying out the mandate of the Constitution of Tennessee. All I am pressing with you is the jurisdictional question that the United States Court would be going to the nth degree, it would seem, in giving the equivalent of the injunction concerning the election of representatives to the Legislature of Tennessee who make the state laws.

* * * * * * *

That power would be assumed by the Supreme Court of the United States to regulate every state in the Union with respect to its local relations, if that power exists, where the state officials fail to carry out their duty. And I think the ergo of it, the conclusion, is that it would pretty well abolish any reserve rights that the states have. It seems to me so drastic a remedy.

* * * * * * *

MR. CHANDLER: We say with the utmost respect that there is no judicial "No Man's Land" in this country of ours. . . . There is no such place.

Chandler resumed his argument, attempting to distinguish the *Colegrove* case, but was again interrupted by Judge Boyd, who pointed out that in the recently decided Oklahoma apportionment case, *Radford* v. *Gary*,[53] the Supreme Court had affirmed the decision of the federal district court, relying on the *Colegrove* case, that it was without jurisdiction. Chandler was forced to agree that the *Colegrove* case and its progeny were "contrary to the position we take here." Judge Martin, however, continued to press him on the Oklahoma case, pointing out that instead of simply dismissing the case, the Court had affirmed the decision below. "Now, that is significant," Martin said, "in view of their manifest statement that denial of certiorari does not mean that they approve of the opinion of the court below; but where they affirm the opinion of the court below, it would seem that that shows they agree with it." Chandler could only reply that "this question ought to be reviewed in the light of changed conditions and ought to be brought down to date and that it is the duty of this Court not to adhere to decisions that are not precisely in point as I see it, but to study this case from its beginning."[54]

Chandler repeatedly stressed the *Dyer* and *McGraw* cases and asserted that the political question concept was "nothing . . . but a red herring drawn across the road to prevent the prevailing of justice." He closed with an appeal to the court to recognize that the interpretation of the Fourteenth Amendment had changed significantly since *Colegrove* and that the case ought to be evaluated in that light. Pointing out that the legislature depends upon the people, Chandler declared that it "is the people whom we represent here, and it is the people to whom we seek to have justice done and great wrongs righted and intolerable conditions relieved. . . . I do not approve of all

[53] 352 U.S. 991 (1957).
[54] Arguments, pp. 36–39.

of the things in the Fourteenth Amendment and all of the things that have happened," Chandler concluded, "but I say this, that the Supreme Court by its unanimous decision in the Brown case, the school integration case, has changed the thrust of this whole question and has put the Colegrove case out of bounds . . . as an authority here because it has changed the approach to this question as to the duties of the Court in dealing with questions of this character."[55]

Hobart Atkins followed Chandler, again emphasizing that the federal courts were the last possible avenue of relief available for those disadvantaged by the Tennessee apportionment system and pointing out that four of the seven justices in *Colegrove* v. *Green* had agreed that there was jurisdiction.[56] Judge Miller questioned Atkins closely on the nature of the remedies available if the court should find it possessed jurisdiction. Miller pointed out that if the court declared the 1901 act invalid, then under the doctrine of the *Kidd* case there could not be a special session to reapportion, since the *Kidd* case had held that in such circumstances the *de facto* doctrine would not apply to the legislators. "The only remedy I can see that could be even thinkable," Miller said, "would be the suggestion that there be an election at large. Whether that could be reasoned out and worked out from a practical basis or not is another question."[57] Judge Martin again interrupted and even more strongly suggested that he felt the court was without jurisdiction to act. "It would be assuming too great a power for the courts of the United States, I think," Martin said. "I am using strong words, but it is because I feel it strongly. I think it would be the usurpation of power."[58]

Z. T. Osborn, following Atkins, argued that the jurisdictional issue was settled in *Smiley* v. *Holm* favorable to the plaintiffs and that, if the 1901 act were invalidated, the legislature could be elected at large. Osborn argued that just as the election of congressmen was not dependent upon state congressional apportionment acts, but could be held at large in their absence, so was the legislature not dependent upon an apportionment act, and, in the absence of a valid apportionment, the legislature could be elected at large.[59]

[55] *Ibid.*, pp. 46–47.
[56] *Ibid.*, pp. 47–50.
[57] *Ibid.*, p. 55.
[58] *Ibid.*, p. 63.
[59] *Ibid.*, pp. 68–83.

Solicitor General Humphreys, in rebuttal for the defendants, again stressed that the *Colegrove* case was against the court's assuming jurisdiction and pointed out that Walter Chandler had admitted that "it stands as a barrier to the relief that he prays, and asks Your Honors either to ignore it or to refine its [meaning] so that [he may] squeeze under it. . . . I submit," Humphreys said, "with all sincerity and due deference that it stands as a barrier because it defines that this Court will not take jurisdiction in cases of this character." Humphreys pointed out also that the *Kidd* case had been dismissed on the authority of the *Colegrove* case and that in the *Radford* case the Court had affirmed the opinion below dismissing the case upon the basis of the *Colegrove* and *Kidd* cases.[60]

Humphreys again emphasized in conclusion that the case raised political questions. He warned the court that if the federal courts held that legislative reapportionment violated the federal Constitution, it would not be "a tune which can be played only here," for all the states would "have to dance to it." All the states "have to dance to the opinion in Brown v. Topeka," he declared, "and it involved just one little school in one little state; and it resulted in a constitutional edict that all of us must bow to, and I say this with all respect: If you ever erected any such federal doctrine, it would eventually result in the total erosion of all state rights. It couldn't help it. It just couldn't help it."[61]

After Humphreys' summation, the court called for any further comments, and Osborn again emphasized the injustice of the apportionment system in Tennessee. He pointed out that remedy by revolution was still an option, since the Tennessee Constitution denounced the doctrine of passive resistance and implied a right of revolution,[62] "but we come to the last of the orderly processes to obtain relief." Judge Martin pointed out that all of the judges were Tennesseans, but that "when it comes to our jurisdiction as judges, we cannot let our desire for justice to force us to take over a power that we think would be a usurpation beyond that conferred upon us."[63] Walter Chandler again declared that, the *Colegrove* case notwithstanding, the

60 *Ibid.*, pp. 85–87.
61 *Ibid.*, pp. 95–96.
62 Osborn was referring to art. 1, § 1 and 2 of the Tennessee Constitution.
63 Arguments, pp. 101, 103.

"right in this matter is what we are trying to get at, the right which we are trying to have prevail here," and that the defendants "won't even deny that there is a great wrong." Judge Martin answered, "I think we have practically said from the bench here that we think the right is on your side, but we may not have the power to right that wrong."[64]

The oral argument had been quite discouraging to Chandler, Atkins, and Osborn. They had been unable to present their arguments in the orderly manner they had planned, and the comments of the judges appeared to foretell defeat. "It is inconceivable to me," one of them said, "that two judges like Martin and Boyd, who know the situation thoroughly, and whose people have suffered under it for sixty years, would be unwilling to try to find a remedy, at least to the extent of letting us present the case on the merits and go to the Supreme Court of the United States with a full record."[65]

On December 21, however, the court issued an opinion granting the motion to dismiss. The court in the course of its opinion admitted that the equal protection clause of the Fourteenth Amendment was violated by the failure of the Tennessee legislature to reapportion. "The inevitable result of this violation of the constitutional mandate is a gross inequality of legislative representation," the court said, "a debasement of voting rights of large numbers of citizens, and hence a denial of the equal protection of the laws guaranteed by the Fourteenth Amendment." The court also stated that the Tennessee legislature "is guilty of a clear violation of the state constitution and the rights of plaintiffs," and that "the evil is a serious one which should be corrected without further delay."[66] Having conceded this much to the plaintiffs, however, the court found that it could go no further, since "there is no doubt that the federal rule, as enunciated and applied by the Supreme Court, is that the federal courts, whether from a lack of jurisdiction or from the inappropriateness of the subject matter for judicial consideration, will not intervene in cases of this type to compel legislative reapportionment." The court also pointed out that the *Kidd* case, raising essentially the same questions, had been dismissed by the Supreme Court, and concluded that even if the court were to invalidate the 1901 apportionment act, it could not fashion

[64] *Ibid.*, p. 109.
[65] Letter, Chandler to Osborn, Dec. 2, 1959.
[66] *Baker* v. *Carr*, 179 F. Supp. 824 (M.D. Tenn. 1959), at 826–28.

68

an effective remedy for the situation.[67] The court therefore granted the motion to dismiss on the grounds of lack of jurisdiction and failure to state a cause of action.

Although the court granted the motion to dismiss, it also granted a motion allowing the intervening petition of Mayor West to be amended and supplemented.[68] The Advanced Planning Division of the Nashville Metropolitan Planning Commission had been set to work on statistical material indicating discrimination against the more populous counties, particularly in regard to the distribution of state aid, but had not been able to complete the compiling of this material before the original complaints had been filed in the federal court. The court's granting of the motion to supplement Mayor West's petition thus allowed the introduction of this material into the record, and the result was a record more complete and perhaps more compelling than it otherwise would have been. Although the granting of the motion to dismiss prevented a trial on the merits, which would have resulted in a fuller record, the material supplementing Mayor West's petition expanded the record beyond the bare legal motions involved. As Walter Chandler pointed out, not a "single case which has been argued against us has been presented to the Supreme Court on the merits and on the record after a full trial. Therefore, only one side of the question, to-wit, the cold, legal proposition, has been presented." The Advanced Planning Division material, however, extended the record in *Baker* v. *Carr* beyond the "cold, legal proposition," and, as Z. T. Osborn later said, "the difference between the Tennessee case and the cases that had gone before is to be found in the detailed preparation of the record and the . . . scope of the carefully documented attack upon the evil involved."[69]

Despite the disappointing loss in the district court, Chandler, Atkins, and Osborn agreed quickly that the case should be appealed. "After we had gone to the trouble to prepare the case so thoroughly," Chandler remarked, "it is shameful to have it disposed of so summarily, and we will drive a little harder before the United States Supreme Court."[70] And as the Tennessee attorneys prepared the

---

[67] *Ibid.*, at 825–28.
[68] B. v. C., Record, pp. 221–23.
[69] Z. T. Osborn, Statement of Mayor Ben West's participation in *Baker* v. *Carr*, Nov. 27, 1961.
[70] Letter, Chandler to Osborn, Dec. 26, 1959.

appeal of *Baker* v. *Carr*, events in other states gave hope for legislative apportionment litigation.

On the state court level, the first significant breakthrough in apportionment litigation came in New Jersey in June, 1960. The New Jersey courts had long held that they possessed the power to invalidate apportionment acts,[71] but in 1951 the legislature failed to reapportion. Asbury Park Press, Inc., located in Monmouth County, filed a suit challenging the validity of the 1941 apportionment act and seeking an injunction against the holding of elections under it. The case was dismissed in the lower court, but an appeal was taken to the New Jersey Supreme Court.

In an opinion announced in *Asbury Park Press* v. *Woolley*[72] on June 6, 1960, the New Jersey Supreme Court rejected the argument that the case involved a political question, and held that the right to equal suffrage and equal representation, guaranteed by the state constitution and by the equal protection clause of the Fourteenth Amendment, could not be denied either by legislative action or inaction. "Inaction," the court said, "which causes an apportionment act to have unequal and arbitrary effects throughout the State is just as much a denial of equality as if a positive statute had been passed to accomplish the result."[73] Distinguishing the *Colegrove* case, the court held that if "by reason of passage of time and changing conditions the apportionment statute no longer serves its original purpose of securing to the voter the full constitutional value of his franchise, and the legislative branch fails to take appropriate restorative action, the doors of the courts must be open to him. . . ."[74]

Citing the *McGraw* case, the court held, however, that it would withhold a declaration on the validity of the 1941 act and any remedy it might enforce until the legislature should have time to act. "Under the circumstances, it is to be presumed that the Legislature contemplates the performance of its constitutional duty to reapportion," the court said, but it proceeded to discuss possible remedies if the legislature failed to act, and suggested to the plaintiffs the type of materials which should be submitted if legislative inaction forced the case to be

---

[71] See *State* v. *Wrightson*, 56 N.J.L. 126 (1893); *Smith* v. *Baker*, 73 N.J.L. 328 (1906); *Botti* v. *McGovern*, 97 N.J.L. 353 (1922).

[72] 33 N.J. 1 (1960).

[73] *Ibid.*, at 11.

[74] *Ibid.*, at 14.

renewed. The court clearly indicated that it was not engaging in mere hollow threats.[75] Thus for the first time a state supreme court had shown its willingness to go beyond invalidating an apportionment act to effecting a positive remedy in the event of the legislature's failure to act.

In Michigan, in contrast to New Jersey, the state supreme court dismissed a suit brought by August Scholle, president of the Michigan AFL-CIO, and joined by the Detroit Americans for Democratic Action and the Detroit Civil Liberties Union as *amici curiae*. The suit challenged the apportionment of the Michigan Senate on equal protection grounds. The dismissal of *Scholle* v. *Secretary of State*[76] by a badly divided court, however, was appealed to the United States Supreme Court, nearly simultaneously with the Tennessee case.

At the same time, another significant case from Alabama was moving up the federal appellate ladder. In July, 1957, the Alabama legislature resolved to deal with the possibility that in Tuskegee, where Negroes outnumbered whites about four to one, Negro voter registration might soon also surpass white registration. Senator Sam Engelhardt, Jr., had long advocated gerrymandering as a method of dealing with Negro voting, particularly since he believed this method would not be susceptible to successful challenge in the courts. Following Engelhardt's suggestion, the legislature passed an act changing the boundaries of the city of Tuskegee from a square shape to a twenty-eight-sided figure "resembling a stylized sea horse." This new boundary excluded from the city all but four or five of the previous four hundred Negro voters in the city.[77]

The Tuskegee boundary legislation was soon challenged in the federal courts by Tuskegee Negroes in *Gomillion* v. *Lightfoot* on the grounds that it deprived them of the equal protection of the laws guaranteed by the Fourteenth Amendment and abridged the right to vote on the basis of race or color in violation of the Fifteenth Amendment. The Negroes, however, lost the case in both the district court and the court of appeals[78] on the grounds that the states traditionally have possessed the power to create, alter, or abolish municipal cor-

[75] *Ibid.*, at 21.
[76] 360 Mich. 1 (1960).
[77] Bernard Taper, *Gomillion versus Lightfoot* (New York: McGraw-Hill, 1962), pp. 11–17.
[78] *Gomillion* v. *Lightfoot*, 167 F. Supp. 405 (M.D. Ala. 1958); 270 F.2d 594 (Fifth Cir. 1959).

porations and that such power is applied as a political function.[79] Judge Wisdom, concurring in the court of appeals, emphasized the political question doctrine as a reason for the federal courts' refusal to intervene, relying particularly on the *Colegrove* and *South* v. *Peters*[80] cases. "I can see no difference between depriving negroes of the right to vote in municipal elections in Tuskegee," Judge Wisdom said, "and not counting at their full value votes cast in certain districts in Illinois in a congressional election or votes cast in certain counties in Georgia in a state election."[81]

The *Gomillion* case was appealed to the Supreme Court, and the Court granted certiorari on March 21, 1960,[82] as preparations for the appeal of *Baker* v. *Carr* were in progress. An ideal "bridging case"[83] was thus assured of a hearing before the Court just as the Tennessee case was appealed. The *Gomillion* case was ideal in that it raised questions that tended to merge the problem of apportionment with the question of racial discrimination in voting. It appeared that the Court would be forced to choose between precedents such as the white primary cases, in which it had rigorously enforced a policy of nondiscrimination in voting, and the apportionment precedents, in which it had maintained a policy of judicial nonintervention. This was particularly true since the *Gomillion* case appeared to raise a more serious equal protection question than a Fifteenth Amendment question, for the Negroes who had been "removed" from Tuskegee by the gerrymander still had the right to vote in county elections. It appeared, therefore, that the gerrymander could more logically be attacked as an attempt to segregate on the basis of race, invalid under the equal protection clause of the Fourteenth Amendment, than as a denial of the right to vote under the Fifteenth Amendment. And if the Court struck down the gerrymander as a denial of equal protection, then it might have some difficulty, when faced with the Tennessee case, in holding that geographical discrimination through districting was valid after having invalidated racial discrimination.[84]

[79] 270 F.2d 594, at 598.
[80] 339 U.S. 276 (1950).
[81] 270 F.2d, at 612.
[82] 362 U.S. 916.
[83] See Samuel Krislov, *The Supreme Court in the Political Process* (New York: Macmillan, 1965), p. 45.
[84] The Court, of course, ultimately held that the Tuskegee gerrymander violated the Fifteenth Amendment, not the equal protection clause of the Four-

Despite the promise of the *Gomillion* case, however, the attorneys in *Baker* v. *Carr* knew it would be difficult to overcome the Court's traditional policy of rejecting cases challenging state apportionment systems. The Court appeared to be continuing this policy when, in December, 1959, just a few weeks before the loss of the Tennessee case in the district court, it affirmed the decision of an Indiana district court to dismiss a suit challenging a state income tax on the grounds that it was passed by a malapportioned legislature.[85] During the winter and early spring of 1960, the attorneys in the Tennessee case labored on a jurisdictional statement that would convince the Court to alter this policy, well aware that all previous cases had been lost at this stage and that the approach to the Court would perhaps be the most crucial stage in the entire litigation.

---

teenth Amendment, thus avoiding the problem of the political question to a certain extent. In my discussion of the *Gomillion* case here, however, I am stating the case as it was perceived by the litigants in the Tennessee case, and I have not intended to present an exhaustive analysis of the case. The latter has been done very well by Professor Jo Desha Lucas in "Dragon in the Thicket: A Perusal of Gomillion v. Lightfoot," in Phillip B. Kurland (ed.), 1961 *Supreme Court Review* (Chicago: University of Chicago Press, 1961), p. 194.

[85] *Matthews* v. *Handley*, 361 U.S. 127 (Dec. 7, 1959); the case below is unreported.

CHAPTER IV

THE APPEAL

THE PRACTICE OF LAW before the United States Supreme Court has altered considerably since the nineteenth century. During much of the nineteenth century a small group of lawyers composing the Supreme Court Bar specialized in practice before the Court and participated in most of the important cases appealed to the Court. In recent times, however, it has become more common for a lawyer who has litigated a case in the lower state or federal courts to carry an appeal to the Supreme Court himself. This means that litigants before the Court are often handicapped by a lack of familiarity with the Court's customs and procedures. The disadvantage is even greater when the federal government is a party to the litigation, since the solicitor general of the United States, who specializes in representing the government before the Court, possesses an expertise in Supreme Court litigation which a lawyer inexperienced in Supreme Court practice cannot hope to match.[1]

In the appeal of *Baker* v. *Carr* to the Supreme Court, however, Mayor Ben West of Nashville believed that a Washington attorney familiar with Supreme Court practice should be retained to insure the best chance of success. After consulting with the American Municipal Association, of which he had been president in 1957–58, West decided in early 1960 to retain Charles S. Rhyne of the Washington firm of Rhyne & Rhyne to participate in the appeal to the Court.

Mayor West's retention of Rhyne brought about a shift in the dominant elements in the litigating coalition supporting *Baker* v. *Carr*. The impetus for the suit in the district court had come from Walter Chandler, who had been responsible for drafting the original

---

[1] Samuel Krislov, *The Supreme Court in the Political Process* (New York: Macmillan, 1965) pp. 52–53.

complaint and who had continued to exert strong leadership in planning strategy at the district court level. With Mayor West's commitment of the technical services of the Advanced Planning Division of the Nashville Metropolitan Planning Commission to the case and particularly with his retention of Rhyne to handle the case before the Supreme Court, the Nashville branch of the coalition became dominant. The crucial legal work on the jurisdictional statement, upon which the case would be won or lost in the Supreme Court, was now primarily the responsibility of Rhyne. Memphis and Shelby County remained second only to Nashville in the financial support of the litigation; Knoxville and Chattanooga contributed little financially, except to defray the expense of printing the record for the appeal.[2]

Rhyne had long been prominent in the activities of the American Bar Association; in 1952, for instance, he introduced a resolution that was passed in the ABA House of Delegates commending the McCarthy subcommittee for "conducting its inquiry in the exposition [*sic*] of Communist activities in a dignified lawyerlike way, with full recognition of all of the constitutional rights of those they call before them."[3] Rhyne served as president of the ABA in 1957–58, and was known for his establishment of Law Day, U.S.A., and the World Peace Through Law program for which he received the Grotius Peace Prize in 1958. He had served for many years as the general counsel of the National Institute of Municipal Law Officers and had been practicing law in Washington since 1937. He considered himself a Democrat until 1952, when he became an independent, and in 1960 he supported for President his long-time friend and classmate at Duke Law School, Richard Nixon.[4]

Rhyne's knowledge of federal procedure and Supreme Court practice added significantly to the fund of legal talent available in the appeal of the Tennessee case. After he had been retained by Mayor West, Rhyne and the members of his firm examined in the Supreme

[2] The foregoing paragraph is based upon my review of the correspondence of the Tennessee counsel in the litigation as well as personal discussions with them.

[3] Quoted in John R. Schmidhauser, *The Supreme Court: Its Politics, Personalities and Procedures* (New York: Holt, Rinehart and Winston, 1961), p. 78.

[4] 18 *Congressional Quarterly* 1670, 1672 (1960). Many newspaper articles in 1969 mentioned Rhyne as a likely nominee for chief justice of the U.S. Supreme Court.

Court library every prior apportionment case that had been appealed to the Court so that they might avoid the mistakes of the previous appellants.[5] Rhyne and his associates ultimately spent thirteen hundred hours in diligent preparations from February, 1960, to the first argument of the case in April, 1961.[6] "I believe we presented the best and most carefully written presentation yet filed in such a case on why the Court should hear the case and grant relief," Rhyne said later. "The basic error made in the other cases was lack of appreciation of the very technical phases of federal jurisdiction. In the other cases they dwelt too much on local angles and such angles do not move the Supreme Court."[7]

Unexpected aid in the appeal of *Baker* v. *Carr* appeared to be in the offing soon after the loss in the district court. The U. S. solicitor general ordered that a copy of the record in the case be sent to Washington for his examination. The solicitor general represents the federal government before the Supreme Court, but in Supreme Court cases to which the government is not a party he may on his own motion participate as *amicus curiae* by filing a brief and arguing orally before the Court. Because the solicitor general is held in high esteem by the Court and is expert in Supreme Court practice, his participation in nongovernment litigation before the Court is highly advantageous to the party he supports and is therefore much sought after. The Justice Department and the solicitor general may therefore experience considerable pressure to enter cases raising policy issues of major public importance.[8]

In 1952, Solicitor General Philip Perlman had intervened as *amicus*

[5] Letter, Charles Rhyne to Walter Chandler, Sept. 2, 1961.

[6] Letter, Rhyne to Z. T. Osborn, April 27, 1961.

[7] Letter, Rhyne to Chandler, Sept. 2, 1961.

[8] Good brief discussions of the solicitor general's role in Supreme Court litigation may be found in Herbert Jacob, *Justice in America* (Boston: Little, Brown and Co., 1965), pp. 71–73; Samuel Krislov, *Supreme Court in Political Process*, pp. 49–50; Robert L. Stern, "The Solicitor General's Office and Administrative Agency Litigation," *American Bar Association Journal*, Vol. 46 (Feb., 1960), pp. 154–58, 217–18. Although the decision to intervene as *amicus curiae* is primarily the responsibility of the solicitor general, in important political cases the decision may involve not only the solicitor general but also the attorney general and the President himself. See Krislov, *Supreme Court in Political Process*, p. 50; for a description of the kinds of pressure brought to bear on the Justice Department to intervene in the restrictive covenant cases, see Clement E. Vose, *Caucasians Only* (Berkeley: University of California Press, 1959), pp. 168–74. For an example of the Justice Department refusing to intervene in *Smith* v. *Allwright*, 321 U.S. 649 (1944), despite pressure from the NAACP,

curiae in *Cox* v. *Peters*,[9] one of the perennial challenges of the Georgia county unit system, but no solicitor general had intervened in any of the challenges to state legislative apportionment systems. Solicitor General J. Lee Rankin's interest in *Baker* v. *Carr*, therefore, understandably aroused considerable enthusiasm among the Tennessee attorneys. "It is rather significant to me that the Solicitor General of the United States would be interested in our case," Walter Chandler said. "Let us hope and pray that the United States Supreme Court will hear one of the apportionment cases or consolidate them all, and that ours will be among those to be considered. This news seems to me almost too good to be true."[10]

Once alert to the possibility of the solicitor general's support, the Tennesseans attempted to gain access to the Department of Justice in order to convince officials of the rightness of their cause and the political advantages to the Republican party, in view of the forthcoming presidential election, if the administration participated in an apportionment case. Their most direct access was through Charles Rhyne, for when Z. T. Osborn informed Rhyne that the solicitor general had ordered up the record in the case, Rhyne immediately telephoned Rankin "and found him to be thoroughly familiar with the case pleaded and argued by us and apparently in the process of determining which of several reapportionment cases to recommend for argument and review by the Supreme Court."

Osborn pointed out that "a national election is in the offing and a voting right case presents the administration with a good opportunity to identify itself with the popular rights of the people, particularly if a voting right case can be found which involves something more than the Negro question." *Baker* v. *Carr*, he continued, might be attractive to the administration because it "involves a flagrant abuse of the rights protected by the Fourteenth Amendment and a debasement of the votes of a geographical class of persons. It also involves the rights of city dwellers with which the Republican Party has had less than the 'edge.' "[11]

In bringing these points to the attention of the Justice Department,

---

relayed through President Roosevelt, see Francis Biddle, *In Brief Authority* (Garden City: Doubleday and Co., 1962), p. 187.
[9] 342 U.S. 936 (1952).
[10] Letter, Chandler to Osborn, Feb. 17, 1960.
[11] Letter, Osborn to Chandler, Feb. 12, 1960.

the litigating coalition found an advantage in being bipartisan, since suggestions coming from Tennessee Republican sources were likely to be better received. Accordingly, Osborn remarked to Hobart Atkins, who had been thinking along the same lines, that Attorney General William G. Rogers himself seemed to be interested in the case and that Atkins and Guy Smith could be of great service if they could persuade Republican Congressman B. Carroll Reece to point out to the attorney general the merits of the Tennessee case compared to other reapportionment cases on their way to the Supreme Court. "We do indeed have the best of all the reapportionment cases so far as I can tell," Osborn continued. "For one thing, our case is plainly to be distinguished from Colegrove vs. Green and for another, we do have the tax matters pretty well pleaded and substantiated by exhibits due to the good work done by the City of Nashville Advanced Planning Division."[12] Atkins discussed the matter with both Smith and Congressman Reece and reported that "Mr. Reece is very enthusiastic about it and thinks we have a good opportunity of having our case heard before the Supreme Court. He suggested the appeal be handled expeditiously from this end."[13]

The Tennesseans were further encouraged when, after the solicitor general entered the *Gomillion* case as *amicus curiae*, the Court granted certiorari in that case, which challenged the Tuskegee gerrymander, on March 21. Commenting on the decision in the Tuskegee case in the court of appeals, Chandler noted that "the long opinions of the different judges will remind you of *Colegrove* v. *Green*, which is under fire again, but the important point is that the United States Supreme Court has accepted jurisdiction of this case, which means to me that the doctrine of *Colegrove* v. *Green* and similar cases is to be reversed." Chandler suggested that Charles Rhyne call "the attention of the Solicitor General to the action of the Supreme Court in the *Gomillion* case, indicating dissatisfaction with the doctrine of *Colegrove* v. *Green*. The *Gomillion* case abundantly justifies the Supreme Court taking jurisdiction of our case."[14] Rhyne, in turn, reported to the Tennesseans that he was "very encouraged about the favorable effect this will have on *Baker* v. *Carr*."[15]

12 Letter, Osborn to Hobart Atkins, Feb. 23, 1960.
13 Letter, Atkins to Chandler, March 12, 1960.
14 Letter, Chandler to Osborn, March 25, 1960.
15 Letter, Rhyne to Osborn, March 29, 1960.

78

Meanwhile work continued on the jurisdictional statement in the Tennessee case. On May 20, after almost four months of drafting, revising, and consulting, Rhyne, Osborn, and Harris Gilbert, the Nashville city attorney, met in Washington to complete the final draft. The crucial jurisdictional statement and record were finally filed with the Supreme Court on June 1.[16]

The objective of the appellants in their jurisdictional statement was to overcome the Court's demonstrated reluctance to hear reapportionment cases. It was therefore essential to distinguish the substantive issues involved in the Tennessee case from *Colegrove* v. *Green* and its progeny and to demonstrate the uniqueness of the issues before the Court in *Baker* v. *Carr*, if the case were to survive beyond this crucial, albeit preliminary, stage. The appellants alleged that a "purposeful and systematic plan to discriminate against a geographic class of persons in their voting rights now exists in Tennessee by the continued enforcement of the statute here challenged." The apportionment system in Tennessee violated the equal protection of the laws guaranteed by the Fourteenth Amendment, they argued, and the discriminatory allocation of state tax funds violated both equal protection and due process. Relying on the *Gomillion* case, the appellants contended that there was no "substantive difference" between that case and the Tennessee case, since geographic and racial discrimination were "equally onerous" and an unequal voice in elections and a complete denial of the right to vote were equally offensive under the Constitution.[17]

The appellants pointed out that a majority of the justices in *Colegrove* v. *Green* had held that jurisdiction existed and the Court had also asserted jurisdiction in the similar cases of *MacDougall* v. *Green* and *South* v. *Peters*. As for remedies, the appellants brought the *Dyer* and *McGraw* cases to the Court's attention to bolster the argument that legislatures would reapportion after a federal court asserted jurisdiction. Moreover, they suggested that if the legislature in Tennessee failed to act under such circumstances, the district court could either enjoin further elections under the invalid apportionment act or declare an election at large.[18]

The heart of the appellants' argument was the contention that the issues in the Tennessee case were unique and the case was therefore

[16] Letter, Osborn to Chandler, June 1, 1960.
[17] Jurisdictional Statement, *Baker* v. *Carr*, Oct. 1961 Term, pp. 6–13.
[18] *Ibid.*, pp. 19–25.

distinguishable from similar cases that the Court had refused to hear in the past. The appellants first argued that their case was unique because of the total lack of any remedies in Tennessee other than federal judicial relief: the state supreme court had refused to act, there was no initiative and referendum in the state, and state constitutional conventions could not afford relief because their authorization and make-up depended on the legislature. In prior cases dismissed by the Court, the appellants argued, one or another alternative remedy had been available to the parties seeking federal judicial relief, and *Baker* v. *Carr* was therefore distinguishable on this ground.[19]

Second, the appellants put forward an ingenious argument by which they sought to distinguish the Tennessee case from *Colegrove* and its progeny regarding the equal protection clause of the Fourteenth Amendment. They conceded that the states possessed the power to define, within federal constitutional limits, the classes of persons possessing the right to vote. But, they argued, if a state declared a policy of equal voting rights, as did Tennessee in its constitution in regard to apportionment, then a denial of equal voting rights by the state would be a violation of the equal protection clause. Thus, as the appellants stated it, they were not "charging inequality of representation under the Fourteenth Amendment," but were claiming "equality in voting rights as provided by the Constitution of Tennessee, and charge that the legislative attempt (successful so far) to deny that equality results in a violation of the equal protection of the laws." This distinction is important, they said, because it "reflects the manner in which the Fourteenth Amendment operates. It does not in itself decree equality of voting rights. It says that if a state policy is to afford equal voting rights (expressed here by the people of Tennessee in their organic law), the attempt by state officers, under color of law, to deny such equality to some of the citizens is a denial of equal protection."[20]

This argument possessed the advantage of stressing the uniqueness of the Tennessee case and allowing the appellants to argue that none of the previously dismissed cases, including *Colegrove*, had involved

[19] *Ibid.*, pp. 17–18.
[20] Reply to Appellees Statement in Opposition and Motion to Dismiss, *Baker* v. *Carr*, Oct. 1961 Term; see also Jurisdictional Statement, pp. 14–16. This argument is contained in both of the above, but since it is most succinctly stated in the Reply, I have drawn the quotation from it.

a statutory or organic command of equal representation as was contained in the Tennessee Constitution. The argument, if accepted, also would have allowed the Court to confine its ruling strictly to those situations and those states where state law required substantially equal population apportionment; the Court could thus stay among the bushes and not be lost among the trees of the political thicket. Finally, the argument suggested that the relief be measured by the Tennessee apportionment provisions, which promised a greater degree of equality of representation in terms of population than could be expected at this point from the Fourteenth Amendment.

The disadvantage of the argument was that it was of doubtful validity and might have endangered the case. In *Nashville, C. & St. L. Ry. Co.* v. *Browning*,[21] a case also arising from Tennessee and cited against the appellants' argument by the Tennessee attorney general, the Court had rejected a similar claim. In that case the railroad had contended that the assessment of the property of public service corporations at a higher rate than other property violated the Tennessee Constitution's requirement of uniformity of taxation and thereby also the equal protection clause of the Fourteenth Amendment. The railroad had thus argued, as did the appellants in *Baker* v. *Carr*, that deviation from a state constitutional norm of equality or uniformity was simultaneously a violation of the equality required by the Fourteenth Amendment. Justice Frankfurter, writing for a unanimous Court, had rejected the argument, saying that the state standards of uniformity in taxation "were not to be insinuated into that meritorious conception of equality which alone the Equal Protection Clause was designed to assure."[22] This lack of merit in the appellants' argument on the equal protection issue might have resulted in the loss of the case, since, as one scholar has noted, the Court could have affirmed the decision of the district court upon finding the appellants' equal protection contentions without merit, and avoided passing upon the merits of an argument based solely on equal protection, uncomplicated by any question of state apportionment standards.[23]

The appellants were joined in urging the Court to hear *Baker* v.

---

[21] 310 U.S. 362 (1940).

[22] *Ibid.*, at 368.

[23] Phil C. Neal, "*Baker* v. *Carr*: Politics in Search of Law," 1962 *Supreme Court Review* (Chicago: University of Chicago Press, 1962), p. 260.

Carr by an *amicus curiae* brief filed by the National Institute of Municipal Law Officers, an organization representing the municipal law officers of over one thousand municipalities. Charles Rhyne was general counsel of this organization. In addition to noting that malapportionment of state legislatures forced "the municipality of 1960 to function in a horse and buggy environment where there is little political recognition of the heavy demands of an urban population,"[24] the NIMLO brief also recited the extensive failure of state legislatures to reapportion and alleged that discrimination against urban areas in the distribution of state tax funds resulted. The brief also called the Court's attention to the *Asbury Park Press* case[25] in which the New Jersey Supreme Court had assumed jurisdiction in an apportionment case.

The Tennessee attorney general's opposing statement and motion to dismiss challenged the heart of the appellants' argument by denying that legislative apportionment involved the right to vote. Pointing out that all votes were counted in Tennessee elections, the attorney general argued that the white primary cases were inapposite and "in no wise support the appellants' premise that inequality of legislative representation is an abridgement of the right to vote guaranteed by the Fourteenth Amendment." The appellants were in reality, he said, "raising a question under the Guaranty Clause which the Court had uniformly held to be unenforceable in the federal courts since *Luther* v. *Borden*." The attorney general contended that the Court has never held that the Fourteenth Amendment required equality of representation in state legislatures. Relying on *Colegrove* and its progeny, he demonstrated that the federal courts had uniformly declined to entertain suits raising such issues, including the *Kidd* case, which had raised the same issues as *Baker* v. *Carr* but which had been dismissed by the Court.[26]

In their jurisdictional arguments, the appellants had contended that the Congress, by providing in the 1957 Civil Rights Act that the federal courts could give equitable and other relief for the protection of civil rights, "including the right to vote,"[27] had reinforced and re-emphasized the duty of the federal courts to protect the right to

[24] Brief *Amicus Curiae* of the National Institute of Municipal Law Officers, *Baker* v. *Carr*, p. 2.
[25] *Asbury Park Press, Inc.* v. *Woolley*, 33 N.J. 1 (1960).
[26] Statement of Opposition and Motion to Dismiss, *Baker* v. *Carr*, pp. 4–8.
[27] 28 U.S.C. 1343 (4).

vote.[28] The attorney general attempted to refute this contention by citing the legislative history of the act, which, he argued, demonstrated that Congress did not consider apportionment to be in the area of civil rights and had not included apportionment within the meaning of the term "right to vote."[29]

"Clearly, we think, the decisions of this Court declare the problem of reapportionment to be a political question which should be addressed to the people of Tennessee and their General Assembly," the attorney general concluded. "The Constitution of Tennessee belongs to its people. They are capable of determining political and governmental issues arising in connection with their state government. They should be permitted to resolve the question of reapportionment in their own way. As this Court said in *Colegrove v. Green*, 'the remedy for unfairness in districting is to secure State legislatures that will apportion properly.' "[30]

Only a few days after the appellants filed their jurisdictional statement, the supreme courts of Michigan and New Jersey announced their decisions in the apportionment cases that had been pending before them,[31] and again the Tennesseans were encouraged. Osborn drew Rhyne's attention to the cases, and suggested that "these developments should be called to the attention of the Solicitor General. In light of his previous interest, these cases may serve to commit him to a course of action in our behalf."[32] Rhyne replied, "We certainly will bring the Michigan and New Jersey decisions to the attention of the Solicitor General who already has our Jurisdictional Statement." The statement "appears to have been very timely filed with the Supreme Court," he continued, "and I feel that all the popular interest now being generated in regard to re-apportionment is going to aid us considerably."[33]

The solicitor general, however, continued to be noncommittal, and as the summer months slipped by, the attention of the country and the litigants in *Baker v. Carr* was increasingly diverted by the heat of the presidential campaign. Charles Rhyne took a prominent

---

[28] Jurisdictional Statement, *Baker v. Carr*, p. 22.
[29] Statement of Opposition and Motion to Dismiss, *Baker v. Carr*, pp. 9–13.
[30] *Ibid.*, p. 25.
[31] *Scholle v. Secretary of State*, 360 Mich. 1 (1960); *Asbury Park Press, Inc. v. Woolley*, 33 N.J. 1 (1960).
[32] Letter, Osborn to Rhyne, June 13, 1960.
[33] Letter, Rhyne to Osborn, June 15, 1960.

part in the Nixon campaign as national chairman of the Volunteers for Nixon–Lodge.[34] To Osborn, at least, it appeared that Rhyne's prominence in the campaign might be useful to the case, and he pointed out to Rhyne that it "comes to my selfish and eager mind that the role you are to play in the campaign should somehow serve to further impress the Solicitor General with the fact that the Tennessee Reapportionment case is, indeed, unique and certainly distinguishable from Colegrove v. Green." Osborn reminded Rhyne to "keep up your contacts" and urged him to talk "from time to time . . . about the rights that majorities ought to have in any democracy which is to long survive."[35]

The hard-fought campaign wore on without any public announcement from the Justice Department about the case. The candidacy of John F. Kennedy, however, could reasonably be interpreted as portending, should he win, a favorable response from the Justice Department. In 1958, Kennedy had denounced the pervasive discrimination against the urban areas under the existing apportionment systems as "the Shame of the States," and had expressed the hope that, given the apparent impossibility of judicial relief, "an aroused public, a vigorous press, and the force of the democratic tradition will create an irresistible demand for justice to the second-class citizens of the city and its suburbs."[36] The Kennedy campaign forces were also aware that the 1960 campaign would be won or lost for the Democrats in the large urban states of the nation, and their most strenuous efforts were therefore concentrated on winning a majority of the metropolitan vote.[37] Kennedy's awareness of the underrepresentation of the urban areas, combined with the political necessities of the 1960 campaign, encouraged the belief that if John Kennedy were elected in 1960 the Department of Justice might be more sensitive to the cause of reapportionment.

On October 18 and 19, in the midst of the campaign, *Gomillion* v. *Lightfoot* was argued before the Supreme Court. A map depicting

[34] 18 *Congressional Quarterly* 1670, 1672 (1960).

[35] Letter, Osborn to Rhyne, Sept. 2, 1960.

[36] John F. Kennedy, "The Shame of the States," *The New York Times Magazine*, May 18, 1958, pp. 12, 40.

[37] Theodore H. White, *The Making of the President 1960* (New York: Atheneum Publishers, 1961), p. 353; Kennedy concentrated on the suburbs of the northern metropolitan areas particularly, where the great expansion of the urban population had occurred.

the gerrymander was brought into the courtroom, and arguments began. Robert L. Carter, the general counsel for the NAACP, opened with the statement that the position of the appellants was simple. "This is purely a case of racial discrimination. The purpose of this legislation . . . was discriminatory. In a manner both callous and deliberate, the state has denied the petitioners their rights solely because they are Negroes." Obviously, Carter said, "Alabama could not openly disfranchise Negroes without violating the Constitution. If it had passed a law that had openly denied Negroes, as such, the right to vote in Tuskegee—or the right to live in Tuskegee—there is little question but that this court would strike that law down as unconstitutional. We contend that the same principle applies when the state does these things covertly. . . ."

When Carter resumed his argument the following day, however, Justice Black quickly asked, "Well, what do you do about Colegrove? Are you asking us to overrule Colegrove?" Carter answered that he was not asking the Court to overrule *Colegrove*, since he rested his case on the fact that racial discrimination in voting was the central issue, but that if the Court found that the *Colegrove* case was a barrier to relief, then it should be overruled. Justice Frankfurter appeared to be more than willing to aid Carter in bypassing the *Colegrove* problem, and through his questioning elicited replies from Carter indicating that the Tuskegee gerrymander was a clear instance of racial discrimination in voting under the Fifteenth Amendment. Assistant Solicitor General Philip Elman, in presenting the government's argument as *amicus curiae*, was also closely questioned. Justice Whittaker pointed out that the Negroes had not been deprived of the right to vote, since they could still vote in the county, and that there was no constitutional provision guaranteeing persons the right to vote in a municipality. Elman replied that the existence of a racial boundary line establishing apartheid was the basic constitutional objection in the case. "I find it inconceivable," he said, "that in the year 1960 any defense of a law establishing a ghetto in the United States could be seriously asserted in this Court."

The counsel for Alabama was James J. Carter, who re-emphasized the legal grounds upon which the state had won the case in the courts below. He pressed the Court with the rule that traditionally the states had possessed the power to alter or abolish the boundaries of municipal corporations without hindrance from the federal courts and also the general rule that the Court would not inquire into the motives of a legislature in passing a particular statute. "You said motive can't be inquired into. Would you say that results can be inquired into?" Chief Justice Warren asked. The Alabama counsel responded by citing the *Colegrove* case and arguing that this "is about as highly political a thing as we can get into—local boundaries," and warned the Court that it would be involved in politics if it attempted to inquire into how and why local boundaries were drawn.[38]

Commenting on the arguments later, Philip Elman pointed out that Frankfurter, "who we thought about with trepidation as we prepared the case, couldn't have been gentler." The sharpest questions had come from Black and Douglas, who, Elman thought, might have been trying to force the case to be perceived as an attack on the *Colegrove* case and the whole doctrine of political questions. But, Elman said inconclusively, "I don't know what they were driving at."[39]

The attorneys in *Baker* v. *Carr* also continued to speculate about the *Gomillion* case and the effect it would have on their case. Osborn noted the arguments in the *Gomillion* case and asked Rhyne if there was anything further they should do in their own case. "Should we remind the Court," Osborn asked, "that the issue in [*Baker* v. *Carr*] is more basic than and actually contains the issue accepted for argument in the Tuskegee case?" Osborn also wondered why the Court had taken no action in the Tennessee case and whether it "will be docketed for argument during the present Term, or whether our case still hangs in the balance and may be the subject of summary dismissal."[40]

The Court had not yet given its answer to Osborn's questions when, on November 8, John F. Kennedy won the presidency by a razor-thin margin of the popular votes. "Knowing how much time and the fine effort you put into the recent national election, and having myself sat with many a loser, I offer my sympathy and congratulations on a job magnificently well done by your particular part of the team," Osborn wrote Rhyne. "You know, of course," he added "that Tennessee went Republican beyond the vote given to President Eisen-

[38] The foregoing paragraphs on the *Gomillion* case are drawn from Bernard Taper's excellent book, *Gomillion versus Lightfoot* (New York: McGraw-Hill, 1963), pp. 83–106.

[39] *Ibid.*, p. 108.

[40] Letter, Osborn to Rhyne, Nov. 9, 1960.

hower, and this is a real compliment to all of you, although my friends and I opposed you mightily."[41]

Six days after the election, the Supreme Court announced its decision in the *Gomillion* case,[42] but the results were somewhat disappointing to the attorneys in the Tennessee case. The majority opinion by Justice Frankfurter invalidated the Tuskegee gerrymander under the Fifteenth Amendment but carefully skirted the political question issue. Frankfurter disposed of the argument that the states have unlimited authority over the boundaries of their political subdivisions by demonstrating that "the Court has never acknowledged that the States have power to do as they will with municipal corporations regardless of the consequences." Legislative control of municipalities, Frankfurter said, "lies within the scope of relevant limitations imposed by the United States Constitution."[43]

Frankfurter also rejected the state's contention that the Court could not intrude under the doctrine of the *Colegrove* case. He pointed out that in the *Colegrove* case the appellants complained of a "dilution of the strength of their votes as a result of legislative inaction," whereas in the *Gomillion* case the petitioners complained that they had been deprived of their votes through legislative action. "When a legislature thus singles out a readily isolated segment of a racial minority for special discriminatory treatment, it violates the Fifteenth Amendment," Frankfurter said. "In no case involving unequal weight in voting distribution that has come before this Court did the decision sanction a differentiation on racial lines whereby approval was given to unequivocal withdrawal of the vote solely from colored citizens. Apart from all else, these considerations lift this controversy out of the so-called 'political' arena and into the conventional sphere of constitutional litigation." Although the Tuskegee gerrymander was in form simply an act redefining the boundaries of the city, Frankfurter concluded, "if the allegations are established, the inescapable human effect of this essay in geometry and geography is to despoil colored citizens, and only colored citizens, of their theretofore enjoyed voting rights. That was not Colegrove v. Green."[44]

Justice Douglas concurred, but noted his adherence to his dissents

[41] *Ibid.*
[42] *Gomillion* v. *Lightfoot*, 364 U.S. 339 (1960).
[43] *Ibid.*, at 344–45.
[44] *Ibid.*, at 346–47.

in *Colegrove* v. *Green* and *South* v. *Peters*, indicating that, if necessary, he remained prepared to discard the political question doctrine
of the *Colegrove* case.[45] Justice Whittaker concurred also, stating his
belief that the Tuskegee gerrymander had not deprived Negroes of
the right to vote under the Fifteenth Amendment, since they could
still vote in the county, but that the gerrymander had instead unlaw-
fully segregated citizens by race, in violation of the equal protection
clause of the Fourteenth Amendment. He also noted that the case
could be decided on the basis of the equal protection clause and still
not involve, as *Brown* v. *Board of Education*[46] had not involved, "the
Colegrove problem."[47]

The counsel in *Baker* v. *Carr* had hoped the *Gomillion* case would
force the Court to face the political question issue squarely, and they
were disappointed when the Court carefully skirted it. "We believe
that action by the Supreme Court in our case has been delayed,"
Rhyne wrote Osborn, "because of the joint influence of the national
elections and the Tuskegee case. With the elections now past and the
decision rendered yesterday . . . in *Gomillion* v. *Lightfoot* . . . we expect a decision in *Baker* v. *Carr* within a week or two." The Tuskegee
case did not shed much light on the Tennessee case, Rhyne continued,
but Justice Frankfurter always insisted "that each case before the
Court must be evaluated and considered on the basis of the facts of
that case alone. In addition, as you know, we need only four Justices
noting jurisdiction." And Justice Douglas had shown his intention to
maintain his stand in *Colegrove* and *South* v. *Peters*. "Because of these
considerations," Rhyne concluded, "we feel the *Gomillion* case is not
determinative of our case, and we continue to believe that the unusual
facts of *Baker* v. *Carr* will be judged on their own merits."[48]

Rhyne's analysis seemed to be substantiated on November 21, when
the Court, a week after the decision in the *Gomillion* case, announced
in a cryptic memorandum decision that in *Baker* v. *Carr* "probable
jurisdiction is noted."[49] The National Institute of Municipal Law Officers had filed a brief *amicus curiae* in the case, but the Department of
Justice had not intervened. Rhyne and the Tennesseans had secured
their Supreme Court hearing on their own.

[45] *Ibid.*, at 348.
[46] 347 U.S. 483 (1954).
[47] 364 U.S., at 349.
[48] Letter, Rhyne to Osborn, Nov. 15, 1960.
[49] 364 U.S. 898.

The Tennesseans, however, continued to hope that the solicitor general would intervene in their case, particularly now that a hearing before the Court was assured, but the outcome of the election in November meant a change in the Justice Department staff for 1961. With the inauguration of the Kennedy administration, the access of Charles Rhyne and the Tennessee Republicans in the coalition would diminish, and new avenues of access through Democrats had to be found.

The new men to be dealt with were Attorney General Robert Kennedy, Byron R. White, the deputy attorney general, and Archibald Cox, the new solicitor general. White had been an All-American halfback and first in his class at the University of Colorado in the late 1930's. He had played professional football with Pittsburgh and Detroit and had been a Rhodes scholar at Oxford, where he met John Kennedy in 1939. Kennedy and White had met again in the South Pacific during the war and in Washington in 1946–47, when White was the law clerk for Chief Justice Vinson and Kennedy was a freshman congressman from Massachusetts. White had led the preconvention Kennedy drive in Colorado in 1960 and served as national chairman of the Citizens for Kennedy and Johnson in the campaign.[50] Cox, a professor of law at Harvard, had served as head of a speech-writing team based in Washington during the Kennedy campaign.[51]

The Tennesseans sought to influence the Justice Department through Tennesseans who had participated in the Kennedy campaign. John J. Hooker, Jr., a Nashville attorney who had been coordinator of Professional Men, Lawyers, Doctors, Scientists, Military Leaders and Mental Health Leaders for Kennedy–Johnson, arranged an appointment for Harris Gilbert, the Nashville city attorney, and Z. T. Osborn with White and Cox in early February, 1961.[52] The results of the conference were greatly encouraging to the Tennesseans. "The talks with the officials . . . were pleasant," Osborn reported, "and we left with the statement of the Solicitor General that the Department would at once conclude work on its brief and, barring some high level policy decision to the contrary, probably undertake to partici-

[50] White, *Making of the President 1960*, pp. 143, 248; 18 Congressional Quarterly 1670–72 (1960).

[51] White, *Making of the President 1960*, pp. 248, 324; 18 *Congressional Quarterly* 1597 (1960).

[52] For a description of Hooker's role in the campaign, see 18 *Congressional Quarterly* 1600 (1960).

pate in argument of the case." There was no need, Osborn remarked, "to elaborate on the real boost our lawsuit would gain if these developments take place."[53]

The Tennesseans, however, took nothing for granted and continued to call their case to the attention of the Justice Department. Osborn, who had discovered President Kennedy's 1958 *New York Times Magazine* article, "The Shame of the States," sent copies of it to White and Cox, "in the thought," he said to his colleagues, "that previous Presidential expression of opinion should not be lightly disregarded."[54] Enclosing the article in a letter to White, Osborn expressed the "hope that the Solicitor General will not only brief the case, but will also appear in argument before the United States Supreme Court. We think his appearance and argument would definitely tip the scales and result in a solution to the [apportionment] problem."[55]

E. William Henry, an attorney in Walter Chandler's firm in Memphis, had also been active in the Kennedy campaign as coordinator of the Nationalities Division of the Democratic National Committee.[56] He also drew the Justice Department's attention to the Tennessee case in a letter to Attorney General Robert Kennedy. "It appears to be widely recognized," he wrote, "that our case involves a question of extreme importance to a number of states, and that similar cases from such other states are now pending in the Federal Courts. Undoubtedly our case will receive the closest attention and the most thorough consideration by the Court if your Department will file a brief *amicus curiae*, and I will appreciate your looking into the matter as a favor to me under the circumstances."[57]

The Justice Department had actually decided to intervene in *Baker v. Carr* during the Eisenhower administration. Solicitor General J. Lee Rankin had authorized the preparation of a brief in the case in the waning months of the Eisenhower administration, but the brief had not been filed when the change of administrations occurred, and Rankin's decision was therefore subject to reconsideration. After discussion with Attorney General Kennedy, however, Solicitor General

---

[53] Letter, Osborn to Ben West, Feb. 7, 1961.

[54] *Ibid.*

[55] Letter, Osborn to Byron R. White, Feb. 10, 1961; Letter, Osborn to Archibald Cox, Feb. 10, 1961.

[56] 18 *Congressional Quarterly* 1599 (1960).

[57] Letter, E. William Henry to Robert Kennedy, Feb. 6, 1961.

Cox reaffirmed his predecessor's decision, and the government's position as *amicus curiae* was continued.[58]

By February 21 the Tennesseans were aware that the solicitor general would definitely file a brief in their behalf, reserving judgment on whether or not to participate in the oral arguments.[59] On March 6, Solicitor General Cox wrote Tennessee Attorney General McCanless that in order that McCanless might take into account "the government's position in your brief in the Supreme Court, I am informing you that the government intends to file a brief *amicus curiae* in *Baker v. Carr*."[60] Charles Rhyne, having seen the draft of the solicitor general's brief, was delighted to inform his colleagues that it "will support us wholeheartedly."[61] And in early April the parties were informed that the Court would hear arguments later in the month and that it had granted one hour to the appellants, forty-five minutes to the solicitor general, and an hour and forty-five minutes to the State of Tennessee.[62]

As the parties in the Tennessee case were writing their briefs and preparing for the arguments that might decide the momentous issue of what standard, if any, the federal Constitution imposed upon legislative representation in the states and the extent to which the federal judiciary could enforce such a standard, the first reapportionment of a state legislature under the threat of affirmative relief from a state court was occurring in New Jersey. The New Jersey Supreme Court had said in the *Asbury Park Press* case that "it is to be presumed that the Legislature contemplates the performance of its constitutional duty to reapportion,"[63] and the court later announced that it would take the matter of reapportionment into its own hands if the legislature had not acted by 5 P.M. on February 1, 1961.

The legislature at first appeared to be prepared to call the court's hand. The speaker of the lower house, in order to block consideration of a reapportionment bill already passed by the state senate, adjourned the house until after the deadline set by the court. But Governor Robert Meyner, who had repeatedly urged the legislature to reappor-

[58] My source for the preceding paragraph prefers anonymity.
[59] Letter, Osborn to West, Feb. 21, 1961.
[60] Letter, Cox to George McCanless, March 6, 1961.
[61] Letter, Rhyne to all counsel, March 7, 1961.
[62] Letter, Rhyne to all counsel, April 3, 1961.
[63] *Asbury Park Press, Inc.* v. *Woolley*, 33 N.J. 1, at 21 (1960).

tion, quickly called a special session to meet during the adjournment. He dispatched state troopers to transport to Trenton an absent legislator whose vote was necessary for passage of a reapportionment bill, and finally was successful in persuading the legislature to reapportion.

Emotions ran high in the debates preceding passage of the bill, with various opponents of reapportionment denouncing the bill as a "sell-out" and the proceedings as "unconstitutional, illegal, arbitrary, capricious, incompetent and irrelevant," but the bill was passed and signed by the governor by 3:13 P.M. The supreme court met at five o'clock sharp, and, being advised of the legislature's action, issued a terse announcement stating that it was "informed that the Legislature had adopted an apportionment bill which the Governor had signed. Litigation, accordingly, appears to be moot and hence the prepared opinion will not be filed."[64]

To a great extent, both state and federal courts had traditionally refused to grant relief in suits challenging state apportionment systems because the courts feared that affirmative judicial relief might be rendered ineffective by legislative defiance. The New Jersey action, however, revealed that the threat of affirmative judicial relief in apportionment cases could be effective in forcing legislative action. But it also revealed the great risks the courts could encounter in the apportionment arena, since without the governor's action in New Jersey there might well have been a direct confrontation between the supreme court and the legislature. The New Jersey experience revealed, therefore, the potential success of the use of judicial power in apportionment cases, and at the same time it revealed the relative dependence of judicial power in such situations upon the acquiescence or support of the nonjudicial branches and the attendant dangers for the judiciary. Considerations of this kind would be among the more important factors being weighed by the United States Supreme Court as the justices examined the briefs and heard arguments in the Tennessee case and decided on the availability of federal judicial relief in apportionment cases.

The Tennessee legislature also met while *Baker* v. *Carr* was pending before the Court. The legislators were aware that the Court had agreed to hear the case, and it was possible that the passage of a reapportionment act, perhaps even of a token nature, might delay the

[64] The above description of the New Jersey reapportionment is drawn from *The New York Times*, Feb. 2, 1961, p. 1.

hearing before the Court or result in the case's dismissal. However, not even the threat of federal judicial intervention could cause the 1961 Tennessee legislature to pass even a token reapportionment act.

Governor Buford Ellington pointed out to the legislature that the Tennessee Constitution with respect to apportionment had not been obeyed since 1901 and that the reapportionment problem was "one that you must and should consider."[65] Although there were reports that rural legislators were considering token reapportionment to head off federal court intervention, Representative Jim Cummings, a leading opponent of reapportionment, apparently expressed the sentiments of most of the legislators when he noted that the problem was before the Supreme Court and "only the good Lord himself and the court" knew what the outcome might be. "It wouldn't make one iota of difference what we do here," Cummings said. "We're going to have to follow the court's directives. We might jump off a deeper precipice than anything we've seen yet. So it's my best judgment that we should not do anything as long as this matter is before the court."[66]

Republican legislators played a prominent role in seeking reapportionment, with Senator Robert Peters, a conservative Republican from Kingsport, leading his party's effort. Peters' reapportionment bill was defeated in the senate, however, by a vote of 12 to 19.[67] The only action the legislature took on apportionment was to establish a joint house-senate committee to determine the number of qualified voters in the state (qualified voters being the apportionment basis required by the constitution) and to authorize a Legislative Council study of the apportionment problem.[68] The Legislative Council study was bitterly denounced by Senator Peters, who charged that the purpose of the resolution authorizing the study was to "undermine the present citizens' reapportionment court case now before the Supreme Court of the United States." It seemed strange, he said, "that when the Supreme Court decides to hear the case on reapportionment and the Justice Department enters the case, the Legislature decides in all piety that something ought to be done."[69]

The minimal response from the Tennessee legislature when the Court granted a hearing in *Baker* v. *Carr* worked to the advantage of

[65] Nashville *Tennessean*, Jan. 6, 1961, p. 2.
[66] Nashville *Tennessean*, Jan. 4, 1961, p. 2.
[67] Nashville *Tennessean*, March 8, 1961, p. 1.
[68] Nashville *Tennessean*, Feb. 24, 1961, p. 1; March 8, 1961, p. 7.
[69] Nashville *Tennessean*, March 17, 1961, pp. 1, 6.

the plaintiffs in the case. The legislature refused to move toward even token reapportionment, and as a result there was nothing to justify even a delay in the litigation. The Tennessee legislature had forfeited its last opportunity to obey the mandate of the Tennessee Constitution free from the compulsion of the federal judiciary.

CHAPTER V

BAKER v. *CARR* BEFORE THE COURT

THE SUPREME COURT heard arguments in *Baker* v. *Carr* on April 19 and 20, 1961, but ordered a reargument for October 9, 1961, during the next term of the Court. In their brief, the appellants recited the failure of the Tennessee legislature to reapportion and the discrimination against the urban areas of the state in both legislative representation and the distribution of state revenues, which they claimed had resulted from the failure to reapportion. Again the Court was reminded that all avenues of relief, other than the federal courts, were either exhausted or unavailable, and again on the substantive issue the appellants sought to invoke in their behalf the apportionment provisions of the Tennessee Constitution. The discrimination under the apportionment act of 1901 was clearly a "denial of the equal protection of the laws under the Fourteenth Amendment to the United States Constitution," they argued, "since the statute which is the source of the forbidden discrimination, when compared with the commands of the organic law of Tennessee, is patently and on its face discriminatory against appellants and an overwhelming majority of the voters." The 1901 act, they said, was "devoid of any justification as a reasonable classification of voters and representatives, because the superior commands of the state constitution deprived the legislature of any discretion to classify voters in relation to the seats in the legislature differently from the proportioning of the seats to the size of the voting population of the several counties and districts."[1]

The appellants argued that *South* v. *Peters*[2] and *Colegrove* v. *Green*[3] could be distinguished because of the Tennessee Constitution's pro-

[1] Brief of Appellants, *Baker* v. *Carr*, pp. 26–28.
[2] 339 U.S. 276 (1950).
[3] 328 U.S. 549 (1946).

visions for equality of representation. In neither of those cases had there existed an "objective measure of equality" as was provided by the Tennessee Constitution in this case.[4] *Colegrove* could also be distinguished because in *Baker* v. *Carr* there was not only jurisdiction but also "no special circumstances, such as impendency of an election (the next for Tennessee is 1962) or the delicacy of relations with Congress; and most importantly there is present what may have been missing for some in *Colegrove*, namely the clearly visible violation of law and the means built into local organic law for applying and measuring a judicial remedy that does not require judicial activity in the legislative field."[5]

The appellants also relied heavily on the white primary cases and especially *Gomillion* v. *Lightfoot*[6] to support the arguments that discrimination against a geographical class of persons was analogous to racial discrimination and that apportionment cases raised political questions no more than cases involving racial discrimination in voting rights. "The inequality practiced in this case was effected by geographically segregating appellants and other voters in some areas of the state from favored voters and areas," they contended, "and discriminating against the former by diluting the value of their votes in comparison with the favored voters." The Fourteenth Amendment, they said, has been "a constant protector of voting rights against discriminatory state action notwithstanding the objection that the subject matter is political."[7]

On the question of what relief could be granted, appellants argued that if the Court would order the district court to vacate its previous order and to deny the motion to dismiss, the legislature would probably reapportion, as the Minnesota, Hawaii, and New Jersey legislatures had done in similar situations. But if the district court were forced to grant further relief in the absence of a legislative response, it could issue a declaratory judgment holding the 1901 act invalid and an injunction prohibiting election officials from holding future elections on the basis of the act. The appellants also argued that the 1957 and 1960 civil rights acts had added "impetus for judicial assistance rather than judicial reluctance in using equitable jurisdiction to protect voting rights," and they cited especially the 1957 act's provision for equit-

[4] Brief of Appellants, p. 28.
[5] *Ibid.*, pp. 33–34.

[6] 364 U.S. 339 (1960).
[7] Brief of Appellants, pp. 28, 31.

able relief from federal courts for "protection of civil rights, including the right to vote,"[8] and the 1960 act's definition of the right to vote, which included "all action necessary to make a vote effective."[9] Under the protection of voting rights provided by these statutes, the district court could issue an injunction against future elections under the 1901 act, which would almost certainly "evoke the necessary action by the Tennessee legislature, if the additional spur is needed to prompt the enactment of the required reapportionment."

The appellants suggested that if the legislature still failed to reapportion, the district court could then either order into effect an apportionment according to the formula in the Tennessee Constitution or order an election at large. "Either measure would be temporary," they said, "and would envisage that the legislature next elected, under either expedient, would provide a suitable apportionment, measured by the state constitutional formula, before the court would relinquish jurisdiction of the case."[10] The Supreme Court had ordered elections at large in *Smiley* v. *Holm*[11] and *Carroll* v. *Becker*,[12] resting its decision on the Article I provision that the members of the House of Representatives be elected by the people of the several states. The Tennessee Constitution similarly provided that the state's house and senate are "both dependent on the people,"[13] providing therefore an analogous basis for an at-large election of Tennessee legislators.[14]

The appellants found *Kidd* v. *McCanless*[15] troublesome because it had raised the same issues as *Baker* v. *Carr*. However, they argued it was distinguishable since the Tennessee Supreme Court's decision in that case rested on state law grounds and therefore its appeal to the United States Supreme Court had not raised the federal questions found in *Baker* v. *Carr*. The *Kidd* case also posed some problems with regard to recommending remedies, particularly the Tennessee court's ruling that, because the Tennessee legislators could not serve as *de facto* officers, invalidation of the 1901 apportionment act would end the existence of the legislature. The appellants argued, however, that even if the Tennessee court's ruling on this point were accepted, the district court could avoid the question by delaying action until the

8 28 U.S.C. 1343(4).
9 Brief of Appellants, pp. 40–41.
10 *Ibid.*, p. 45.
11 285 U.S. 355 (1932).

12 285 U.S. 380 (1932).
13 Tenn. Const., art. 1, § 3.
14 Brief of Appellants, pp. 46–47.
15 200 Tenn. 273 (1956).

legislature reapportioned, while putting the legislature on notice that the 1901 act was to be invalidated.[16]

During oral argument, Charles Rhyne was questioned closely from the bench about the contention that the legislature had violated the Fourteenth Amendment when it disregarded the Tennessee constitutional guarantee of equal representation. Rhyne pointed out that the legislature had not properly apportioned under the Tennessee Constitution even in 1901, and that "since that time, they have not done anything but vote down every bill that has proposed the reapportionment of the state." Justice Frankfurter interrupted to question Rhyne on the relation of the apportionment provisions of the Tennessee Constitution to the equal protection clause of the Fourteenth Amendment.

JUSTICE FRANKFURTER: Mr. Rhyne, what is the bearing of these provisions in the Tennessee Constitution on the Federal Constitution?

MR. RHYNE: Well, the right to vote, Mr. Justice Frankfurter, is created by the state. And this defines the right to vote. It is a vote given in equality insofar as representation [is concerned].

JUSTICE FRANKFURTER: What about a statute?

MR. RHYNE: Well, I think if it was a statute conferring the right to vote in equality, and then there were some state action that came along and wipes it out—you see, what we have here is a constitutional provision.

JUSTICE FRANKFURTER: I know. That is my contention. What difference does it make whether it is in the constitution or any other expression or action by the state?

MR. RHYNE: I think it makes a lot of difference, Mr. Justice Frankfurter, because the legislature comes along by this 1901 statute and takes away what the constitution gave to the people of the State of Tennessee.

JUSTICE FRANKFURTER: Well, suppose it does not offend the Federal Constitution? I am not denying it doesn't. All I am saying is you stressed that fact that it is incorporated in the state constitution.

MR. RHYNE: Well, I think, if Your Honor please, that it does offend the equal protection of the laws clause of the 14th Amendment.

JUSTICE FRANKFURTER: That is what we are arguing.

16 Brief of Appellants, pp. 42–44.

MR. RHYNE: And I think it is quite important that it is in the constitution of Tennessee, and that we have this statute [which] takes away what the people gave to themselves in Tennessee.[17]

Frankfurter's questions prompted the appellants to file a supplemental memorandum before the reargument of the case, which modified somewhat their reliance on the Tennessee Constitution's provisions as the standard for legislative apportionment in Tennessee under the Fourteenth Amendment. The Tennessee Constitution's provisions, the memorandum said, "constitute part of the facts and legal background in determining, in relation to the Fourteenth Amendment, the intended meaning of voting rights in Tennessee, the extent of the violation of these rights, and the standard or measure for remedial action in restoring the rights violated." When a state such as Tennessee creates a system of representation based on equal voting rights, the memorandum continued, the voting rights in that state take on a "measured meaning, which is obviously within the parameters of the Fourteenth Amendment, though that Amendment did not compel adoption of that particular measure and might allow some other reasonable measure, if changed by appropriate action." But having adopted such a standard of equality, the dilution of equal representation is outside the discretion of the state legislature under the state constitution, and "at the same time makes unreasonable classifications of voters which violate the equal protection guaranty of the Fourteenth Amendment. The violation of the Fourteenth Amendment would be demonstrable by its grossness without the aid of the state constitutional provisions, if these did not exist. But because they exist, the state constitutional provisions assist in demonstrating that on its face the inconsistent legislative action . . . is discriminatory, unequal treatment."[18] Thus, the state constitution's apportionment provisions, rather than being absorbed by the Fourteenth Amendment as was argued in the jurisdictional statement, had now become significant be-

---

[17] Oral Argument before the United States Supreme Court in *Baker* v. *Carr* (Washington, D. C.: Ward & Paul, 1962), pp. 5–6. Hereinafter cited as Argument. Unfortunately, copies of the transcript of the second argument are not available, and excerpts of the reargument published in newspapers are therefore relied on herein. In quoting from the transcript of the first argument, I have corrected obvious errors of spelling and punctuation without following the pedantic custom of indicating each instance where this has been done.

[18] Supplemental Memorandum for Appellants, *Baker* v. *Carr*, pp. 2–3.

cause they facilitated evaluation of the unreasonableness of the classification of voters under the 1901 act, which violated the Fourteenth Amendment.

The appellants also contended in their supplemental memorandum that the Tennessee constitutional provisions "provide the courts with a yardstick which saves the courts the more difficult judgment of determining in the case of this state (as distinct from cases which might arise in other states) how much of a departure from mathematical equality the Fourteenth Amendment permits, and what is a suitable standard for compliance in judging remedial action to be taken by the state."[19] While having softened their dependence on the state constitutional provisions in their equal protection argument, the appellants thus still insisted that relief should be conditioned by these provisions.

In attempting during the first argument to distinguish *Colegrove* v. *Green* from the Tennessee case, Charles Rhyne admitted that "we have a major problem of distinguishing what we consider to be a misunderstood decision." He pointed out, however, that four of the justices voted in *Colegrove* that jurisdiction existed, and contended that while in *Colegrove* there had been "no fundamental law requiring equality of congressional districts," the Tennessee constitutional provisions required such equality in the Tennessee case. In addition, Rhyne argued that Justice Frankfurter's opinion in *Colegrove* had been based substantially on the exclusive power of Congress to correct the malapportionment of congressional districts, while no such power existed in relation to state legislative apportionment. But again Justice Frankfurter interrupted Rhyne's argument.

> JUSTICE FRANKFURTER: Does that imply, Mr. Rhyne, that the Congress has said that as to federal voting rights, it could not be unconstitutional to have what you call second-class citizens—there is greater constitutional protection for states and state voting?
>
> MR. RHYNE: No. I am trying to distinguish between a federal voting right and a state voting right, because we have a state voting right here. I am merely saying—
>
> JUSTICE FRANKFURTER: You are suggesting that there is exclusive remedy in Congress. Does that mean that Congress can establish second-rate voters with reference to national interests?
>
> MR. RHYNE: I am not arguing with your opinion. I am merely distinguishing it from this case, Mr. Justice Frankfurter.

19 Ibid., p. 4.

JUSTICE FRANKFURTER: I am merely suggesting the implication of your distinguishing it.

MR. RHYNE: I would say that I do not intend to distinguish it on that basis. I think that all voters should be equal in federal elections and in state elections.

JUSTICE FRANKFURTER: I can understand you saying the decision is wrong and you would object to it. I cannot understand the distinction you make, because it would not lead to that conclusion in that under the United States Constitution Congress would have the power to differentiate on voting rights, but that state voters have greater rights than anybody has under the federal Constitution with regard to federal rights.

MR. RHYNE: I do not come to that conclusion.

JUSTICE BLACK: You distinguished on the grounds that only three members of the Court agreed to it.

MR. RHYNE: That is right.

JUSTICE BLACK: Four members thought there was jurisdiction—but one of the four thought that relief should not be granted on equitable grounds.

MR. RHYNE: That is true.

JUSTICE FRANKFURTER: You say that. But you also said I relied—the opinion relied on the specific congressional power.

MR. RHYNE: And it did. I would say insofar as Colegrove is concerned. I will just make the one distinction that it [held] . . . four [to] three for jurisdiction.

JUSTICE FRANKFURTER: That I can understand.

MR. RHYNE: Now, in the Gomillion case, it is true that Colegrove was distinguished on the basis that you had affirmative action in Gomillion. Now, we have affirmative action here. This 1901 act was invalid when it was adopted, and over and over again, since 1901, the Tennessee legislature has rejected any reapportionment time and time again.

JUSTICE WHITTAKER: What difference would it make if it were affirmative action or non-action?

MR. RHYNE: As to jurisdiction, Mr. Justice Whittaker, I would agree that it does not make any difference; I think that non-action can be just as bad as affirmative action. But that distinction was made in Gomillion. And I wanted to point out that we have the affirmative action here in this case.[20]

---

[20] Argument, pp. 22–25.

Questions from the bench also indicated great interest in the nature of the relief which might be granted, if the appellants won a favorable decision. This was to be expected, since the anticipated difficulty of judicial relief for malapportionment had influenced judicial reluctance to speak to the apportionment question. Charles Rhyne, following the appellants' brief, suggested that all the Court need do was to hold that jurisdiction existed, reverse and remand the case to the district court, and "on that point alone, on that action alone, we feel that the legislature of Tennessee must be presumed, once this Court has declared the law, to follow the law, and that it will go ahead and perform its legislative action."

[MR. RHYNE:] Now, we have some history to back us up. Recently in New Jersey, the New Jersey Supreme Court held that it had jurisdiction, and it waited to enter its order until the legislature could act, and the legislature did act.

In Minnesota, a federal district court held that it had jurisdiction,[21] and it waited for the legislature to act, and the legislature did act.

JUSTICE BLACK: What case was that?

MR. RHYNE: McGraw v. Donovan. It is cited in our brief, Mr. Justice Black.

Now, we feel—

JUSTICE FRANKFURTER: You might cite Illinois.

MR. RHYNE: Well, they have not done so well out in Illinois.

JUSTICE FRANKFURTER: They agreed to reapportion.

MR. RHYNE: Well, I could cite some others, likewise. In Wisconsin and in other states, it is true that some of them have.

But if on finding that jurisdiction exists, and reversing the district court, there is any further relief that is required, we feel that there are several other alternative steps that we merely want to mention to demonstrate to this Court that there are judicial things that can be done to cure this malignant cancer....

The first thing that we would suggest is that all of the state officials who have anything to do with elections be enjoined from conducting any further elections under the 1901 Act. And then we think that the Governor would call them into special session and they would go ahead and perform their legislative function.

JUSTICE HARLAN: Supposing they don't do that? Then what would you do?

21 Here Rhyne was incorrect. The federal district court in the Minnesota case, *McGraw v. Donovan,* 159 F. Supp. 901 (D. Minn. 1958), had withheld its decision regarding all issues in the litigation, including jurisdiction.

MR. RHYNE: Well, in tandem with that, Mr. Justice Harlan, we would suggest the possibility of a declaratory judgment that the 1901 Act is invalid. If you couple the two together, we certainly think that the legislature would act.

JUSTICE WHITTAKER: What about the suggestion that it will be time enough to meet that situation when it arises?

MR. RHYNE: I like that suggestion, Mr. Justice Whittaker.

* * * * * * *

JUSTICE BLACK: Why do we have to anticipate what steps they take at all?

MR. RHYNE: I don't think you do, Mr. Justice Black. I think all you need to do is reverse and remand. I say I am merely mentioning these to demonstrate that there are a lot of things that a court of equity can do to cure this situation, or to assist the legislature in moving to do its duty.[22]

Throughout both the first and second arguments of the Tennessee case, Rhyne stressed that the federal courts offered the only realistic avenue of relief for the Tennesseans. As he said during the reargument of the case, the appellants were "at the end of the road." If there were no federal judicial remedy for the apportionment situation in Tennessee, "these people are consigned to second-class citizenship for the rest of their lives." The apportionment situation in the states had become "a great national tragedy," Rhyne concluded. "There is nothing in the Constitution of the United States that ordains that state government must be an agricultural commodity."[23]

The position of the government as *amicus curiae* was presented in two briefs filed by the solicitor general, one filed prior to the first argument and the second a revised brief filed before the reargument of the case. Although these briefs contained some significant differences, the main thrust of both, and the policy the solicitor general urged upon the Court, was primarily aimed at securing a decision upon the narrowest possible grounds; that is, the Court was urged to decide only that jurisdiction existed, to reverse the district court's decision and remand the case for a trial on the merits, while avoiding any ruling on the substantive question of what standard state legislative apportionment systems were required to meet under the Fourteenth

[22] Argument, pp. 26–29.
[23] Anthony Lewis, "High Court Urged by U.S. to Speed Reapportionment," *The New York Times*, Oct. 10, 1961, pp. 1, 85.

Amendment. As stated in the government's second brief, the question of whether particular apportionment systems violated the Fourteenth Amendment "must be pricked out case by case."[24]

The government's brief on reargument, however, contended that when a state "arbitrarily and unreasonably apportions its legislature so as to deny the real meaning of the right to vote, *i.e.*, effective participation in democratic government, both the equal protection and due process clauses are violated." The government urged on the other hand that the Court need not decide at this time the extent to which the state could weight representation in favor of some individuals as opposed to others without offending the Fourteenth Amendment. Constitutional evaluation of state apportionment systems was subject to rational analysis and judicial determination, the brief continued, and several tests could be applied to determine whether a particular apportionment system conformed to constitutional standards. The first consideration was the extent to which the apportionment embodied equality of representation by population, since political equality was "one of the fundamental ideals of American life" and any "serious departure from apportionment according to population . . . certainly any departure affecting both houses of a legislature—is subject to question, although the divergence might be shown to have a rational justification."[25]

It was conceded that factors other than numerical equality could be valid bases of representation, but such factors were capable of rational statement and analysis. "If the State can point to neither rhyme nor reason for a discriminatory apportionment," the brief argued, "save that it is an anachronism, the apportionment should be held to violate the Fourteenth Amendment."[26] The government admitted that representation of political subdivisions, recognition of "geographic and other minority interests," or population shifts since the last reapportionment were rational justifications for deviations from numerical equality, if reapportionment occurred periodically. Also, a complaint of underrepresentation in a state legislature "may be less serious in a State which provides for legislation by referenda initiated by a reasonable number of voters" or where the people were able to call con-

---

[24] Brief of the United States as *Amicus Curiae* on Reargument, *Baker* v. *Carr*, p. 25.
[25] *Ibid.*, pp. 25–26.
[26] *Ibid.*, p. 28.

stitutional conventions, although it was conceded that where minorities were underrepresented, such political remedies might not be effective. "A study of State constitutions does show . . . ," the government argued, "that the acceptable bases for any serious departure from the basic ideal of political equality are amenable to identification and articulation. Consequently, where a serious malapportionment is challenged under the due process or equal protection clause, the initial step is to inquire whether it has any asserted justification or coherent purpose beyond the perpetuation of past political power."[27]

As for the Tennessee apportionment system, the government argued that there was no rational justification for its gross discrimination against the urban areas of the state. "So gross a departure from the basic ideal of political equality, affecting both branches of the legislature, requires some rational justification. None has been suggested by the appellees." The Tennessee Constitution's apportionment provisions, "coupled with the passage of sixty years from the last apportionment," demonstrated that there was "no rational basis whatever for the present allocation of seats in the Tennessee legislature." The continued use of the 1901 apportionment act by the legislature, therefore, "results from the indifference of the incumbents or their determination to retain unwarranted power, and not from any rational policy." There were in addition no political remedies by which the appellants could change the situation in Tennessee, since there was no initiative and referendum. *Baker* v. *Carr*, the government argued, was thus indistinguishable from *Gomillion* v. *Lightfoot*. "We recognize the breadth and importance of the States' political power to apportion representation in its legislature, but we submit that to exalt this power into an absolute is to misconceive the reach and meaning of the Fourteenth Amendment. It is unsound to distinguish *Gomillion* from the present case on the ground that it arose under the Fifteenth Amendment. The Fourteenth Amendment protects the right to vote . . . and arbitrary geographical distinctions are scarcely less invidious than discriminations based upon race."[28]

Citing the famous footnote 4 of the *Carolene Products* case,[29] the

27 *Ibid.*, pp. 28–32.
28 *Ibid.*, pp. 43–48.
29 *United States* v. *Carolene Products Co.*, 304 U.S. 144 (1938). In footnote 4 in his opinion for the Court in this case, Justice Stone advanced what was to become known as the doctrine of preferred freedoms. This doctrine was the

government argued that judicial intervention to remedy legislative malapportionment was necessary in order to protect underrepresented individuals who could not protect themselves, because of the dilution of their votes, in the political process. Such individuals "who are denied the right to vote or who are grossly under-represented cannot protect their franchise by voting," the government contended, and therefore there was "a special reason for the courts to exert all the power they possess for the vindication of these constitutional rights."[30] Judicial intervention was also necessary because malapportionment of state legislatures was resulting in malapportioned congressional districts and was also undermining state and local governments since it was partly the cause of the growing dependence of urban areas on the federal government. The Court was therefore urged by the government to remedy the situation in order to preserve the health of the federal system.[31]

The government urged that the case could be properly decided by the Court without passing on the substantive issues; all the Court need hold was that the jurisdiction of the federal courts extended to challenges of state apportionment systems. Malapportionment violated the "personal" right of the appellants to vote, which, as the white primary cases established, was protected by the Fourteenth Amendment. The appellants thus had standing to bring a suit to vindicate their personal rights.[32] The Court had also held in *Smiley* v. *Holm, Carroll* v. *Becker, Koenig* v. *Flynn*,[33] and *Colegrove* v. *Green* that federal court jurisdiction extended to suits involving apportionment. Citing the fact that four of the seven justices in *Colegrove* had held that jurisdiction existed, the government argued that it and its largely *per curiam* progeny were precedents for the proposition that federal courts may refuse to exercise their equitable discretion in apportionment cases, but did not deny that federal jurisdiction existed in such cases. "The citation of the *Colegrove* decision," the government contended, "to support rejection of attacks on state apportionment systems must, therefore, we believe, mean reliance on the only holding of the pre-

basis for the idea that the Court's primary role should be the protection of the open political process and of "insular minorities."

[30] Brief of the United States, p. 35.
[31] *Ibid.*, pp. 36–43.
[32] *Ibid.*, pp. 50–52.
[33] 285 U.S. 375 (1932).

vailing majority in that case, *i.e.*, that an injunction was not justified in the circumstances. It cannot be assumed that the Court intended to settle this important issue of federal judicial power in accordance with the view of the minority of the Court in *Colegrove* v. *Green* by citing *Colegrove* in *per curiam* decisions, without the benefit of full briefing or oral argument."[34] Federal jurisdiction was also not affected, it was argued, by the contention that malapportionment resulted from legislative inaction, since the holding of elections under a statute commanding malapportionment *was* action, and, in any case, the "character of the controversy is not changed nor its justiciability altered by the vintage of the legislation under which the State officials propose to act."[35]

Colegrove v. *Green*, according to the government, was also distinguishable from the Tennessee case. First, *Colegrove* dealt with congressional districts, not state legislative districts. Second, the Court had held that Article I of the Constitution conferred upon Congress the exclusive power to remedy defects in congressional districts, but such a ruling was inapplicable to state legislative apportionment, since the Court had never held that the Congress possessed exclusive power to enforce the Fourteenth Amendment. Also, since *Colegrove*, the passage of the 1957 and 1960 civil rights acts, protecting the right to vote, had emphasized that "the election process is not to be regarded as exclusively political in nature." These acts, the government contended, indicated the intent of Congress and "the national consensus" that "the right to vote should be afforded federal protection to the fullest possible extent" and that "its protection should principally take the form of judicial action." Finally, it was argued that in *Colegrove* there may have been a political remedy, but no such political remedy existed in Tennessee.[36]

Also, because the Tennessee case did not raise any question under the guaranty clause, its issues were not similar to those in *Luther* v. *Borden*.[37] The government argued that the appellants were not attacking the legitimacy of the Tennessee legislature nor were they attacking the validity of any of its prior acts. The Tennessee Supreme Court had ruled in *Kidd* v. *McCanless* that an invalidation of the 1901

[34] Brief of the United States, p. 59, note 30.
[35] *Ibid.*, p. 60.
[36] *Ibid.*, pp. 62–65.
[37] 7 Howard 1 (1849).

act would result in the destruction of the legislature, but the government suggested that this problem could be avoided by the district court's ruling the act invalid only for the next election. In any case, the *Kidd* ruling was not binding on the federal courts. "The consequences to follow," the government said, "would depend upon federal law."[38]

The government recommended several methods by which the district court could frame an appropriate remedy. The legislature might act if the court held that jurisdiction existed, but if the legislature failed to respond to this minimal assertion of judicial power, the court could then hold that the present apportionment violated the Constitution, but withhold relief, as the New Jersey Supreme Court had done in the *Asbury Park* case.[39] If the legislature still failed to act, the court could, by combining some of the most overrepresented districts and thus releasing representatives to be assigned to the underrepresented areas, effect relief with a minimum of judicial intrusion into the state political process. Or, the government suggested, the court could declare an election at large, or order into effect weighted voting in the legislature, or order election officials to retain existing districts but provide for the election of one representative from the least populous districts and an increasing number of representatives from the other districts in proportion to their population.[40]

Thus, the government concluded, "we submit that this case should be approached, like other cases of alleged constitutional violation, by ascertaining whether courts have jurisdiction over the issue presented. If they have jurisdiction, the constitutional issue should then be adjudicated. If a constitutional violation is found, then the question of a remedy should next be considered. We do not think the premise that the federal courts possess no appropriate remedies can be accepted at this early stage in the proceedings. . . . The fact that in this area devising a proper remedy may call for a delicate and resourceful exercise of federal judicial power does not affect the court's jurisdiction or call for refusal to act."[41]

The course the government urged upon the Court in its brief resulted in almost continuous questioning of the solicitor general during

[38] Brief of the United States, pp. 66–68.
[39] *Asbury Park Press, Inc.* v. *Woolley*, 33 N.J. 1 (1960).
[40] Brief of the United States, pp. 74–84.
[41] *Ibid.*, pp. 84–85.

the first argument of the case. Opening with a brief summary of the government's position, Solicitor General Cox was almost immediately interrupted by Justice Stewart.

JUSTICE STEWART: As I heard it, none of your three points had to do with the basic substance of this case—whether or not this is a violation of the 14th Amendment.

MR. COX: Well, I think that is involved to this extent: a court of law—

The court below had jurisdiction if the complaint states a claim under the Fourteenth Amendment, whether the complaint is well founded or not.

JUSTICE STEWART: Yes, sir.

MR. COX: But at least if it is not patently frivolous. We think the point is involved at least to the extent that we should show that this isn't a futile, silly fact. But it does not seem necessary or, indeed, even appropriate for the Court to rule now whether there has or has not been a violation of the Fourteenth [Amendment] if it decides that there is a substantial claim. Then there [will be] jurisdiction and there ought to be a ruling by the lower court.

JUSTICE STEWART: That is right. There has to be implicitly a ruling that the allegation of this complaint alleged a violation of the Fourteenth Amendment.

MR. COX: There has to be an allegation that they alleged [a] violation but not a determination that what they allege is a violation, if I may put it that way. In other words, whether the complaint states a cause of action is different from the question whether the court has jurisdiction of the subject matter.

*   *   *   *   *   *   *

JUSTICE WHITTAKER: Mr. Solicitor, if we should take your view, need we do more than hold that the complaint states a cause of action and the district court must exercise it?

MR. COX: Must exercise its jurisdiction.

JUSTICE WHITTAKER: Yes.

MR. COX: I think all you need hold is that the case is within the jurisdiction of the Federal courts and that the court below must go on and determine whether this complaint states a cause of action; in other words, adjudicate the merits of the claim that there is a violation under the Fourteenth Amendment.

JUSTICE WHITTAKER: Well, I—

MR. COX: Let me perhaps, by using an example—

I can make a little clearer the point that I have in mind. Let us suppose that the apportionment of Vermont were such that it was in proportion to population except that every town—they have the New England system of town government—was entitled to at least one representative, but, because of the present distribution of population, that would not result in a representation in ratio to the population. Such an allegation that this violated the Fourteenth Amendment would be within the jurisdiction of the Federal court, but it might well be held when one got to the merits that the Fourteenth Amendment didn't require an absolutely equal apportionment of seats, and that, although the complaint was within the court's jurisdiction, it should be dismissed on the merit[s].

As I said to Justice Stewart, I do want to repeat, I am arguing here, of course, that this isn't a frivolous complaint and the thrust of my argument is necessarily that there is on the face of the complaint a violation of the Fourteenth Amendment.

THE CHIEF JUSTICE: Didn't the court hold both general jurisdiction and it had no general jurisdiction and also that it did not state a cause of action?

MR. COX: I thought not, Mr. Chief Justice. I thought the court did rest on two grounds which it didn't clearly distinguish: one, that there was no jurisdiction—

THE CHIEF JUSTICE: Yes.

MR. COX: And, two, that, even if there was Federal jurisdiction, jurisdiction over the subject matter, that this was not an appropriate case for the exercise of the powers of the court of equity.

Here again I have another—

THE CHIEF JUSTICE: A very fine line.

MR. COX: Yes. They run together.

THE CHIEF JUSTICE: Yes.

MR. COX: I think the difference does go to the heart of this case.

THE CHIEF JUSTICE: Yes.

MR. COX: I was about to develop my point, that the complaint does sufficiently allege deprivation of the Fourteenth Amendment rights under color of State law to bring the case within the general jurisdictional statute.

The right to be free from hostile or capricious discrimination by a State in defining the class of people entitled to vote or in the exercise of the franchise is a Federal right protected by the Fourteenth Amendment. It is also a right enforceable by the courts. Both points have been adjudicated on many occasions in cases such as Nixon and Herndon, the Texas jaybird case and others of that type.

The closest precedents involved do involve racial discrimination, but I suggest the Fourteenth Amendment proscribes other arbitrary and capricious distinctions affecting the right to vote.[42]

Although Solicitor General Cox turned to other matters, Justice Stewart later returned to the question of what Cox proposed that the Court do in the case.

JUSTICE STEWART: You are suggesting, Mr. Solicitor, that, as to a good many things, if we agree with you, we should decline to decide here whether we should send it back to the three-judge court for a decision, as I understand it.

MR. COX: That is correct.

JUSTICE STEWART: But you are suggesting that we should decide, I suppose, that this is a case in which equitable jurisdiction should be exercised.

MR. COX: That is what I am suggesting.

JUSTICE STEWART: Or are you suggesting that if the Court, after a hearing, would find that all these things that you tell us are true, then we should say it should exercise equitable jurisdiction? Or are you suggesting we leave it all up to the district court?

MR. COX: I think there are two possible views, and I would press them both on the Court.

The normal practice is, of course, to consider the question of remedies after you have dealt with the merits, as Justice Whittaker suggested, and it would seem to me entirely proper for the Court to say there is jurisdiction of the subject matter. We don't need to go beyond that now.

Now in a number of cases, including Colegrove v. Green, and, no doubt, some of the per curiams, although I can only speculate about them, the Court has gone ahead and said, "Is there so little chance that an equity court could usefully contribute here that the bill should be dismissed for want of jurisdiction now?"

And I wouldn't object very much to anyone taking that view. That is, if there is clearly nothing the Court can usefully do, it might as well say so and be done with it. But I think all we need show at this stage is that one can't properly come to the conclusion that there is clearly nothing the courts can do at this stage. That may turn out to be....

JUSTICE BRENNAN: Let me get this clear.

You are not urging upon us that, on the face of these pleadings, a

[42] Arguments, pp. 31–35.

case is presented which, if proved, indicates that something should be done?

MR. COX: That something—

JUSTICE BRENNAN: Should be done in the way of equitable relief.

MR. COX: I would say I was urging—

No, I am not pressing quite that far. I would say that it shows that something should be done, if possible, but that the Court should not finally determine at this stage whether it is possible.

JUSTICE WHITTAKER: Mr. Solicitor, specifically are you urging that if there is jurisdiction in the district court as you contend there is, then this is not a proper case for it to withhold the hand of equity?

MR. COX: I am urging that this is not a proper case for it to rule now that it should withhold the hand of equity.

What I am suggesting is this, that the proceedings in the district court, after all, may go through a number of stages. First will be a ruling on jurisdiction. Then one might deal with the merits. Then there might be a hearing on what relief, if any, was appropriate.

I think the Court has power at any one of those stages to say, "Now that all the facts have been laid in front of us, and we have studied them, we know more than we did before about the possibilities of granting relief," and I would say it was possible at any of those stages, and the Court shouldn't prejudge the question, that the district court could conclude that there wasn't any useful relief that could be administered.

I don't think it will turn out that way, but I don't see any occasion to decide that in advance.

JUSTICE WHITTAKER: Well, if there is a clear constitutional right that is being violated, and if these parties have standing to raise the question, then is there not both power and duty in the courts to enforce that constitutional right?

MR. COX: Yes.

JUSTICE WHITTAKER: Well, if there is then, once you concede the power, then how could there be a case of justifiable equitable withholding of the hand?

MR. COX: Well, because there may be a case where the court of equity just couldn't work out any sensible form of equitable relief.

JUSTICE STEWART: The majority of the Court in Colegrove v. Green.

MR. COX: I was just going to say let me use Colegrove v. Green as an example. In Colegrove v. Green there apparently were only two choices. One would be to hold the election at large.

Now there the disease might well be worse than the cure.

JUSTICE STEWART: Vice-versa.

MR. COX: It undoubtedly would be worse. I think my point has been made for me.

* * * * * * *

MR. COX: The other possible remedy in Colegrove v. Green would have been to redraw the Illinois [congressional] districts on the map. Now I don't see how a court could embark on such a task as that, that there are just too many possibilities and that is too much involved in the political process, that it is something that a court really shouldn't undertake to do.

JUSTICE WHITTAKER: What is? What is too much involved in the political process that a court shouldn't undertake to do?

MR. COX: Attempting to lay out 30 equally apportioned—whatever the number is—30 districts for the election of congressional representatives on the map of Illinois, with nothing to start with except the outline of the map and the figures on voting population.

JUSTICE BLACK: May I ask you, with reference to your suggestion at this point as amicus curiae, if we were to hold that jurisdiction [exists and] stopped there . . . the next thing would be that it would be right back on us, on the basis of the motion to dismiss on the ground that they failed to state a cause of action?

Do I understand that it is your suggestion that we stop short of holding that there is nothing alleged in here to justify relief if the facts were established, and we hold jurisdiction [exists]?

MR. COX: My suggestion was that the Court did not have to rule on that question at this stage, that it could send it back for the guidance of the lower court, and I presume that the court could decide whether it wished to decide it on the papers or whether it wished to take further testimony.

JUSTICE BLACK: But there would still be the question whether it stated a cause of action. The two things are different—jurisdiction and stating a cause of action.

MR. COX: Jurisdiction, yes. I think that question does not need to be determined now.

JUSTICE BLACK: If we didn't—

MR. COX: It would be argued in detail in the three-judge court.

JUSTICE BLACK: And it was dismissed on that ground, and then it would come back.

MR. COX: And whichever way it went, it might well come back.

JUSTICE BLACK: Not whichever way it went, because if they held it stated a cause of action, they would hold a trial. If they were to hold it doesn't state a cause of action, it seems to me the claim of the plaintiffs then would be dismissed and come right back.

MR. COX: It could come back immediately if it were dismissed below, which seems unlikely on the basis of the court's opinion, but I don't think it fully went into this question, and this Court, what I was trying to suggest earlier was, that this Court might want the benefit of a full exploration of the point by the three-judge court before it decides. I would think this a matter that this Court should determine on the basis of how sure it feels or what doubts it has about [whether] the complaint does state a cause of action.

JUSTICE WHITTAKER: Didn't the—

MR. COX: The point I was seeking to make, Justice Whittaker, is that the problem of remedy here differs very greatly from case to case, that there may be cases dealing with apportionment where we couldn't concede—let me say simply for the purpose of argument, if you will—that it would be so far removed from a judicial function that the Court should not embark on the task.[43]

Although Solicitor General Cox avoided committing the government on the question of the extent to which state legislative apportionments had to be based on population, he did admit under questioning by Justice Stewart that in his opinion both houses of a state legislature need not be apportioned on a population basis under the Fourteenth Amendment.

JUSTICE STEWART: Mr. Counsel, what if a State with 95 counties . . . decided to set up a unicameral legislature giving simply one representative to each county. Could that be attacked under the Fourteenth Amendment?

MR. COX: I think a question under the Fourteenth Amendment would be presented.

I am not suggesting, clearly not suggesting or intending to suggest that the Fourteenth Amendment requires the apportionment of representatives in both houses of the legislature in ratio to the population. It is quite plain that that is not a requirement of the Fourteenth Amendment. Our history makes it plain. There are other considerations—geographical distribution, historic association, political subdivisions and things of that kind that may be taken into consideration.[44]

In the Tennessee case, however, the solicitor general contended that there was no rational basis for the existing apportionment system.

43 *Ibid.*, pp. 50–57.
44 *Ibid.*, pp. 36–37.

Following the government's brief, he urged that the Tennessee Constitution's apportionment provisions were important in evaluating the rationality of the existing apportionment system in Tennessee, and that the system deviated so grossly from those provisions as to support a conclusion that the Tennessee system was not based on any rational considerations. On this point also, Cox was subjected to close questioning by the Court.

[MR. COX:] Now I say that where the apportionment that the State has departs from the only ostensible basis on which the apportionment is based, by that degree it is such an egregious area that it stands on the face of it as arbitrary and capricious.

JUSTICE BRENNAN: That is to say, Mr. Solicitor, that Tennessee did not have to adopt, as it did, the constitution and basis of apportionment.

MR. COX: That is true.

JUSTICE BRENNAN: But if it did it did not so far depart from it as to—

MR. COX: No, I don't think I even have to go quite that far. I think if Tennessee came in at the trial on the merits of this case and showed some other rational foundation for what it has done, that then the complaint—

I don't like, as the amicus, to talk my friends out of court, but at least my argument would be consistent with dismissing the complaint at that stage.

All I say is having an ostensible basis and what you do comes up with no resemblance to it, that that at least puts the burden on you of coming forward with an explanation.

Now let me make it plain that this is not a claim that there is a Federal right to have Tennessee follow the Tennessee constitution. The only Federal right I am speaking of is the right to have some rational basis for the apportionment. And we say at this stage that on the face of it this is so egregious—

JUSTICE BRENNAN: . . . because it departs on the face of it so far from the constitutional basis which they set up.

MR. COX: On the face of what we have in front of us at this stage.

JUSTICE FRANKFURTER: You had occasion in this Court, Mr. Solicitor, in which it was conceded that there was a complete departure from the express and explicit and formally defined terms of the Tennessee constitution on taxation in making a difference between railroad and other property for purposes of taxation, and this Court said that doesn't make any difference.

So that the fact that Tennessee has written something into its constitution doesn't give it less power than if it deleted it from the constitution and then came here.

MR. Cox: Except it would seem to me that here in Tennessee, or at least I urge Your Honor, that the ostensible basis was following the Tennessee constitution. Tennessee hasn't—

JUSTICE FRANKFURTER: So it was in the tax case. It stopped for a time, but then it became settled practice to disregard the provisions in the Tennessee constitution. That is the Brownsville case, 310.[45]

*   *   *   *   *   *   *

[JUSTICE FRANKFURTER:] According to your statement, Tennessee has a right to be irrational in not having anything in its constitution and making differentiations as a matter of history. Then I don't see what difference it makes whether it is written in the constitution or disregarded in the constitution.

MR. Cox: Well, I would argue that one could infer from that that this hadn't been done rationally. That is what it boils down to.

JUSTICE FRANKFURTER: Rational.

MR. Cox: Well, perhaps where it is entirely irrational the results don't conform to the Fourteenth Amendment.

JUSTICE WHITTAKER: Mr. Solicitor, do I properly gather that the argument you have been making here the last three or four minutes, and particularly in your answers to Mr. Justice Stewart and Mr. Justice Brennan, that you are proceeding on a due process basis?

MR. Cox: I hadn't sought to distinguish between due process and equal protection.

It would seem to me the requirement of a rational basis for the discriminations to [conform to] the equal protection clause, and if there is a bad enough lack of rationality, then, as I understand it, it goes to due process, too.

*   *   *   *   *   *   *

The equal protection clause requires a reasonable classification, and I suppose that that means one has something rational behind it. And I was seeking to argue that here, on the basis of what we have, there is not a frivolous claim, that this classification running against the voters in the underrepresented counties is not a rational classification. I would think it was also bad enough to violate the due process clause.

JUSTICE WHITTAKER: I understand.[46]

[45] Justice Frankfurter was apparently referring to *Nashville, C. & St. L. Ry.* v. *Browning*, 310 U.S. 362 (1940), rather than to "Brownsville."
[46] Arguments, pp. 38–41.

116

During the reargument, Justice Frankfurter "peppered counsel with questions and comments," questioned whether there was any workable standard under which the courts could evaluate state apportionment systems, and observed that it would be difficult to enforce any decision against recalcitrant legislatures. When Solicitor General Cox argued that the legislature would act if the Court only held that federal judicial jurisdiction existed, Frankfurter retorted, "You would push them into something you can't legally make them do?" Justice Whittaker, however, said that even if the Court "couldn't tell the legislature exactly what to do, does that mean you can't tell them that what they're doing is wrong?" Certainly not, replied Cox, adding that the Court could expect the legislatures to obey the law because "by and large the people in this country recognize that representative democracy depends on compliance with law." Frankfurter, still indicating concern over the prospect of judicial intrusion in apportionment, asked Cox if he thought a reapportionment decision would be easier to enforce than the desegregation decision. "I would doubt that it would be," Cox replied.

Frankfurter also expressed the opinion that "the mere fact that there's a rotten situation doesn't mean a court should act," and Cox conceded in his argument that the Court "does not carry the whole burden of government." In conclusion he declared, "There are wrongs which can be righted only by the people or their legislatures. But judicial inaction through excessive caution or a fancied impotence in the face of admitted wrong and crying necessity might do our governmental system, including the judicial branch, still greater damage." A positive decision by the Court would lead to reapportionment by the state legislatures, Cox said, while a negative decision would lead to an acceptance of legislative malapportionment and the stifling of reform.[47]

The most compelling argument the appellants possessed in *Baker* v. *Carr* was that apportionment and voting were indivisible and that gross discrimination in apportionment was as offensive constitutionally as the denial of the right to cast a ballot. The State of Tennessee accordingly set out to convince the Court that apportionment and

[47] The paragraphs above on the reargument of the case are drawn from Anthony Lewis, "High Court Urged by U.S. to Speed Reapportionment," *The New York Times*, Oct. 10, 1961, pp. 1, 85; and Nashville *Tennessean*, Oct. 10, 1961, pp. 1, 2.

voting were not indivisible and that the case should not be viewed as a voting rights case. The Tennessee attorney general thus began his brief by asserting that the appellants were without standing to maintain the suit, since they had suffered no personal injury but were complaining of a public wrong. The appellants complained, he said, "not of discrimination, but of a wrong suffered by all of the voters of Tennessee." And he argued in addition that the municipalities that had entered the case were without standing since they had no interests of their own to assert because municipalities or their officers could not sue for the benefit of third persons, including their taxpayers.[48]

The issues in the case, the attorney general said, involved not the right to vote, but whether or not Tennessee possessed a republican form of government. The appellants were thus asking the Court, "in the guise of citizens denied the right to vote," to enforce the guaranty clause of the Constitution. The white primary cases and the other precedents relied upon by the appellants were thus inapposite, since the right to vote under the Fourteenth Amendment was not involved, but cases such as *Luther* v. *Borden*, in which the Court had held the guaranty clause unenforceable by the courts, were in point and were adverse to the appellants' position.[49]

The attorney general also relied heavily upon *Colegrove* v. *Green* and subsequent apportionment cases which the Court had refused to enter. "Can it be seriously contended that this Court has not reached the issues presented by the present appeal?" he asked. "Has not the Court said that such actions cannot be maintained? Has not the Court held that issues relating to apportionment of members of state legislatures do not present substantial federal questions? Has not the Court ruled that the type of relief here prayed cannot be granted? It is respectfully submitted that the Court has not acted erroneously in deciding the foregoing cases."[50]

The attorney general also stressed that, according to the *Kidd* case, a decision invalidating the 1901 apportionment act would destroy the legislature of Tennessee. Surely, he said, the federal courts' equity powers would not be exercised to bring about such a result in which the "basic framework of constitutional government in Tennessee

[48] Brief of the Appellees, pp. 15–16.
[49] *Ibid.*, pp. 20–31.
[50] *Ibid.*, p. 40.

would be destroyed." The appellants were in effect asking "this Court to destroy the government of the State of Tennessee."[51]

Relying on remarks by the Court in previous cases, particularly by Justice Frankfurter,[52] to the effect that in a healthy democracy the people acted through the elected branches of government to maintain their rights, rather than appealing to the judiciary for protection, the attorney general insisted that the proper remedy for malapportionment was through the political processes. He insisted that the avenues of relief for malapportionment in Tennessee were not closed, and pointed out that the 1953 constitutional convention in Tennessee had resulted from continuous public pressure for change. "The authorization for the holding of the convention was brought about by an aroused and enlightened public," the attorney general said. "The same goal can, and will be [attained] in connection with reapportioning legislative seats." To suggest, he said, "that no avenue of relief is open is to suggest that the citizenry of Tennessee is incapable of self-government. This postulate we unequivocally reject."[53]

In his supplemental brief filed after the first argument of the case, the attorney general contended that, because the district court had held that there was no cause of action, the Court could not, as the solicitor general urged, decide only the jurisdictional issue and remand the case for trial. The Court was required to determine whether there was a cause of action, and there was none because the distribution of political strength for legislative purposes raised no issues under the Fourteenth Amendment, nor did it affect personal rights sufficient to confer standing on appellants. In any case, discrimination that resulted from passage of time and shifts in population could not be "purposeful and systematic" discrimination. He also contended that there was no discrimination in the distribution of state tax revenues, since there was no constitutional "requirement that the State return to a city or county an amount of tax funds equal to that collected in that city or county."[54]

Emphasizing again the harm that would be done if the federal judi-

---

[51] *Ibid.*, p. 45.
[52] Frankfurter's remarks in *Colegrove* v. *Green*, 328 U.S., at 556; and *Minersville School District* v. *Gobitis*, 310 U.S., at 599, were particularly relied on.
[53] Brief of Appellees, p. 53.
[54] Supplemental Brief of Appellees, p. 12.

ciary entered the apportionment arena, the attorney general argued that the solicitor general and the appellants "would have the federal courts coerce the legislature." He reminded them that "the Union came into being as the result of grants of power from the several sovereign states. It must also be remembered that the Tenth Amendment is still in force and effect. If the citizens of the United States wish to abandon the principle of separation of powers, and also our dual system of government, they should do so by the amending process."[55]

During the first argument of the case, Assistant Attorney General James Glasgow was closely questioned by Justice Whittaker about whether invalidating the 1901 apportionment act would destroy the Tennessee legislature.

> JUSTICE WHITTAKER: It is true, is it not, Mr. Glasgow, that Tennessee could tomorrow repeal this constitutional provision that affords the core of this case, couldn't it?

> MR. GLASGOW: I think the constitution could be amended and those provisions eliminated, yes, sir.

> JUSTICE WHITTAKER: Well, as long as it is there, is it to be ignored? What does it mean? Why is it? I don't follow that. It is there now; and it means something. Are you complying with it?

> MR. GLASGOW: In a sense, no, sir, it has not been complied with in regard to the reapportionment of the legislature since 1901.

> JUSTICE WHITTAKER: But it is still there.

> MR. GLASGOW: Yes, sir.

> JUSTICE WHITTAKER: And it gives to a citizen in Davidson County the right not to have his vote, or in Shelby County, not to have his vote diluted by somebody out in another county, doesn't it?

> MR. GLASGOW: No, sir, I do not think that it means that, because I think that the case of Kidd v. McCanless shows that our court does not attach that significance to those provisions. . . . we think that whatever the state court says about those things is controlling. . . . We think that that is the situation with which this Court is confronted on the basis of the Kidd case.

> JUSTICE WHITTAKER: But is there any case in Tennessee that holds this constitutional provision does not mean that Tennessee must reapportion every ten years as its words say?

55 *Ibid.*, p. 29.

Mr. Glasgow: The only case, if Your Honor please, is Kidd v. Mc-Canless.

Justice Whittaker: The court below, the three-judge court, here said that on the averment of this bill, as I read it, that a discrimination was being practiced. But they could not do anything about it for want of power. Isn't that what they said?

Mr. Glasgow: That is true, they said that.

Justice Whittaker: Now, is that not substantially also the Kidd case? Is that not the grounds of it also?

Mr. Glasgow: The ground of the Kidd case as I read it is that the lower court held the act unconstitutional, and the Supreme Court said that the trial court erred in holding it unconstitutional because to do so would in effect place Tennessee without a state legislature....

Justice Whittaker: If your argument is right, it appeared a while ago you said that the state legislature is competent to determine the election and competency qualifications of its own members. If that is right, then nothing could happen towards the future compliance with the statute which would in any way undermine the validity of the present legislature, nor in any way affect the validity of the laws it had enacted since 1911.

Mr. Glasgow: Well, I think that surely follows.

Justice Whittaker: Then how is it true that if it were now held that Tennessee, in order to accord equal protection of the laws to each citizen, must comply with its constitutional provision—how could it then be said that this would leave Tennessee without a present legislature or undermine the validity of the laws it had enacted since 1911?

Mr. Glasgow: Well, in regard to the validity of the laws that have been enacted since 1911, I dare say that the courts would not invalidate those laws. But if the argument which is advanced here is correct, that the legislature or the apportionment provision expired in 1911, then it must be that everything that has been done since 1911 is invalid. As a matter of theory, I do not see how it could be any other way. And I think that was the problem that was in the minds of the Tennessee court.

Justice Whittaker: That could not be true, could it—or could—Mr. Glasgow, if your argument is sound that the legislature is competent to determine the election qualifications of its own members, and they have done that time after time since 1911. If that argument is good, then they were properly elected in the past. Is that not so?

Mr. Glasgow: That is true.

JUSTICE WHITTAKER: Well, would that mean that the courts could not do anything about the future with respect to requiring compliance with the Tennessee Constitution?

MR. GLASGOW: Well, it is our insistence, may it please the Court, in that regard that the question is a political question, it is one that the courts have refused for many, many years to [adjudicate] and that being true it is not a proper area for the judiciary.[56]

Assistant Attorney General Jack Wilson, who shared the burden of the argument for the State of Tennessee with Glasgow, also stressed the potentially disastrous effects that an invalidation of the 1901 act would have on the state.

[MR. WILSON:] What would be the effect of a declaration by the Federal district court that the apportionment statutes of Tennessee are unconstitutional?

The appellees connected with the government of the State of Tennessee take the position that the effect would be, and must of necessity be, that the government of the State of Tennessee is operating unconstitutionally.

I submit that there could be no other reasonable conclusion. The Federal district court, let us say, makes that declaration, enters its decree. What does the State of Tennessee and its government do? It is operating unconstitutionally. Can it, aside from the rule in Luther v. Borden . . . upon the declaration being entered . . . what may the State of Tennessee do as to, let us say, the operation of its polls?

If the government is operating unconstitutionally, may it continue to sentence defendants in criminal courts? May it? May it continue to pay its school teachers? It is an unconstitutional government at that time. May it pay its judges? May it maintain its hospitals for the mentally ill? What happens to the State of Tennessee upon that declaration?

Well, for all practical purposes—

I pause here to say that this is not theoretical, may it please the Court, this matter, when you are directly connected with the operation of a State government.

Suppose the State of Tennessee had planned to execute a defendant in a capital crime on the day following the declaration [of] the three-judge district court? What would the Attorney General of Tennessee advise the warden of the State penitentiary as to carrying out that execution? Frankly, I don't know. I hope the question doesn't arise.

The question will not arise if no such declaration is made by the Federal district court, and that is one reason why, and an important reason why from a practical standpoint, that we say the Federal

[56] Arguments, pp. 83–86.

district court should not enter any such decree. This is a matter for
settlement by the citizens of Tennessee.[57]

During the reargument, Assistant Attorney General Wilson, in
response to questions from Chief Justice Warren and Justice Brennan,
denied that he was arguing against the need for increased urban representation. "Urban counties ought to have more representation," he
said. "I'm not arguing that. I'm arguing the problem." But Wilson
denied that there was a valid Fourteenth Amendment question raised
in the Tennessee case. Justice Black asked if it would be a denial of
the right to vote if a legislature were to say that a rural vote was worth
ten times an urban vote. Wilson replied that this would be morally
wrong, but not a denial of voting rights. "Would it be a reasonable
classification?" Black asked. "It would not be a denial of due process,"
Wilson replied.

Wilson warned the Court that if it held that legislative apportionment raised justiciable questions under the Fourteenth Amendment,
it would also have to decide cases challenging the apportionment of
city councils and local units of government. "In the city of Nashville,
whose honorable mayor [Ben West] is a party to this suit, citizens
are clamoring for equal representation on the City Council. And what
does the honorable mayor say?" Wilson asked. "He says, 'We are
working on it.' " These comments produced laughter from spectators
and from the justices.

Again emphasizing that the appellants could assert no personal
rights in the case, Wilson contrasted this to a case in which, if the
right to vote were denied, someone could be arrested. In an apportionment case, he asked, "Who would you indict? Members of the
Legislature? They are not parties to the action."

Justice Whittaker asked if there was an allegation that rural legislators in Tennessee voted as a bloc against urban legislators. Wilson
answered that although that was "the clear implication," it was untrue.
"Isn't it strange," he asked, "that there never has been a campaign for
governor where this is the issue? The people can decide the issue. No
candidate has ever made this an issue. When one does, the legislature
may take action. Shouldn't political ills be handled politically? Let it
not be said that the channels of reform in Tennessee are closed."
Wilson argued that even if the legislature continued to refuse to reap-

---

[57] *Ibid.*, pp. 102–104.

portion, the legislature's offense would not be as grave as that of the federal courts if they intervened in the field of apportionment. "Is it worse for the Legislature of Tennessee not to reapportion," he asked, "or for the Federal courts to overstep their age-old boundaries?"[58]

After the Court had noted probable jurisdiction in the Tennessee case, the Tennesseans began to receive many requests for permission to intervene as *amici curiae* from individuals and groups in other states. Individuals or groups who perceive their interests to be affected by litigation pending in the courts often use the *amicus curiae* brief to gain access to the courts and express their views on the issues involved. The rules of the Supreme Court require an outside party to seek the consent of both parties in pending litigation before intervening as *amicus curiae*. Lacking such consent, however, the outside party may petition the Court for permission to intervene and, with the Court's permission, file an *amicus* brief in the case without the consent of both parties involved.[59]

Since all of the individuals and groups requesting permission to intervene as *amici curiae* in *Baker* v. *Carr* intended to support the appellants, Attorney General McCanless refused his permission to all of them. The appellants also, however, had some initial misgivings about allowing very many *amicus* briefs to be filed in the case. When a group of Mississippians requested permission to intervene, for example, Z. T. Osborn pointed out to them that one of the problems raised by their request "is presented by Mr. Justice Frankfurter's 'political thicket' fear as expressed in Colegrove v. Green." Osborn thought it "might be a mistake to flood the Court with briefs and further alert them to the many lawsuits which would probably arise if they grant relief in our case."[60] The Mississippians replied that the Supreme Court was aware of the number of lawsuits that would arise as a result of a decision favorable to the appellants in *Baker* v. *Carr* and argued that their intervention would aid the Tennessee case, since "there is perhaps no great admiration for . . . the State of Mississippi by the U. S. Supreme

[58] These excerpts of the reargument are drawn from Lewis, "High Court Urged to Speed Reapportionment," pp. 1, 85; and Nashville *Tennessean*, Oct. 10, 1961, pp. 1, 2.

[59] For good discussions of the role of the *amicus* brief in Supreme Court litigation, see Clement E. Vose, "Litigation as a Form of Pressure Group Activity," *The Annals of the American Academy of Political and Social Sciences*, Vol. 319 (Sept., 1958), p. 20; and Samuel Krislov, "The Amicus Curiae Brief: From Friendship to Advocacy," 72 *Yale Law Journal* 694 (1963).

[60] Letter, Osborn to Upton Sisson, Dec. 1, 1960.

Court for obvious reasons unnecessary to discuss. If then it could be appropriately pointed out to the court that Mississippi may not be as bad a state as is generally considered, if its control were placed in the hands of the majority, rather than the small minority which has controlled it for many years . . . this would carry favorable weight with the court, all of which would enure to the benefit of the Tennessee case."[61]

Osborn finally agreed that the "Supreme Court already knows well enough the number of cases which might arise in light of a favorable verdict in our case. We are not going to lessen this knowledge—or increase it—by refusing to consent to the filing of amicus curiae briefs."[62] Walter Chandler also favored granting the Mississippi group permission to intervene, saying that he thought "it should be very beneficial to us to have as many petitions as possible to intervene as *amicus curiae*, and I would favor the intervention of Mississippi where apportionment has been very disadvantageous to Negroes, for instance."[63] Because Attorney General McCanless would not give his permission to outside parties to intervene as *amicus curiae*, all those wishing to file briefs had to petition the Court. The Court ultimately granted its permission to the Mississippi group, the National Institute of Municipal Law Officers, Governor J. Howard Edmondson of Oklahoma, August Scholle (the president of the Michigan AFL-CIO), a group of citizens active in challenging legislative apportionment in Kansas, a New York group seeking reapportionment in that state, and the mayor of St. Matthews, Kentucky, a suburb of Louisville which was underrepresented in the Kentucky legislature.

The brief filed by the National Institute of Municipal Law Officers drew the Court's attention to the successful use of judicial power by the New Jersey Supreme Court in the *Asbury Park Press* case. It also cited the many state court decisions which held that apportionment was not a political or nonjusticiable issue.[64] The NIMLO brief warned that the failure of the Court to "restore the Appellant Tennessee voters their sacred rights in a democratic society" would completely

---

[61] Letter, Sisson to Osborn, Dec. 9, 1960.

[62] Letter, Osborn to Charles Rhyne, Dec. 16, 1960.

[63] Letter, Walter Chandler to Rhyne, Dec. 16, 1960.

[64] Brief *Amici Curiae* of the National Institute of Municipal Law Officers, pp. 8–9, 10–11. In discussing the *amici* briefs, points covered in these briefs which were also covered by the briefs of the primary parties or the solicitor general will not be discussed.

"shock and dishearten" citizens of every city in America. "If the Court fails to grant relief in a case as outrageous as the case at bar," it said, "little doubt exists that the continued, oppressive voting discrimination herein complained of will remain to flourish and to grow worse."[65]

Governor Edmondson of Oklahoma had led an initiative movement for reapportionment of the legislature in 1959, but the initiated proposal had been defeated by the voters in a referendum election.[66] Intervening in his own behalf in the Tennessee case, the governor argued that the denial of equality in apportionment was more serious than in the case of segregation because of the greater number of persons affected by malapportionment. He also contended that malapportionment resulted in financial discrimination against urban areas and in the increasing financial dependence of local governments on the federal government. "There . . . can be no question that not only does discrimination exist," he said, "but that irreparable injury to democracy, representative government and the very moral fiber of our people is clear and imminent."[67]

The governor pointed out that there had been a reapportionment of the Oklahoma legislature as a result of the Tennessee case. Although this reapportionment had alleviated the situation only slightly, Edmondson argued that the fact that the legislature had acted at all "shows that the retention of jurisdiction is a potential source of relief alone" and "may be the spur that will give fair representation throughout the country. It confirms contentions of Appellants and results reached" in New Jersey, Minnesota, and Hawaii.[68]

Edmondson also contended that the availability of the initiative and referendum was not sufficient to guarantee relief from malapportionment. Describing the failure of the initiative proposal he had supported in his state, the governor argued that the inability to amend proposals once proposed, the expense and difficulty of explaining complex proposals to the public, as well as other factors, made the use of the initiative and referendum "at most a possible means of relief but ex-

[65] *Ibid.*, p. 12.
[66] The Oklahoma situation is discussed in *Inventory of Work on Reapportionment by State Leagues of Women Voters* (Washington, D. C.: League of Women Voters of the U.S., 1960), p. 12.
[67] Brief of J. Howard Edmondson, Governor of the State of Oklahoma, as *Amicus Curiae*, p. 10.
[68] *Ibid.*, p. 13.

tremely impractical."[69] The federal courts must thus afford relief, he said. "If truly representative government is to survive, this Honorable Court offers the only apparent hope. This Court is the last resort. It might even be said this Honorable Court is duty bound to act!"[70]

The Kansas intervenors as *amici curiae*—J. P. Harris, Peter Mac-Donald, John McCormally, and Ernest W. Johnson—were residents of Reno and Johnson counties who were preparing to attack the apportionment of the Kansas legislature in a state court suit. Harris, Mac-Donald, and McCormally were the board chairman, publisher, and editor of the Hutchinson *News* who in 1965 would win a Pulitzer Prize for their efforts to force reapportionment in Kansas. Their *amicus* brief traced the history of apportionment in Kansas and contended that the current apportionment presented a "picture of gross mathematical underrepresentation of the four large metropolitan counties. . . . It has been said that if a popular basis lies behind the scheme of representation in American states, it lies behind it by as much as fifty years."[71] The right of "equal representation in the making of our laws is absolute," they argued, and denial of such equality either by deliberate action or inaction was a "denial of equal protection of the laws guaranteed by the Fourteenth Amendment of the Federal Constitution, if this clause is held to mean anything at all." The validity of all laws was a justiciable issue, and this was particularly so "where the boundaries of constitutional authority are exceeded and the sacred rights guaranteed the citizens are denied."[72]

The *amicus* brief filed by Mayor Bernard Boling and the City of St. Matthews, Kentucky, sought to present to the Court the plight of the suburban areas, which were even more seriously underrepresented in state legislatures than urban areas. The brief cited the representation of Jefferson County (Louisville) in the Kentucky legislature as an example. The total population of the county was over 600,000, and it received eleven seats in the lower house of the legislature, yet nine of these seats were assigned to Louisville, leaving the representation of the population of the rest of the county, including St. Matthews, at only two seats for a population of 300,000.[73] The explosive expan-

[69] *Ibid.*, p. 14.
[70] *Ibid.*, p. 18.
[71] Brief for J. P. Harris, Peter MacDonald, John McCormally, and Ernest W. Johnson as *Amici Curiae*, pp. 21, 23.
[72] *Ibid.*, p. 39.
[73] Brief of the City of St. Matthews, Kentucky, *Amicus Curiae*, pp. 2–5.

sion of the suburbs, the brief said, had thus resulted in gross underrepresentation of suburban areas.

The brief contained in addition the novel argument that the right to equal representation was one of the unenumerated rights guaranteed by the Ninth Amendment of the Constitution, a right "derived from the Great Legislator of the Universe," the brief said, quoting John Adams. "The natural rights of the citizens of this country are not fixed as of the date we adopted the Constitution," the argument continued. "For the Court to hold that this right of reapportionment and equal representation is not an unenumerated right and, therefore, does not exist, is to expose the citizens to a type of tyranny the Constitution was adopted to protect us against."[74]

The brief filed by John F. English and the Nassau County, New York, group also emphasized the underrepresentation of the suburbs in the state legislatures. The brief pointed out that Nassau County, with a population of more than 1,200,000, had only six assemblymen, while thirty-one upstate counties with a combined population almost equal to Nassau County's possessed thirty-one representatives.[75] "As a practical matter," the brief said, "a rural upstate legislator is not faced with the problems which are attendant on explosive growth of population such as has taken place in the suburbs. He has not been and will not be sympathetic to these problems, e.g., aid to education, housing, air and water pollution, and the like. This will inevitably mean either that these problems will find no solution or that suburban eyes will turn increasingly to the Federal Government."[76]

The brief was addressed specifically, however, to "those who believe that a free people must find vindication of their most vital interests not so much through the intervention of courts as through 'the vigilance of the people in exercising their political rights.' "[77] The brief then proceeded to attack Justice Frankfurter's judicial self-restraint position as expressed in several of his opinions.[78] "The

[74] Ibid., pp. 9–10.
[75] Brief as Amici Curiae for John F. English, et al., p. 2.
[76] Ibid., p. 3.
[77] Ibid., p. 4.
[78] The brief cited particularly Minersville School District v. Gobitis, 310 U.S. 586, at 600 (1940); American Sash & Door Co. v. American Federation of Labor, 335 U.S. 538, at 556 (1949); Kovacs v. Cooper, 336 U.S. 77, at 97 (1949); and Dennis v. United States, 341 U.S. 494, at 517, 525, 552 (1951).

philosophy espoused by these opinions is indeed daring. But it presupposes more than an informed electorate. It also contemplates that the democratic process shall not be 'impaired or restricted,' that legislative judgment will indeed be 'controlled by public opinion,' and that the 'alertness' and 'vigilance' of the people over their representatives will not be frustrated by grossly unfair apportionment." The brief contended that Frankfurter's position was dependent, in short, upon the assumption that representative institutions would be representative. It would be a mockery, the brief said, "to inform us that the vindication of our most vital interests lies with the legislature and then to permit such an apportionment of legislative districts as to make such vindication impossible." Citing Frankfurter's remark in the *Colegrove* case that the people must rely on pressure on their legislatures to force redistricting of congressional districts, the brief asked, "Where is the remedy for unfairness in districting the state legislatures themselves if one man's vote is worth fourteen times that of another's? *Quis custodiet ipsos custodes?*" If the suggestion were to be taken seriously that courts should exercise restraint in interfering with legislation affecting interests "we prize so highly as those afforded by the Bill of Rights," the brief concluded, "the courts must assure that the legislatures are not so districted as to be unresponsive to public opinion."[79]

The Mississippi group had filed suit in the state courts challenging the apportionment of that state's legislature.[80] Their brief filed in the Tennessee case argued that the discrimination against the more populous areas in their state was "perhaps the most brazenly calculated discrimination of human suffrage rights ever presented to a court."[81] They attacked especially the oft-heard theory that rural people were superior to urban dwellers in the responsible exercise of political power, noting that while it was true that "nature, in her partiality, designates here and there an individual as the favored recipient of her special endowment," it was rare to find that "she allocates such an

[79] Brief as *Amici Curiae* for John F. English, *et al.*, p. 6.
[80] This case was *Fortner v. Barnette*, No. 59,965, Chancery Court, First Judicial District, Hinds County, Mississippi; see also *NCR*, Vol. 50 (July, 1960), p. 368. The *National Municipal Review's* name was ultimately changed to *National Civic Review* which is cited hereafter as *NCR*.
[81] Brief for Marvin Fortner, W. D. Alberts, J. K. Milner, Cline Allen, Jr., Carl Stanton, and Sam Maxwell as *Amici Curiae*, p. 24.

array of special talents within the confines of rural areas to the exclusion of urban areas." On the whole, the brief continued, "it may be safely assumed that the destiny of the several states will be protected and preserved as well through equal representation as it will by dominant rural minority control." If it was conceded that minorities should control our institutions, then "under what conceivable theory can the advocates of democracy criticize totalitarianism, and most especially today when the whole world is literally on fire?"[82]

The *amicus* brief of August Scholle, president of the Michigan AFL-CIO, was prompted by the current appeal of *Scholle* v. *Secretary of State*,[83] in which the Michigan Supreme Court had dismissed his challenge of the apportionment of the Michigan Senate. Because Michigan's Constitution provided for the initiative and referendum, Scholle's brief especially attacked the solicitor general's contention that the availability of the initiative and referendum in a state might support a refusal of equitable relief by a federal court. According to the solicitor general's argument, the brief said, a denial of equal protection or due process of law would be "immune from judicial redress if arguably subject to future repeal by political means." The proposition, said the brief, was "astonishing and erroneous." If accepted, such a proposition would mean an abdication of the judicial function, and leave aggrieved parties, such as the Negroes in *Brown* v. *Board of Education*,[84] "to theoretical political remedies of the offending states."[85] It would mean that where the initiative and referendum as well as methods for constitutional revision were available, no law, however offensive, could be challenged in the courts. Rejecting the solicitor general's position, Scholle's brief argued that malapportionment was a violation of the Fourteenth Amendment no matter what constitutional provisions a state might possess. "In short, we believe the doctrine of 'one man–one vote' is the basic principle to be necessarily derived from the Fourteenth Amendment and from the voting rights cases, and necessarily to be applied to all states and to all 'state action.' "[86]

[82] *Ibid.*, pp. 13–14.
[83] 360 Mich. 1 (1960).
[84] 347 U.S. 483 (1954).
[85] Brief of August Scholle, *Amicus Curiae*, p. 9.
[86] *Ibid.*, p. 15.

Once the arguments of the primary parties as well as those of the *amici* had been presented, the Court faced the problem of deciding the momentous issue of whether or not federal judicial power would be brought to bear on the problem of state legislative apportionment. The choices for the Court ranged from affirming the decision of the district court, and thus reaffirming the previous policy of nonintervention in such cases, to declaring that federal judicial action in such cases was appropriate and then attempting to spell out the standards to which state apportionment systems must conform under the Fourteenth Amendment.

If the Court decided in the plaintiffs' favor, however, it would probably avoid spelling out the Fourteenth Amendment standard that would govern in such cases. Neither the appellants nor the solicitor general had urged such a course upon the Court, but had on the contrary urged a much narrower course of action—that of determining that jurisdiction existed and remanding to the district court for a trial on the merits. Although some of the *amici* briefs had argued more or less specifically for a straight population, "one man, one vote" standard, the Court would nevertheless have to reach out to decide the issue if it chose to decide the issue. The broadest decision to be expected from the nature of the arguments presented by the appellants and the solicitor general was therefore one in which the Court found that jurisdiction existed, that a nonfrivolous question was raised under the Fourteenth Amendment and therefore a cause of action had been stated, and that the Tennessee apportionment system discriminated so grossly and irrationally as to offend the Fourteenth Amendment.

Aside from the questions of whether malapportionment offended the Fourteenth Amendment and whether federal judicial action was appropriate, the question undoubtedly weighing heavily on the justices' minds, as their interrogation during oral argument indicated, was whether or not the federal courts could effectively afford remedies in such cases, particularly in the face of massive legislative resistance. The justices were no doubt troubled by expressions such as that of the speaker of the lower house of the Pennsylvania legislature, who declared that there was no legitimate federal authority to force reapportionment of state legislatures and even "if the Supreme Court should say [such authority exists], the only possible way to do it would be for the President to declare martial law, send in troops, hold guns at the legislators' heads and force them by sheer might."[87] In few other cases in its history had the Court faced a decision on a question fraught with such potential danger to its authority and to the effective use of federal judicial power.

[87] Bascom M. Timmons, "Tennessee Case Is a Complex One," Nashville *Tennessean*, March 28, 1961, p. 1.

CHAPTER VI

BREAKTHROUGH: THE COURT DECIDES

"ONE THING IS CERTAIN," Walter Chandler remarked following the reargument of *Baker* v. *Carr* in October, 1961. "Everyone has done his best, and I cannot help but feel that we will win." He thought that the appellants had produced a record in the case "full enough to justify the most incisive decision that it would be possible for the United States Supreme Court to write in our favor."[1] Solicitor General Cox, however, commented that counsel "will have to keep our fingers crossed for many months, I fear."[2] And in this prophecy he was correct, for the Court's decision in the Tennessee case did not come down until more than five months later, on March 26, 1962.

Both Chandler and Z. T. Osborn, who commented on "the folly of speculating what a Supreme Court, jury or a woman will do," were able to make, upon the basis of impressions gained during the oral arguments, reasonably accurate predictions about the final outcome of the case. Osborn was convinced that the Court would decide the case in their favor, and that "we will have a 6–3 or 7–2 split of the court." Only Justices Frankfurter and Clark, he said, expressed "die-hard opposition to our side of the case. Justices Black, Douglas, Harlan, Stewart, and Brennan seemed plainly to favor our side. Chief Justice Warren really didn't make enough comment or take enough part in the questioning to justify speculation as to his stand."[3] Chandler also believed the decision would be favorable by a 6 to 3 vote. "I think that, if we win, we will get six votes, and that we will lose Frankfurter, Clark and Harlan." Chandler added that he could not believe "that Black, Douglas, Brennan and Warren will be against us,

[1] Letter, Walter Chandler to Hobart Atkins, Oct. 16, 1961
[2] Letter, Archibald Cox to Atkins, Oct. 18, 1961.
[3] Letter, Z. T. Osborn to Haynes M. Miller, Jan. 31, 1962.

and I think that Whittaker and Stewart are young enough to be bold enough to fight for the right."[4]

The appellants' counsel began to speculate on possible lines of action they might take once the Court's decision came down. Osborn suggested that the best strategy, in the case of a favorable decision, would be to abandon the federal courts and resort again to the state courts. He was convinced that the Tennessee Constitution's provisions would provide a greater degree of equality of representation than any standard the United States Supreme Court might require under the equal protection clause of the Fourteenth Amendment. He thought that if more than five justices favored the appellants, the risk increased that the opinion would have a statement that voters may be classified without offense to the Fourteenth Amendment. "I think Frankfurter is too influential," Osborn said, "and really that his position is too sound for us to expect more than a bare majority of the court to hand down a ruling that any form of reapportionment than exact mathematical equality is offensive to the Fourteenth Amendment. Indeed if we obtain an opinion limiting itself to sustaining our jurisdictional contention, the fact that our complaint states a cause of action under the Fourteenth Amendment and that we are entitled to some form of relief, I will feel that we have been very lucky and most successful."[5] Since Osborn believed that a majority of the Court would not support a Fourteenth Amendment standard requiring equality of representation to the degree guaranteed by the Tennessee Constitution, he suggested a return to the state courts, where it was possible the state constitution's provisions would be enforced.

The Tennesseans did not intend to abandon the fight even if, despite their expectations, they lost in the Supreme Court. Realizing the need for alternative plans in case of an adverse decision, they had agreed by February, 1962, to seek injunctions in the state courts against the holding of elections in twenty-nine of the small counties possessing one representative each in the legislature, and to seek court orders consolidating these counties with neighboring counties for representation purposes before the 1962 primary elections.[6] Walter Chandler apparently expressed a commonly held feeling among ap-

[4] Letter, Chandler to Osborn, Nov. 16, 1961.
[5] Letter, Osborn to Chandler, Jan. 30, 1962.
[6] Chattanooga *Times*, Feb. 19, 1962.

pellants' counsel when he declared that he was "committed to fight as long as I can hobble to Nashville and Washington."[7] But on March 26, 1962, the Supreme Court finally announced its decision in *Baker* v. *Carr*,[8] confirming the Tennesseans' hopes for victory and eliminating the necessity of further contingency planning.

Justice Brennan wrote the majority opinion which was concurred in by Chief Justice Warren and Justices Black, Douglas, Clark, and Stewart. After reciting the history of the case and the decision of the court below, Brennan stated that the Court would limit its opinion to holding that jurisdiction existed, that the complaint stated a justiciable cause of action, and that the appellants possessed standing to maintain the action.[9] The Court's decision thus adhered largely to the narrow grounds urged upon it by the appellants and the solicitor general.

Brennan carefully distinguished the issue of jurisdiction from questions of justiciability. Questions of jurisdiction were determined, he said, by inquiry into whether or not a cause arises under the Constitution, laws, or treaties of the United States or whether or not a cause is a "case or controversy," as required by Article III of the Constitution, or whether or not a cause falls within one of the jurisdictional statutes enacted by Congress. Justiciability, on the other hand, requires inquiry into whether "the duty asserted can be judicially identified and its breach judicially determined, and whether protection for the right asserted can be judicially molded." Since the cause of action in *Baker* v. *Carr* arose under the Constitution—the complaint having alleged a violation of the Fourteenth Amendment—and since the district court did not consider this claim unsubstantial or frivolous, "it should not have dismissed the complaint for want of jurisdiction of the subject matter."[10]

Citing *Smiley* v. *Holm*, *Wood* v. *Broom*, and similar cases, Brennan noted that an "unbroken line of our precedents sustains the federal courts' jurisdiction of the subject matter of federal constitutional claims of this nature." *Colegrove* v. *Green* was not contrary to this holding, since four of the seven participating justices in that case had held jurisdiction existed, and none of the *per curiam* progeny of

[7] Letter, Chandler to Osborn, Feb. 1, 1962.
[8] 369 U.S. 186 (1962).
[9] *Ibid.*, at 198.
[10] *Ibid.*, at 198–99.

Colegrove had been "dismissed for want of jurisdiction over the subject matter."[11] Both *MacDougall* v. *Green* and *South* v. *Peters*, Brennan added, had been decided on grounds that plainly indicated that the Court had accepted the existence of jurisdiction over the claims presented. "We hold," Brennan therefore said, "that the District Court has jurisdiction of the subject matter of the federal constitutional claim asserted in the complaint."[12]

Brennan next considered the State of Tennessee's argument that the appellants lacked standing to maintain the suit. Again relying on the cases he had cited to sustain jurisdiction, Brennan held that the appellants possessed standing and that *Colegrove* was a case in point, since it had "squarely held that voters who allege facts showing disadvantage to themselves as individuals have standing to sue."[13] The appellants were asserting that the 1901 apportionment act "disfavors the voters in the counties in which they reside, placing them in a position of constitutionally unjustifiable inequality vis-a-vis voters in irrationally favored counties." The right to vote, free of arbitrary impairment by the state, had been "judicially recognized as a right secured by the Constitution, when such impairment resulted from dilution by a false tally . . . or by a refusal to count votes from arbitrarily selected precincts . . . or by a stuffing of the ballot box. . . ."[14] It was not necessary to hold that the appellants' allegations were true to hold that they possessed standing, since if "such impairment does produce a legally cognizable injury, they are among those who have sustained it."[15]

Brennan then turned to the issue of justiciability. He held that the "claim pleaded here neither rests upon nor implicates the Guaranty Clause" and that the lower court had "misinterpreted Colegrove v. Green and other decisions of this Court on which it relied."[16] In order to clearly outline the doctrine of political questions, Brennan reviewed the Court's decisions involving political questions to demon-

---

[11] *Ibid.*, at 202.
[12] *Ibid.*, at 204.
[13] *Ibid.*, at 206.
[14] Here Brennan cited *United States* v. *Classic*, 313 U.S. 299; *United States* v. *Mosley*, 238 U.S. 383; *Ex parte* Siebold, 100 U.S. 371; *United States* v. *Saylor*, 322 U.S. 385, in which the Court had sustained federal prosecutions for interference with the right to vote in federal elections through the means listed.
[15] 369 U.S., at 208.
[16] *Ibid.*, at 209.

strate that the doctrine did not apply to cases challenging state apportionment systems. Cases involving political questions, he said, had held that judicial power was particularly limited in cases concerning foreign relations, the dates of duration of hostilities, the validity of the enactment of a congressional statute or how long a constitutional amendment remained open for ratification, and the status of the Indian tribes, and also in cases arising under the guaranty clause.[17] A review of these cases revealed, Brennan concluded, that prominent "on the surface of any case held to involve a political question is found a textually demonstrable constitutional commitment of the issue to a coordinate political department; or a lack of judicially discoverable and manageable standards for resolving it; or the impossibility of deciding without an initial policy determination of a kind clearly for nonjudicial discretion; or the impossibility of a court's undertaking independent resolution without expressing lack of respect due coordinate branches of government; or an unusual need for unquestioning adherence to a political decision already made; or the potentiality of embarrassment from multifarious pronouncements by various departments on one question."[18]

The issues in the Tennessee case, Brennan said, had none of the characteristics of political questions. "We have no question decided, or to be decided, by a political branch of government coequal with this Court. Nor do we risk embarrassment of our government abroad, or grave disturbance at home if we take issue with Tennessee as to the constitutionality of her action here challenged. Nor need the appellants, in order to succeed in this action, ask the Court to enter upon policy determinations for which judicially manageable standards are lacking." Judicial standards under the equal protection clause, he continued, "are well developed and familiar, and it has been open to courts since the enactment of the Fourteenth Amendment to determine, if on the particular facts they must, that a discrimination reflects *no* policy, but simply arbitrary and capricious action."[19] Brennan emphasized that the cases decided by the Court arising under the guaranty clause were held to raise political questions, not because "they touch on matters of state governmental organization," but for other reasons. He cited *Gomillion* v. *Lightfoot* to demonstrate

17 *Ibid.*, at 210–29.
18 *Ibid.*, at 217.
19 *Ibid.*, at 229–31.

that cases involving such challenges to "matters of state governmental organization" were justiciable under other provisions of the Constitution.[20]

After reiterating that jurisdiction existed, and after distinguishing each of the post-*Colegrove per curiam* opinions in which similar suits had been dismissed or affirmed, Brennan concluded that the "complaint's allegations of a denial of equal protection present a justiciable constitutional cause of action upon which appellants are entitled to a trial and a decision. The right asserted is within the reach of judicial protection under the Fourteenth Amendment." The decision of the district court was reversed and the cause "remanded for further proceedings consistent with this opinion."[21]

Three of the justices—Douglas, Clark, and Stewart—wrote concurring opinions. Justice Douglas' opinion added very little to what the Court had already said. In discussing the question of whether a state might weight some votes heavier than others in its apportionment system, however, Douglas said, "Universal equality is not the test; there is room for weighting,"[22] and he indicated that the test under the equal protection clause was whether or not "invidious discrimination" existed. It would seem that Justice Douglas did not think that the standard for state apportionment systems must be population alone.

Justice Clark believed that the Court should have declared that a violation of the equal protection clause existed and proceeded to award relief. Taking "the law of the case from *MacDougall* v. *Green*,"[23] in which the Court had said that a state could "assure a proper diffusion of political initiative as between its thinly populated counties and those having concentrated masses," Clark believed the test under the equal protection clause was one of "rationality." And in this respect he found the Tennessee apportionment act of 1901 to be lacking, since it was a "crazy quilt" which admitted of "no policy whatever."[24] Since there was discrimination among counties equal in population, Clark said, "the plan is neither consistent nor rational. It discriminates horizontally creating gross disparities between rural areas themselves as well as between urban areas themselves, still maintaining the wide vertical disparity . . . between rural and urban."[25] No one, Clark added, "not even the State nor the dissenters has come

[20] *Ibid.*
[21] *Ibid.*, at 236.
[22] *Ibid.*, at 244–45.

[23] 335 U.S. 281 (1948).
[24] 369 U.S., at 254, 257.
[25] *Ibid.*, at 256.

up with any rational basis for Tennessee's apportionment statute."[26]

Nevertheless, Clark felt that the Court should not intrude in the field of apportionment, even if shown a denial of equal protection, unless no other political remedies were available, such as the initiative and referendum. But, lacking such remedies, the people of Tennessee were stymied, he said, "and without judicial intervention will be saddled with the present discrimination in the affairs of their state government."[27] The relief the Court should provide in this case should not partake of an assertion of jurisdiction to force legislative action, for that, Clark felt, "would be nothing less than blackjacking the Assembly into reapportioning the State." Clark recommended rather that the Court consolidate the most overrepresented districts and award the seats that would be released to the most underrepresented counties, thus loosening "the strangle hold now on the Assembly and permit it to redistrict itself."[28]

In conclusion, Clark directed his attention to the dissenting opinions of Justices Frankfurter and Harlan and declared that it was proper for the Court "to practice self-restraint and discipline in constitutional adjudication, but never before in its history have those principles received sanction where the national rights of so many have been so clearly infringed for so long." He added, "National respect for the courts is more enhanced through the forthright enforcement of those rights rather than by rendering them nugatory through the interposition of subterfuges. In my view the ultimate decision today is in the greatest tradition of this court."[29]

Justice Stewart felt constrained to deliver a short concurrence because of the "separate writings of my dissenting and concurring Brothers" which strayed "so far from the subject of today's decision as to convey . . . a distressingly inaccurate impression of what the Court decides." Stewart thus reiterated twice that the Court had decided only that jurisdiction existed, that a justiciable cause of action had been alleged, and that the appellants had standing to maintain the action. The merits of the case were not before the Court, he said, and "the proper place for the trial is in the trial court, not here."[30]

Justices Harlan and Frankfurter both delivered lengthy dissents. Justice Frankfurter, in what was to be his last major opinion as a jus-

[26] *Ibid.*, at 258.
[27] *Ibid.*, at 259.
[28] *Ibid.*, at 260.

[29] *Ibid.*, at 262.
[30] *Ibid.*, at 265–66.

tice, declared in the opening his delivery from the bench: "Today the court begins a process of litigation that it requires no prophet to say—and Cassandra was sometimes right—will outlast the life of the youngest member of this court."[31] The majority, in Frankfurter's view, had cast aside a uniform series of precedents, which "reflected the equally uniform course of our political history regarding the relationship between population and legislative representation," and was engaged in a "massive repudiation of the experience of our whole past in asserting destructively novel judicial power." The Court had sustained a "hypothetical claim resting on abstract assumptions" because it had not attempted to formulate any remedy "that would not invite legislatures to play ducks and drakes with the judiciary." Frankfurter declared that "to charge courts with the task of accommodating the incommensurable factors of policy that underlie these mathematical puzzles is to attribute, however flatteringly, omnicompetence to judges." The Court's decision, in effect, empowered "the courts of the country to devise what should constitute the proper composition of the legislatures of the fifty states."[32]

The *Colegrove* case had indicated the Court's concern over the problems involved in the adjudication of apportionment cases—problems related to the involvement of the judiciary in legislative matters, problems in shaping appropriate standards in such cases, and problems in affording relief. These considerations, Frankfurter argued, had led the Court to uniformly refuse to hear such cases since the *Colegrove* decision in 1946. "The Colegrove doctrine, in the form in which repeated decisions have settled it, was not an innovation," he said. "It represents long judicial thought and experience. From its earliest opinions this Court has consistently recognized a class of controversies which do not lend themselves to judicial standards and judicial remedies."[33] And the same factors that were present in past cases raising political questions were also present in *Baker* v. *Carr*. Indeed, this case, Frankfurter believed, involved "a Guarantee Clause claim masquerading under a different label."[34]

Nor could the appellants assert a denial of the right to vote, Frankfurter argued, since they were able to vote, and the talk of debase-

[31] *The New York Times*, March 27, 1962, p. 20.
[32] 369 U.S., at 267–69.
[33] *Ibid.*, at 280.
[34] *Ibid.*, at 297.

ment and dilution of their right to vote was "circular talk," because these terms had no content unless the value of a vote was first defined. The Court, in Frankfurter's opinion, had been asked in reality to "choose among competing bases of representation—ultimately really, among competing theories of political philosophy—in order to establish an appropriate frame of government for the State of Tennessee and thereby for all of the States of the Union."[35] Representation according to population, he said, was not so universally accepted as to be the only standard to which the states must conform under the Fourteenth Amendment. Population had never been so accepted in Great Britain, in the colonial system in America, or in the system established by the Constitution, nor was it exclusively practiced by the states during the time of the adoption of the Fourteenth Amendment or at the present time.[36] "The stark fact is," Frankfurter said, "that if among the numerous widely varying principles and practices that control state legislative apportionment today there is any generally prevailing feature, that feature is geographic inequality in relation to the population standard."[37]

The Court had thus plunged into an area in which judicially discoverable or administrable standards were lacking, an area epitomized by partisan politics, and it "will add a virulent source of friction and tension in federal-state relations to embroil the federal judiciary in them."[38] The lack of adequate standards could not be remedied by resort to the Tennessee Constitution's provisions, Frankfurter continued, because the applicable standard was not the state constitution but the standard of the equal protection clause. Nor could the lower court provide a satisfactory remedy, because the enjoining of a state election would "paralyze the critical centers of the State's political system and threaten political dislocation whose consequences are not foreseeable." Nor could the court "itself remap the State" because "the same complexities which impede effective judicial review of apportionment a fortiori make impossible a court's consideration of these imponderables as an original matter." An election at large would be "a matter of sweeping political judgment having enormous political implications" which made such a remedy improper for judicial judgment and administration. Finally, the invalidation of the 1901 act would, according to the *Kidd* case, "deprive the State of an effective

---

[35] *Ibid.*, at 300.
[36] *Ibid.*, at 301–21.
[37] *Ibid.*, at 321.
[38] *Ibid.*, at 324.

law-based legislative branch." *Baker* v. *Carr* was therefore "unfit for judicial action," Frankfurter concluded, and the district court's decision should have been affirmed.[39]

Justice Harlan, who joined Justice Frankfurter's dissent, also filed his own dissenting opinion. He began his oral dissent by declaring that *Baker* v. *Carr* "is the most important decision rendered by this court, in its potential consequences, since I have had the privilege of being here."[40] Harlan's principal argument was that the equal protection clause did not require that "state legislatures must be so structured as to reflect with approximate equality the voice of every voter."[41] So long as "there exists a possible rational legislative policy for retaining an existing apportionment," he argued, "such a legislative decision cannot be said to breach the bulwark against arbitrariness and caprice that the Fourteenth Amendment affords." The standard was therefore whether an apportionment was based upon *any* rational policy, and, to Harlan, under this standard the apportionment of the Tennessee legislature under the 1901 act was rational. One need not search far, he said, "to find rationality in the Legislature's continued refusal to recognize the growth of the urban population that has accompanied the development of industry over the past half century. The existence of slight disparities between rural areas does not overcome the fact that the foremost apparent legislative motivation has been to preserve the electoral strength of the rural interests notwithstanding shifts in population."[42] Harlan found this legislative policy rational and therefore in conformity with the equal protection clause. Thus while Harlan agreed with Frankfurter that the courts should not enter the apportionment arena, he also felt that upon the merits of the case the standard imposed by the Fourteenth Amendment was one of rationality. Since Tennessee's apportionment system met this test, the decision of the district court should be affirmed.

The Court's decision in *Baker* v. *Carr* opened the doors of the federal courts to litigants challenging state apportionment systems, but without establishing the standard by which the lower courts were to measure the validity of apportionment systems under the Fourteenth Amendment. The Court avoided this ultimate issue perhaps because

[39] *Ibid.*, at 325–30.
[40] Chattanooga *Times*, March 27, 1962, p. 4.
[41] 369 U.S., at 332.
[42] *Ibid.*, at 348, Appendix to the opinion of Mr. Justice Harlan.

the standard imposed by the Fourteenth Amendment was not fully argued in *Baker* v. *Carr*. Indeed, both the appellants and the solicitor general had attempted to narrow the issues to those upon which the Court ultimately decided the case. More important, however, the opinions of the justices and their subsequent positions on this issue revealed that at the time of the decision of *Baker* v. *Carr* there was no majority in favor of any ultimate Fourteenth Amendment standard for apportionment.

With Frankfurter and Harlan dissenting from the Court's acceptance of jurisdiction in the case, and with Justice Whittaker not participating, the six majority justices were able to agree only on the issues of jurisdiction, standing, and cause of action. Justice Clark favored a rationality test as the Fourteenth Amendment standard, and in the 1964 apportionment cases[43] continued to adhere to this position. Justice Black, although not expressing his views in *Baker* v. *Carr*, had consistently argued in favor of substantially equal population as the standard in similar cases such as *Colegrove* v. *Green* and *South* v. *Peters*, and it is not likely that he would have supported any other standard in *Baker*; he remained consistent with this position by voting in favor of the equal population standard in the 1964 cases. Justice Douglas had joined Black in cases such as *Colegrove*, and although he emphasized "room for weighting" in his concurrence in the Tennessee case, it is doubtful that he would have accepted a Fourteenth Amendment standard, such as Clark's rationality test, which allowed any great deviation from population; Douglas also voted in favor of the population standard in the 1964 cases. Chief Justice Warren and Justice Brennan had never expressed their views in apportionment cases, but in the 1964 cases they ultimately supported the equal population standard along with Black and Douglas. Justice Stewart did not commit himself in the Tennessee case, but in the 1964 cases vehemently opposed the population standard.

In *Baker* v. *Carr*, if all of the justices had supported the same position that they ultimately supported in the 1964 cases, there would not have been a majority in favor of the population standard, since only Chief Justice Warren and Justices Black, Douglas, and Brennan would have voted in favor of such a standard. It is not likely that Justice Stewart would have supplied the fifth vote for a standard he so

[43] *Reynolds* v. *Sims*, 377 U.S. 533 (1964).

vehemently opposed two years later. Even if some of the justices who voted in 1964 for the population standard were willing in 1962 to support a rationality test—perhaps Warren, Douglas, and Brennan—there still would not have been a majority on the merits, since Justice Clark advanced such a test but admitted that he was not "able to muster a court to dispose of the case on the merits."[44] Since a majority could not be mustered for Clark's rationality test, such a test could perhaps have been agreed on by Warren, Brennan, Douglas, and Stewart, but a majority in favor of such a test could only have been secured with the highly unlikely adherence of Justice Black. It seems highly probable, therefore, that a majority in favor of any standard did not exist on the Court when *Baker* v. *Carr* was decided.

Since the Court had left the question of the standard for apportionment undecided in the Tennessee case, personnel changes on the Court were crucial to future apportionment litigation. Two such changes occurred in 1962. Justice Whittaker, who did not participate in the decision in *Baker* v. *Carr*, announced his retirement on March 29, ending five years on the Court.[45] Justice Frankfurter suffered a stroke and collapsed at his desk at the Supreme Court on April 5,[46] and ended his long and distinguished career on the Court with the announcement of his retirement on August 28. President Kennedy appointed Byron R. White, his deputy attorney general, to succeed Justice Whittaker, and Arthur J. Goldberg, his secretary of labor, to succeed Justice Frankfurter. The personnel of the Court thus changed at a crucial time, when the standard required of state apportionment systems under the equal protection clause was still in doubt. White's and Goldberg's votes supporting the equal population standard in the 1964 apportionment cases converted the minority in favor of that standard in the Tennessee case to a majority.

The reaction to the Court's decision in *Baker* v. *Carr* was generally favorable. Of sixty-three leading metropolitan daily newspapers, thirty-eight favored the Court's disposition of the case, ten opposed it, and the remainder expressed neutral or confused opinions.[47] Editorial support was generally based on metropolitan newspapers'

[44] 369 U.S., at 261.
[45] *The New York Times*, March 30, 1962, p. 1.
[46] *The New York Times*, April 6, 1962, p. 1.
[47] These figures are drawn from Chester A. Newland's excellent article, "Press Coverage of the United States Supreme Court," *Western Political Quarterly*, Vol. 17 (March, 1964), pp. 15, 29.

desire for increased urban representation in state legislatures, particularly for their own communities, while opposition was generally mild and based on opposition to increased federal intrusion into state affairs.[48]

Officials of the national government also approved the decision. Attorney General Robert Kennedy called it "a landmark in the development of representative government." The democratic process, the attorney general said, "has been distorted because there has been no effective judicial remedy for the failure of some states to provide substantial equality of representation in the legislature. We hope that as a result of the decision the state legislatures will recognize their responsibilities and take action to make voting and representation more equitable without the need for further litigation."[49]

The American Municipal Association, the U. S. Conference of Mayors, the Unitarian Fellowship for Social Justice, and the Industrial Union Department of the AFL-CIO were among the groups which early expressed support for the Court's action. In the United States Senate, Senator Kenneth Keating of New York said that the decision would "meet with the approval of everyone who believes in giving full significance to the equal protection clause of the Fourteenth Amendment."[50] Senator Keating was joined in his support of the decision by his Republican colleague Senator Barry Goldwater of Arizona, who characterized it as a "proper decision." Speaking as a conservative, Goldwater noted that "there are those who say that the conservatives' political strength will be reduced if the cities gain more representation in the legislatures." But, he said, "I don't agree with that. There are proportionately just as many conservatives in the metropolitan as in the rural areas."[51]

The most outspoken early critic of the Court's decision was Senator Richard Russell of Georgia, who characterized *Baker v. Carr* as "another major assault on our constitutional system." He continued, "The true protection of our rights as citizens and the cornerstone of our great civilization is founded in the system of checks and balances which the majority of the Supreme Court has set out to destroy." If the people really cared for their freedom, Russell warned, "they

[48] *Ibid.*, pp. 29–30.
[49] *The New York Times*, March 28, 1962, p. 22.
[50] *Ibid.*
[51] *The New York Times*, March 29, 1962, p. 17.

will demand that Congress curtail and limit the jurisdiction being exercised by this group before it is too late."[52] Senator Russell's criticism of the decision may well have been at least partly a response to the fact that on the day the Tennessee case was decided, a suit was filed in federal court seeking to invalidate the Georgia county unit system.[53] This suit, filed by Morris B. Abram, representing James O'Hear Sanders, chairman of Active Voters of Atlanta, was ultimately successful in the Supreme Court and marked the beginning of the end of the county unit system in Georgia.

Unlike President Eisenhower, who refused to endorse the Court's 1954 desegregation decision, President Kennedy in his news conference on March 29 stated his complete support of the Court's decision in *Baker v. Carr.* In response to questions, the President noted that the "Administration made clear its endorsement of the principles implicit in the court decision as a friend of the court. . . . Quite obviously, the right to fair representation that each vote count equally is, it seems to me, basic to the successful operation of a democracy." This equality of representation should be brought about by the "responsible groups involved in the states," but in the Tennessee case "for many years it was impossible for the people involved to secure adequate relief through the normal political processes." The problem was not confined to Tennessee, however, but was evident in Massachusetts and other states, the President said, and there was "just no sense of a Senator representing 5,000,000 people sitting next to a Senator representing 10,000 people and then when no relief comes to say the court is taking action where it should not. It's the responsibility of the political groups to respond to the need and—but if no relief is forthcoming, then of course it seemed to the Administration that the judicial branch must meet a responsibility."[54]

This presidential endorsement of the Court's decision was of great importance. The Court was entering a field where the methods of judicial relief were still uncertain and the possibilities of resistance, if not defiance, from state legislators were great. A presidential refusal to endorse the decision, or outright opposition to it, would have inflicted immeasurable damage to enforcement of the Court's mandate, for this was the beginning of a judicially supervised revolution

[52] *The New York Times*, March 28, 1962, p. 1.
[53] *The New York Times*, March 27, 1962, p. 21.
[54] *The New York Times*, March 30, 1962, pp. 1, 12.

in the political systems of the states, and the President's support was vital to its success.

Reaction to *Baker* v. *Carr* among political leaders in Tennessee was predictable, although the reaction of rural political leaders was unexpectedly mild. Among the state's congressmen, only one, Representative Robert A. ("Fats") Everett of the Eighth Congressional District, publicly opposed the decision. The Court, Everett said, had amended the Constitution and deprived "the people of Tennessee of their rights to specify how they should be represented in the General Assembly."[55] Senator Estes Kefauver, however, called the decision a landmark and expressed confidence that the people of the state and their political leaders would "cooperate fully in bringing this problem to a reasonable solution," and Republican Congressman Howard Baker of the Second Congressional District declared that "this will mean a great deal to Tennessee and I am delighted with the decision."[56] He urged the governor to call a special session of the legislature immediately to reapportion properly.

Congressman Baker's enthusiasm for the decision reflected the general conviction among Republican leaders that the Court's action would ultimately increase the strength of their party in Tennessee, since East Tennessee, where they were strongest, had long been underrepresented in the legislature. Guy L. Smith, former chairman of the Republican State Executive Committee, publisher of the Knoxville *Journal*, and a supporter of the apportionment litigation since the initiation of *Kidd* v. *McCanless*, declared that the Tennessee case was "the beginning of a revolution, politically, in this state." The first result, he said, "will be to give representation to urban populations as well as to give representation to Republicans. It may well be the beginning of a real two-party system in Tennessee."[57]

There were no initial vows of defiance from rural politicians. State Representative James H. Cummings of Woodbury, who was an acknowledged rural leader in the legislature and opponent of reapportionment, said that he was "at a complete loss" about what would happen next, but that the legislature would not be able to agree on any "wholesale" changes in the districts. "If the courts are

---

[55] Knoxville *News-Sentinel*, March 27, 1962, p. A–2.

[56] Chattanooga *Times*, March 27, 1962, p. 4.

[57] Knoxville *Journal*, March 27, 1962, p. 1; Chattanooga *Times*, March 27, 1962, p. 9.

going to take jurisdiction, I hope they will lay out the legislative districts themselves," he said, "because we can't agree on it here in Tennessee." Cummings also predicted that "we will be running back and forth between Nashville and Washington for the next several years."[58] Perhaps the most extreme response from a rural leader was the comment that the "Supreme Court already has shoved integration down our throats, and now it is trying to do the same with reapportionment. . . . Apparently its formula is more Negroes and less money for rural areas."[59]

While the appellants' attorneys hailed the decision as a great victory, they were also aware of the narrowness of the Court's decision and the difficulties ahead. Soon after the Court's decision, therefore, all of them met in Washington to decide what would be done when the case was remanded to the three-judge court. From the opinions of the justices, they concluded that the governing standard in the federal court would be the equal protection clause of the Fourteenth Amendment and not the apportionment provisions of the Tennessee Constitution. This meant that apportionment on a strict population basis would probably not be required. They still hoped, however, that the three-judge court would use the Tennessee Constitution as a guide in granting relief.

They further concluded that all of the county election commissioners in the state would have to be joined as parties-defendant in the case, that the exhibits in the case would have to be updated to conform to the 1960 census, and that they should discard their arguments based on discrimination in the distribution of state revenues, except as background information. They agreed that expert use of federal procedure was now more vital than ever in the lower court, since "if we flunk there, all is lost."

The attorneys agreed that the question of relief was now their most important problem, and they decided that they should seek alternative forms of relief depending on the responsiveness of the legislature, including the possibility of a declaratory judgment holding the 1901 act invalid, an injunction against the holding of elections under the 1901 act, a court-ordered election at large, and court-administered re-

[58] Knoxville *News-Sentinel*, March 27, 1962, p. A–2; Chattanooga *Times*, March 27, 1962, p. 4.
[59] Chattanooga *Times*, March 27, 1962, p. 4.

apportionment under a special master or by the court itself. Although the attorneys acknowledged the importance of presenting an acceptable plan for reapportionment to the court, they also agreed that any court-ordered reapportionment should be made temporary, to be superseded whenever the legislature properly reapportioned.

These plans, of course, precluded Z. T. Osborn's idea that they should return to the state courts for relief. As Charles Rhyne said later, a return to the state courts would "indicate our lack of confidence in the Federal courts and would be changing horses in midstream," and "would run directly into *Kidd* v. *McCanless*." The Tennessee apportionment litigation would therefore remain in the federal courts, but the attorneys concluded that "study of the opinions gives a sober feeling about the difficulty of the hurdles that lie ahead in implementing the decision."[60]

What action would ultimately be taken, however, depended upon whether or not the governor convened a special session of the legislature. Both Governor Ellington and Attorney General McCanless were initially noncommittal. McCanless stated to the press that without studying the Court's opinions it was "impossible to say what we will do."[61] And four days following the decision the governor indicated that he opposed calling a special session of the legislature because he doubted that "any stop-gap reapportionment" would satisfy anyone and would "just get another court fight going." He had received only two telegrams and one personal call urging a special session, the governor said, while he had received "about 500 asking me to go slow." The governor also indicated that he felt it had been the state's duty to defend the suit "only up to now" and that the rural legislators ought to assume the defense of the suit on remand from the Supreme Court.[62] A few weeks later the attorney general announced that he would not petition the Supreme Court for a rehearing in the case because he did not "believe any useful purpose would be served."[63] The

---

[60] The foregoing paragraphs on the conference held by the appellants' counsel in *Baker* v. *Carr* are based on a memorandum apparently prepared to summarize the major conclusions of the conference. It is in the files of Hobart Atkins and is not dated, although I have established that the conference itself occurred on April 6, 1962.

[61] Chattanooga *Times*, March 27, 1962, pp. 1, 2.

[62] Knoxville *News-Sentinel*, March 30, 1962, p. 3.

[63] Chattanooga *Times*, April 18, 1962, p. 1.

case was thus expedited considerably; a petition for rehearing would have delayed for some time the remand of the case to the three-judge court.

By mid-April, some six months after the Supreme Court announced its decision, some legislators from the less populous areas of Tennessee were reported to have second thoughts about waiting to see what action the federal court would take. Some of the legislators became convinced that almost any minimal reapportionment would be more defensible in the federal court than the 1901 act, and also that under a reapportionment by the legislature the less populous areas might fare better than under a court-ordered plan. Justice Clark's opinion, suggesting that a lower court could combine some of the most over-represented districts, particularly disturbed some of the legislators, since it was a concrete suggestion that they feared the federal court might accept and order into effect before the November elections. Support for a special session thus increased. As one legislator said, "If we are going to have reapportionment, I'd rather it be done on Capitol Hill than down there at Eighth and Broad," where the federal district court was located in Nashville.[64]

Governor Ellington, on April 24, indicated that he had abandoned his initial opposition to a special session and noted that a majority of the legislators had indicated that they preferred to act before the federal court hearing. "I never got into anything where there were so many ramifications," the governor said. "Some in the city are very rabid on this subject just as some on the other side are rabid." The governor suggested that reapportionment along lines of a "federal plan" would be most satisfactory. "If it would be accepted to re-apportion the House on population and the Senate on the area basis, I think a majority of [the legislators] would go along with it. If something along that line could be worked out, then they would like to have a constitutional convention in 1965. It is getting to a point where a majority of them want to do something."[65]

The governor's proposal, however, drew immediate criticism from Hobart Atkins and Walter Chandler. Atkins indicated that he felt the governor's proposal would not conform to the Fourteenth Amendment, arguing that one "can't discriminate between the House and

[64] Fred Travis, "Rural Bloc Shifts Views," Chattanooga *Times*, April 16, 1962, p. 4.
[65] Chattanooga *Times*, April 25, 1962, pp. 1, 2.

the Senate. The people must have equal representation in both houses."[66] And Chandler warned that anything less than "complete reapportionment" would force the plaintiffs to "carry on the pending case to conclusion."[67] Despite this criticism, Governor Ellington announced on May 2 that he would call a special session of the legislature to convene on May 29 to consider reapportionment. Confessing that he had failed to gain the agreement of the legislators and interested groups on any plan, he stated that reapportionment was "a legislative responsibility" and that he felt "it is certainly my responsibility to call a special session and give the membership an opportunity to reapportion itself before the Federal Court would be forced to take action."[68]

At a pre-trial conference on May 7, the attorneys involved in *Baker v. Carr* met before Judge Miller in the federal district court in Nashville in an attempt to settle technical and procedural issues before the trial of the case on the merits. The attorney general had renewed his motion to dimiss the suit on the grounds that indispensable parties were not joined, but, upon the statement of plaintiffs' counsel that all county election commissioners were being joined as parties-defendant, Judge Miller overruled the motion to dismiss on this ground. The attorney general then agreed to stipulate that the 1960 census figures accurately reflected the numbers of qualified voters in each county and also that the legislature had not been reapportioned since 1901.[69]

The Tennessee Farm Bureau Federation, through its attorney Edwin Hunt, made a motion to intervene in the suit. The plaintiffs opposed the motion, suggesting that the status of *amicus curiae* would be appropriate for the Farm Bureau, but not the status of intervenor which would allow its full participation in the suit, including the

[66] *Ibid.*, p. 2.

[67] Chattanooga *Times*, April 26, 1962, p. 1.

[68] Knoxville *News-Sentinel*, May 2, 1962, p. 1.

[69] Pre-Trial Conference before Judge William E. Miller, Nashville, May 7, 1962, Transcript of the Proceedings, Vol. I, pp. 33–36, 55, 62–63. It should be noted that the three-judge court in its original decision in *Baker* v. *Carr* had not ruled upon the defendants' motion to dismiss on the grounds that indispensable parties were not joined, but had dismissed the suit for lack of jurisdiction and failure to state a cause of action. The Supreme Court specifically noted in its decision that it was not ruling on this motion to dismiss (359 U.S. 186, at 198, note 16), and the attorney general thus renewed the motion on remand of the case. The plaintiffs, seeking to avoid dismissal of the suit on this ground, joined all county election commissioners as parties-defendant, at the cost of about four thousand dollars. See the Chattanooga *Times*, April 18, 1962, p. 1.

right of appeal.[70] Hunt argued, however, that "rural voters, when their interests are to be affected, should have representation in the case and be heard to no less extent than the urban voters."[71] In overruling the plaintiffs' objections to the intervention of the Farm Bureau, Judge Miller indicated some of the problems he foresaw in the litigation. The court would "want and must have all of the help it can possibly get," Miller said. While the Supreme Court had settled some of the issues in the case, others remained open, the most significant of which was "the appropriate remedy in the event the legislature does not act and does not remove the discrimination in accordance with the requirements of the Fourteenth Amendment." That problem, he said, "has plagued me from the very start much more than the question of jurisdiction and justiciability, and I think I made that clear during the argument at the time."

That did not mean there was no remedy, Miller added, because if the court had jurisdiction to declare an act unconstitutional, a remedy to enforce the ruling must be found. Otherwise such a ruling would be an "idle ceremony," and it "would make the courts look ridiculous if they assumed jurisdiction and then threw up their hands and said that they were helpless to do anything about it, and I do not believe that this court, whether it is constituted by a single judge or three judges, would ever admit helplessness and its inability to afford an appropriate remedy." But the question of remedy remained a serious problem, Miller said, and the court would need "a lot of help and a lot of enlightenment from every possible source," and for that reason he thought the Farm Bureau should be allowed to intervene. Miller also noted that the attorney general was in a "somewhat ambiguous position as to his duties as to the extent to which he should go in this litigation," and the intervention of the Farm Bureau would thus make "this controversy a more real controversy."[72]

Despite the Supreme Court's decision, therefore, Judge Miller was still faced with the problem of implementing a decree invalidating the 1901 act, and it was evident that he was much concerned about how this could be done. The attorney general advised Miller that the special session of the legislature would convene on May 29 and urged that any further action by the court be delayed until the expiration of

[70] *Ibid.*, Vol. I, pp. 5–32; Vol. II, p. 59.
[71] *Ibid.*, Vol. II, pp. 59–60.
[72] *Ibid.*, pp. 61–62.

152

the session on June 17. Miller agreed only to stay proceedings until June 11, on which date he indicated he would hear a motion to invalidate the 1901 act. The legislature was thus put on notice that it must act and act quickly or face a federal judicial remedy.[73]

The legislators meeting in the special session were inundated with plans for reapportionment. It soon became apparent that Speaker of the House James L. Bomar and Senate Speaker William D. Baird were seeking a reapportionment which would not conform to the state constitution's provisions but which, they hoped, would satisfy the federal court while retaining as many of the 1901 districts as possible. Defending his plan to reapportion the senate largely on an area basis, Baird argued that if "I didn't think with all my heart that what we are trying to do was the best thing for Tennessee, I wouldn't be here." He argued that domination of the legislature by the urban areas would mean domination by organized labor. The Tennessee right-to-work law would never have been passed by such a legislature, he said. "If organized labor ever gets control of the Legislature of Tennessee, they will repeal the 'Right to Work' law quicker than a minnow can swim across a dipper." If that happened, he warned, "you can forget about industry coming to Tennessee." Baird added that it was usually "the urban areas that send the liberals and the extremists and the educated cranks to the Legislature." In rural areas, people knew their representatives, he said, while in the city candidates appeared on television and ran newspaper ads, but the people did not know them, and as a result the urban people were "lucky if they don't get a smooth-talking crackpot."[74] In response to a question about whether or not his plan conformed to the Tennessee Constitution, Baird remarked, "We're not concerned with the state constitution. Our concern is that we pass a bill that meets the requirements of the federal court."[75] A rural legislator, asked the mood of his colleagues, perhaps best summed up the prospects during the special session. "Most of them feel just as I do—they're going to take care of their districts. You can't expect any other kind of action in a legislature. If the federal court hadn't stepped in, it would have stayed the way it was, from now on."[76]

[73] *Ibid.*, pp. 28, 63.
[74] Chattanooga *Times*, May 31, 1962, pp. 1, 5.
[75] Nashville *Tennessean*, May 31, 1962, p. 1.
[76] Nashville *Tennessean*, May 30, 1962, pp. 1, 2.

On June 6 the legislature passed and sent to the governor the "Baird–Bomar plans" for reapportioning the senate and house, as well as legislation authorizing a limited constitutional convention in 1965 to consider revision of the state constitution's apportionment provisions if approved by the voters in a referendum.[77] Somewhat surprising was the support of the Bomar plan by fifteen of the nineteen house Republicans, whose party stood to gain substantially more representation in the legislature from a reapportionment more closely reflecting population than the Bomar plan.[78] Although the representation of the more populous areas of the state was increased by these bills, neither the house nor the senate was apportioned on a population basis under their provisions. On June 7, however, Governor Ellington signed the reapportionment bills and the bill authorizing the limited constitutional convention. But the governer signed the convention bill before he signed the reapportionment bills, thus assuring that the constitutional convention, if approved by the voters, would be composed of delegates elected on the basis of the 1901 apportionment of the legislature and not on the basis of the 1962 acts. The strategy of the legislators from the less populous areas to reapportion sufficiently to satisfy the federal court and then to change the state constitutional provisions to allow greater geographic representation, with the aid and acquiescence of Governor Ellington, was thus completely, and not unexpectedly, successful.[79]

On June 11 the three-judge federal court heard arguments on a motion by the plaintiffs for a summary judgment that the 1962 acts were invalid and a simultaneous motion of the attorney general to dismiss the suit. Court of Appeals Judge Paul Weick replaced Judge John D. Martin, who had died since the three-judge court originally heard *Baker* v. *Carr*. The court at this point allowed the Tennessee Labor Council, AFL-CIO, to intervene in the case. Walter Chandler characterized the 1962 acts during the hearing as not being a "new deck of cards" but simply "a reshuffle of the old deck." He argued that the matter of reapportionment was right back where it had started. "Our intention was to have every voter represented on an equal basis. Juggling with voting should be ended. The Constitution

[77] Knoxville *News-Sentinel*, June 6, 1962, p. 1.

[78] Chattanooga *Times*, June 6, 1962, pp. 1, 12.

[79] Ed Topp, "Short-Changed in Remap," Chattanooga *Times*, June 10, 1962, p. A-5.

should be the supreme document of the state." While the plaintiffs asserted the 1962 acts were invidiously discriminatory and irrational, Attorney General McCanless contended that the gross inequities that had existed under the 1901 act had been removed and that the 1962 acts contained no invidious discrimination. In any case, he said, "I don't believe it was the intention of the Supreme Court that the Federal Court act as auditor of acts passed by legislatures. The court should not undertake to correct any inequities it finds."[80]

After considering the case for eleven days, the court announced on June 22 that it found the 1962 acts not in conformity with the standards required by the Fourteenth Amendment.[81] The court inferred from the language of the several opinions of the Supreme Court justices in the Tennessee case that "if a state legislative classification for apportionment purposes is wholly irrational and arbitrary, supported neither by the standard of the state nor by any other standard, it is outside the permissible limits of the Fourteenth Amendment." The Supreme Court, the judges thought, had determined at least *sub silentio* that "invidious discriminations were present in the 1901 reapportionment statute and that it fell short of the standards of the equal protection clause."[82]

The court then considered the 1962 acts passed by the legislature. It found the act reapportioning the house[83] to be not as offensive to the Fourteenth Amendment as the act reapportioning the senate.[84] The court accepted the validity of the state constitutional provision that assigned one representative in the house to any county possessing two-thirds of the qualified voters necessary to entitle it to a representative. The court also accepted the extension of this provision to the assignment of representatives to floterial districts. The application of this provision, the court said, "at least in one house of a bicameral legislature, cannot, in our opinion be characterized as per se irrational or arbitrary," since the court felt that the state "has the right, if it sees fit, to assure that its smaller and less populous areas and communities are not completely overridden by sheer weight of numbers." However, the court found that the house reapportionment contained de-

---

[80] Knoxville *News-Sentinel*, June 12, 1962, p. A-2.
[81] *Baker v. Carr*, 296 F. Supp. 341 (M.D. Tenn. 1962).
[82] *Ibid.*, at 344–45.
[83] Public Chapter No. 1, Extraordinary Session of 1962.
[84] Public Chapter No. 3, Extraordinary Session of 1962.

viations from equality of population not justified by the application of the two-thirds rule. For example, Fayette County, with a population of 11,652, was assigned one direct representative, while Loudon County with a population of 14,054 was not assigned any direct representative, but shared instead a floterial representative with Blount County, which had a population of 32,849. Anderson County, with a population of 33,554, was assigned one representative, but, although it had a population that was 12,000 more than the ratio entitling it to one representative, it was not permitted to participate in the selection of a floterial representative.[85]

These objections to the house reapportionment were relatively mild, however, compared to the court's view of the senate reapportionment, which it found to be "devoid of any standard or rational plan of classification which we are able to discern." The judges found there was "no pretense of equality or substantial equality in numbers of qualified voters," nor were the districts "equal or even remotely equal in area." The act, the court said, quoting Justice Clark, was a "crazy quilt" and was "inexplicable either in terms of geography or demography."[86] The population spread per district ranged from 35,773 in the twenty-first district to 92,777 in the sixth district. But the population variation among districts was not exclusively a function of discrimination against urban areas, the court noted, but included discrimination against the rural areas of East Tennessee in contrast to the rural areas in West and particularly Middle Tennessee. The act also followed no discernible policy of area representation, the court said, since the districts varied in square miles from 3,577 to 1,025; nor was the act based on the equal representation of counties, since the districts contained a range of from two to six counties; and although the discrimination against urban counties was great, the court noted that even in this the act was not consistent, since in Hamilton County (Chattanooga) the ratio of senator to population was one to 71,489 but in Knox County (Knoxville) the ratio was one to 92,772. "We conclude," the judges said, "that the Act reapportioning the Senate of Tennessee is utterly arbitrary and lacking in rationality. Its only consistent pattern is one of invidious discrimination."[87]

The court next considered the problem of remedies. It dismissed

85 296 F. Supp., at 345–46.
86 *Ibid.*, at 346–47.
87 *Ibid.*, at 348.

the possibility of invalidating the 1962 acts and giving the legislature, elected on the basis of the 1901 act, another chance to reapportion properly, since the legislatures elected under the 1901 act had consistently "defaulted in their duties and responsibilities in regard to apportioning the state for over fifty years," and since it would be "incongruous" for the court to invalidate the 1962 acts while leaving in effect the much more offensive 1901 act. The court also rejected the idea of reapportioning by judicial decree. The court decided instead to allow the 1963 legislature to be elected on the basis of the 1962 acts and to remedy the defects in those acts. The standard required of the legislature, the court said, was that "apportionment in at least one house shall be based, fully and in good faith, on numbers of qualified voters without regard to any other factor." Thus if the two-thirds rule were applied in the apportionment of the house, the senate would have to be based on numbers of qualified voters, or if the senate were based on area or other factors, the house would have to be based on numbers of qualified voters. The remand of the case by the Supreme Court had not been "an idle gesture," the court warned, and "if the General Assembly fails to act or if it should act in a manner violative of the Fourteenth Amendment, this Court will be under a clear and unmistakable duty to take such steps as will effectively accomplish the enforcement and vindication of the constitutional rights of the plaintiffs." Although not bound by the interpretation of the *de facto* doctrine in the *Kidd* case, in which the Tennessee Supreme Court had held that an invalidation of the apportionment acts would result in the destruction of the legislature, the court decided that it would "express our views as to the 1962 statutes and expressly withhold final judgment on all issues, including the declaration of invalidity, the issuance of an injunction, or otherwise, until the General Assembly has acted at its 1963 session." But the court again warned that the case could be reopened by any of the parties or on the court's own motion, and that a final order would be entered not later than June 3, 1963.[88]

The court had thus declared the defects in the legislature's product, yet avoided any chance of a direct confrontation between the legislature and the federal judiciary by leaving the remedying of the defects in the hands of the legislature. Both sides in the case expressed satisfaction with the ruling. Attorney General McCanless said that he was

[88] *Ibid.*, at 348–50.

"gratified that the court handled the decision in this manner. We had urged the court to permit the newly apportioned legislature itself to correct any inequities, and that is what the court did." Z. T. Osborn also expressed satisfaction on the part of the plaintiffs, saying, "I am delighted with the ruling. I like it. I think it is the type of ruling we should have been granted." And Walter Chandler noted that if the 1963 legislature failed to act, "we will ask the federal court to reopen the pending suit and take all necessary steps to complete reapportionment according to the constitution." Senate Speaker Baird also accepted the court's decision gracefully, noting that he still felt as he had from the beginning that one house could be based on factors other than population and the court had agreed. "I have said I did not think the courts could require a higher standard than that applied to the federal Congress," he said. "It is asinine to think about applying higher standards to Tennessee than that." The house reapportionment, Baird thought, was rational, but because of the application of the two-thirds rule in the house, the senate, according to the court, must be based on population, since "when you apply the two-thrids rule, obviously it leaves a deficit that has to come out of somebody's hide." Baird also expressed the hope that the constitutional convention authorized by the legislature would change the apportionment provisions of the state constitution to allow one representative to be assigned to each county. "I understand," he said, "that's what they're going to try to do."[89]

Thus ended the first installment of reapportionment in Tennessee under the supervision of the federal judiciary. The assertion of federal judicial power had not been defied, and the legislature had responded, although inadequately, to the threat of judicial action. The federal court, on the other hand, had avoided attempting to reapportion the state by judicial decree or any other action that might have produced a direct confrontation with the legislature, while at the same time it had vigorously maintained its jurisdiction to review the reapportionment of the state and had given credibility to its power to act if the legislature failed to respond.

The results of the Supreme Court's decision in *Baker* v. *Carr* were similar throughout the nation, as apportionment suits were filed in both federal and state courts in thirty-three states during the spring

[89] Nashville *Tennessean*, June 23, 1962, pp. 1, 2.

and summer of 1962. "The rush through the door unlocked by *Baker v. Carr,*" one observer remarked, "has been staggering."[90] But another observer noted that in contrast to "the hostile response which greeted the segregation decisions in the South, the apportionment decision has met with general support throughout the country and, indeed, has proved to be a highly popular one."[91]

The action of the three-judge court in Tennessee had not, of course, precluded the possibility of considerable deviation from equal popu- lation representation in one house of the legislature, and the leaders in the less populous areas were hopeful, as Speaker Baird had indicated, that the constitutional convention would legitimate a "federal plan," allowing one house to be based on factors other than population. There was extended litigation challenging the proposal for a constitu- tional convention, since delegates would be elected on the basis of the 1901 apportionment act, but the state courts and the United States Supreme Court refused to invalidate the proposal,[92] and on November 6, 1962, the convention was authorized by a state-wide majority of approximately ten thousand votes.[93] The convention, to meet in 1965, could be expected to alter the apportionment provisions of the Ten- nessee Constitution in accordance with the desires of the less populous areas. Tennessee thus seemed to be moving toward a compromise be- tween area and population as the basis of legislative representation, but when the convention met in the summer of 1965 the delegates found the road to such a compromise blocked. In 1964, the United States Su- preme Court had spoken again on the question of apportionment. The equal protection clause of the Fourteenth Amendment, said the Court, required districts as nearly as practicable of equal population in *both* houses of a state legislature. The standard had at last been defined.

[90] Arthur L. Goldberg, "The Statistics of Malapportionment," 72 *Yale Law Journal* 96–97 (1962).

[91] Thomas I. Emerson, "Malapportionment and Judicial Power," 72 *Yale Law Journal* 79 (1962).

[92] *West* v. *Carr,* 378 U.S. 557 (1964); the decision of the Tennessee Supreme Court in the case is reported in 212 Tenn. 367 (1963).

[93] Knoxville *News-Sentinel,* Nov. 29, 1962, p. 4. The vote was 216,877 for the convention to 206,390 against.

CHAPTER VII

REYNOLDS v. SIMS:

THE REVOLT OF THE LOYALISTS

THE CONSTITUTIONAL CONVENTION which assembled in Montgomery, Alabama, in May, 1901, met to write a constitution that would make Alabama safe for rule by white, conservative Democrats. To accomplish this, the convention felt duty bound to systematically disenfranchise Negroes and lower-class whites and apportion the legislature to favor the conservative Democratic stronghold, the Black Belt. The purpose of such arrangements was to insure that the Negro, whom the president of the convention declared to be "descended from a race lowest in intelligence and moral perceptions of all races of men,"[1] would no longer participate in the political process in Alabama, and to diminish the possibility of a successful populist uprising from which the Black Belt politicians had only recently saved the state, many convention delegates believed, by their ability to cast their area's Negro vote for conservative Democrats. The government of the state was thus to be returned, in the opinion of the convention, to the virtuous, intelligent, economically better-off, white citizens.[2]

Concerning the apportionment of the legislature, the principal issue in the convention was whether to base apportionment on the number of white inhabitants or on the total number of inhabitants in the state. The northern section of the state had traditionally insisted upon the number of white inhabitants as the basis because of its smaller Negro population, while the Black Belt because of its large Negro population had traditionally insisted upon the total number of inhabitants as the proper basis of legislative apportionment. North Ala-

---

[1] Malcolm Cook McMillan, *Constitutional Development in Alabama, 1798–1901: A Study in Politics, the Negro, and Sectionalism,* James Sprunt Studies in History and Political Science, Vol. 37 (Chapel Hill: University of North Carolina Press, 1955), p. 268.

[2] *Ibid.*, chap. 18, pp. 281–309.

bama had won this conflict in the convention of 1819 which wrote Alabama's first constitution, but the constitution of 1867 based legislative apportionment upon the "whole number of inhabitants" because of the Radicals' dependence upon the Negro vote during Reconstruction, and the 1875 constitution had continued to base apportionment on the whole population.[3]

The Birmingham *Age-Herald*, reflecting the interest of North Alabama, suggested that the 1901 convention base the apportionment of the legislature either on votes cast or upon white population. "Justice in this respect is very important if the new constitution is to endure a long time," it said. "The present representation is greatly unjust, and the elimination of the Negro vote would make it notoriously so."[4] The Black Belt and South Alabama, however, insisted upon the retention of the whole population as the basis of legislative apportionment and, as the price for surrendering their controlled Negro vote, which would result from disenfranchising Negroes, insisted that such a provision should not be subject to constitutional amendment.[5] The Alabama Constitution of 1901 thus provides that senators and representatives are to be apportioned on the basis of population, except that each county shall have at least one representative in the lower house, and that "such basis of representation shall not be changed by constitutional amendment."[6]

The convention also provided for an apportionment of the legislature which under the constitution's provisions for decennial reapportionment would theoretically remain in effect until 1911. The 1901 apportionment of the legislature, however, was to remain unchanged for over sixty years. Thus, as one student of Alabama constitutional development has said, "instead of abolishing the inequality of representation in the state legislature, the convention actually consolidated and made more permanent the power of the Black Belt oligarchy in that body."[7]

By 1960, senate districts, which the Alabama Constitution requires

[3] *Ibid.*, pp. 36, 136, 201–202.

[4] *Ibid.*, quoted at p. 252.

[5] *Ibid.*, p. 307.

[6] Section 284, Alabama Constitution; the other provisions relating to legislative apportionment may be found in §§50, 197, 198, 199, 200, and 201.

[7] McMillan, *Constitutional Development in Alabama*, p. 307. In 1903 a new county, Houston, was created by the legislature, resulting in the addition of one more representative to the lower house of the legislature. The number of representatives in the lower house thus became 106.

to be "as nearly equal to each other in the number of inhabitants as may be," ranged in populations from a low of 15,417 in the sixteenth senatorial district (Lowndes County) to a high of 634,864 in the thirteenth district (Jefferson County). Representative districts revealed similar disparities in population in addition to those necessitated by the constitution's provision for at least one representative per county (see Appendix B, Tables I and II). The bias in favor of South Alabama built into the apportionment of 1901 was also aggravated by the fact that northern Alabama increased in population during the next sixty years at a more rapid rate than the rest of the state.[8] North Alabama's Jefferson County (Birmingham), with a population in 1960 of 634,864 electing seven representatives and one senator, was the most disadvantaged county in the state in terms of its population, but urban counties outside North Alabama, particularly Montgomery and Mobile, were similarly disadvantaged.

There were occasional efforts between 1901 and the 1960's to persuade the legislature to reapportion. One of the more notable of such efforts was made in 1939 by Governor Frank M. Dixon, who chided the legislature on its failure in this field and pointed out that as "long as those of us who have been elected to make and enforce the laws ignore the constitution which we are sworn to uphold, I fail to see how we can in good conscience ask obedience on the part of others." Governor Dixon's proposals for reapportionment were rejected by the legislature, however, in votes that found the rural, less populous North Alabama counties voting with similar South Alabama counties to maintain their advantage over the more urban, industrialized counties of both sections of the state.[9] On three separate occasions the legislature also attempted to change the status quo by submitting to the electorate constitutional amendments that would have allowed every county to have one senator, but on each of these occasions the amendments were defeated by the voters.[10]

The Alabama Supreme Court, like courts in other states, held that the question of reapportionment was a legislative matter and refused

[8] See Hallie Farmer, *The Legislative Process in Alabama: Legislative Apportionment* (University: Bureau of Public Administration, University of Alabama, 1944), pp. 18–19.

[9] *Ibid.*, pp. 27–29.

[10] See the Transcript of Hearing before Judges Richard T. Rives, Daniel H. Thomas, and Frank M. Thompson, Jr., at Montgomery, Ala., April 14, 1962, p. 6.

to intervene,[11] and a federal court challenge of the apportionment system was dismissed in 1956.[12] The Alabama Constitution does not provide for the initiative and referendum, and the proposal of constitutional amendments or a call for a constitutional convention is dependent upon legislative action. In Alabama, therefore, as in many other states, there appeared to be no effective avenue of relief to those seeking change in the state's apportionment system.[13]

The Supreme Court's 1954 decision against segregation in public schools struck Alabama like a thunderclap. The effects of the decision in Alabama politics were many, but perhaps the most prevalent was the infection of almost all public and many private issues with racial overtones. Issues and political careers turned upon the omnipresent and overriding racial issue. Political success depended upon insistence that the Court's decision was illegitimate and assurances that it would never prevail in Alabama. And federal law and federal courts became targets of the fear and hatred thus aroused.

Those who opposed the lawlessness that seemed to receive official encouragement from the state's political leaders, those who believed that the time for justice to the Negro had come and who remained loyal to the national Democratic party in the face of the Dixiecrat orientation of the state Democratic party, found the 1950's and 1960's in Alabama a time of trial, frustration, and dwindling influence. In a state well on the road to selective secession, those who resisted increasingly came to feel themselves to be outsiders in their state and strangers in their hometowns.[14]

Charles Morgan, Jr., a graduate of the University of Alabama and its law school, a practicing Birmingham attorney and a loyalist Democrat, was among those who had become deeply disillusioned by the trend of events in Alabama. A liberal possessing a profound belief in political and civil liberties and justice for the Negro, Morgan found

[11] See *Waid* v. *Pool,* 255 Ala. 441 (1951); and *Bonds* v. *State Department of Revenue,* 254 Ala. 553 (1950).

[12] *Perry* v. *Folsom,* 144 F. Supp. 874 (N.D. Ala. 1956).

[13] A good analysis of the apportionment problem in Alabama before *Reynolds* v. *Sims* may be found in James E. Larson, *Reapportionment in Alabama* (University: Bureau of Public Administration, University of Alabama, 1955).

[14] I have based the two paragraphs above largely on Charges Morgan, Jr., *A Time to Speak* (New York: Harper & Row, 1964), and upon impressions gained from interviews conducted during June, 1965, with those active in the apportionment litigation in Alabama.

himself progressively alienated by the lawlessness and denial of basic human liberties he saw in the state. He became convinced that if the state were to progress, the conservative Black Belt's political dominance in the state had to be changed, which meant the Alabama legislature had to be reapportioned. Sixty years after the convention of 1901, Morgan said later, "most of Alabama's people lived from industrial Birmingham north to the Tennessee boundary—political power still resided south, in the rural Black Belt. And most of that power lay outside Mobile, South Alabama's largest, most progressive and most underrepresented city." Although other factors had worked to retard the state's progress, he said, "there was no doubt in my mind that Black Belt domination in Montgomery was the vital political underpinning to a system designed to curb the influence of all the state's Negroes and a major part of its more progressive white population."[15]

Morgan was aware in the summer of 1961 that the Tennessee case, *Baker* v. *Carr*, was pending before the United States Supreme Court and that the best hope for reapportionment in Alabama would be a similar suit in the federal courts. However, there was no overt support for reapportionment among the Birmingham business and industrial leadership, the "Big Mules," who had often been found in alliance with Black Belt politicians. Also, because the federal courts had become bogeymen of Alabama politics, a suit in federal court involving the much abused Fourteenth Amendment might be received publicly with something less than enthusiasm.[16]

As a result of the 1960 census, Alabama lost one of its congressmen, necessitating congressional redistricting. In the summer of 1961, Black Belt leaders in the legislature proposed that Jefferson County be "chopped up" and shared among four congressional districts. This brought agonized protests from the leadership of Birmingham, and from the conflict emerged threats by Birmingham leaders to file suit to force reapportionment of the legislature. Although Morgan did not believe the Birmingham leaders were serious in their threat, he took advantage of the situation. He secured from the Young Men's Business Club, an organization composed of the younger, more progressive business and professional men of Birmingham, approval of a reapportionment suit to be filed in behalf of several of the YMBC's members, with M. O. Sims heading the list. "Although it seemed ludi-

[15] Morgan, *A Time to Speak*, pp. 102–103.
[16] *Ibid.*, pp. 103–105.

crous," Morgan said later, "fear of extremist reaction had come to pervade the community so thoroughly that even asking a federal court for the protection of our own constitutional rights was considered 'unwise' by some people. Again I was urged, by conservative and liberal alike, to exercise care and caution—in effect, to do nothing." But, he continued, "I ignored their advice and when the chop-up debate reached a crucial point filed suit in the U.S. District Court in Montgomery, a beleaguered institution presided over by Frank M. Johnson, Jr."[17]

Public understanding, if not support, for the suit was not ignored. Morgan and the other attorneys who ultimately intervened as plaintiffs in the suit were careful to draft their complaints and other legal papers filed in the case with an eye toward favorable publicity. As one of them said later, "Many of the legal documents filed in the case read more like press releases than legal documents."[18] From the beginning the apportionment suit received important newspaper support from the Birmingham *News*, which the plaintiffs' attorneys kept well informed throughout the litigation. In order to avoid any allegation that the suit was self-serving, the attorneys agreed that if the suit resulted in reapportionment, none of them would seek election to any of the seats opened up through their efforts.[19]

Joined by George Peach Taylor, David Baker, Robert Loeb, and Kenneth Howell—all young Birmingham attorneys—Morgan filed the complaint in the federal district court on August 12, 1961. Named as defendants were Bettye Frink, the secretary of state; the county probate judges of Lowndes, Jefferson, and Montgomery counties, who were sued as representatives of all probate judges in the state; Republican and Democratic state party officials; and the attorney general.[20] The complaint alleged that the plaintiffs were being deprived of their

[17] *Ibid.,* p. 105. The other YMBC members who were plaintiffs in the suit were Fred A. Beam, Wylie Johnson, G. R. Southard, Miles S. Lee, Paul Friedman, William Lindsay Williams, William P. Shaw, Jr., Prentice W. Thomas, Richard D. Tannehill, Paul M. Byrne, David R. Baker, Charles Morgan, Jr., and George Peach Taylor.

[18] Interview with David J. Vann, June 18, 1965, Birmingham, Ala.

[19] Morgan, *A Time to Speak,* p. 107; interviews with David J. Vann, June 18, 1965, Birmingham, Ala.; and John McConnell, Jr., June 12, 1965, Mobile, Ala.

[20] Amended Complaint, filed Aug. 12, 1961, in the Federal District Court for the Middle District of Alabama, Northern Division, Montgomery, Ala. Hereinafter cited as Complaint. In Alabama, the county probate judges, in addition to other administrative duties, play an important role in the administration of elections.

right to free and equal elections under the Fourteenth Amendment and the constitution of Alabama by the failure of the Alabama legislature to reapportion since 1901. Alleging that under the existing apportionment system 23.3 percent of the people could elect more than 50 percent of the members of the house of representatives and that 25 percent could elect over 50 percent of the members of the senate, the complaint asserted that the result was a "distortion and emasculation of the constitutional system established, defined and guaranteed by the Constitution of the United States" and that "a minority now rules Alabama by virtue of its control of both Houses of the Legislature, contrary to the rudimentary principles of representative government."[21] Pointing out that from past performance no reapportionment could be expected by the legislature, that constitutional amendments or conventions were similarly dependent upon legislative action, and that the state courts had refused to take action, the complaint declared that "all forms of relief for plaintiffs have been heretofore exhausted and that this Honorable Court is the last and only authority to which the people of Alabama may look for relief."[22]

The complaint relied primarily upon the apportionment provisions of the Alabama Constitution for the standard upon which relief should be based. Although alleging a violation of the Fourteenth Amendment, the complaint had little to suggest in regard to what standard was imposed upon state legislative apportionment systems by the federal Constitution. Specifically the complaint alleged that the apportionment act of 1901 violated the due process clause of the Fourteenth Amendment, the guaranty clause, and the right to vote guaranteed by both the Alabama and United States constitutions. The complaint requested that the court grant relief either by ordering an election at large for the legislature or by reapportioning the legislature by court order.[23]

Federal Judge Frank M. Johnson, Jr., in whose court the complaint was filed, had arrived on the federal bench in spite of the considerable handicap of being a Republican in an overwhelmingly Democratic state, for he was a native of Winston County, which had supported its staunch Unionist principles by seceding from the state of Alabama when the state seceded from the Union and by remaining generally

21 Complaint, p. 18.
22 Ibid., pp. 20–21.
23 Ibid., pp. 25–26.

Republican since the Civil War. Johnson had graduated from the University of Alabama Law School and had established himself as an attorney in Montgomery prior to his appointment to the federal bench by President Eisenhower in 1955. As a federal judge, Johnson had encountered his share of the difficulties faced by all southern federal judges following the school desegregation decision. Perhaps his most publicized difficulty had occurred in 1958 when George C. Wallace, his friend and former classmate who was then a state circuit court judge, refused to make voting records available to the U. S. Civil Rights Commission for their examination to determine if discrimination against Negro voters was occurring. Johnson ordered Wallace to surrender the records, but Wallace announced he would go to jail rather than comply, although he later allowed the records to fall into the hands of the commission. Johnson refused to sentence Wallace for contempt, despite the latter's much publicized assertion that he was in contempt of the federal court. "This Court," Judge Johnson had said, "refuses to allow its authority and dignity to be bent or swayed by such politically-generated whirlwinds."[24] Wallace responded by calling Johnson an "integrating, scallawagging, carpetbagging, bald-faced liar."[25]

Now Judge Johnson had to wrestle with the problem of legislative apportionment. Most of the defendants filed answers or motions to dismiss shortly after the complaint was filed, with the exception of the probate judge of Jefferson County, who admitted the allegations of the complaint and pledged to obey any order the court might issue.[26] The other defendants adopted positions similar to that of Attorney General Gallion, who asserted that the court lacked jurisdiction, that the complaint failed to state a claim upon which relief could be granted, that indispensable parties had not been sued, that the suit was a suit against the state in violation of the Eleventh Amendment of the Constitution, and that the attorney general of Alabama had nothing to do with the administration of elections or the apportionment of the legislature.[27]

On September 7, Chief Judge Elbert Tuttle of the Fifth Circuit

[24] Jack W. Peltason, *Fifty-Eight Lonely Men* (New York: Harcourt, Brace & World, 1961), p. 12.

[25] Morgan, *A Time to Speak*, p. 106.

[26] Answer of J. Paul Meeks, Judge of Probate, Jefferson County, Sept. 21, 1961.

[27] Answer of Attorney General Gallion, Sept. 1, 1961.

Court of Appeals designated Judge Johnson, Circuit Court Judge Richard T. Rives, and District Court Judge Daniel H. Thomas as the three-judge court to hear the case. The attention of all parties in the case, including the judges, was of course directed toward *Baker* v. *Carr*, which was pending before the Supreme Court. It was hoped that the Court's decision in the Tennessee case would provide the answer to the question of jurisdiction and the standard, if any, imposed upon state legislative apportionment by the Fourteenth Amendment. Accordingly, on September 7, Judge Johnson wrote his colleagues on the three-judge court pointing out that since "this is a case seeking to have this Court reapportion the State of Alabama and since the case is patterned very closely after the Tennessee case which is now pending before the Supreme Court of the United States and is to be submitted . . . in October of this year, it is my idea that we should delay any setting or rulings on the question of jurisdiction until action on the part of the Supreme Court in the Tennessee case."[28] Judge Johnson's colleagues apparently agreed, since the court took no action in the Alabama case until after the decision of *Baker* v. *Carr*.

During this period of judicial inaction, however, the plaintiffs in the case received important additional support. On November 1 an intervening complaint was filed in the case on behalf of the director of District 36 of the United Steel Workers and the presidents of locals of the Steel Workers in Birmingham, Etowah County, and Mobile.[29] The intervention of the Steel Workers was important because it gave the litigation support from areas outside Birmingham and a group other than the Young Men's Buisness Club; also, it put the litigation on a firmer financial basis. The members of the YMBC had become concerned after the filing of their complaint that they might ultimately have the costs of litigation awarded against them, placing upon them a financial burden they felt they could ill afford to bear, and the Steel Workers' intervention was therefore somewhat joyously received by Charles Morgan and the YMBC group.

Finally, the Steel Workers' intervention meant the litigation would also be aided by the union's attorney, Jerome A. Cooper. Cooper, a native of Alabama and a graduate of Harvard and Harvard Law

[28] Letter, Frank M. Johnson, Jr., to Judges Rives and Thomas, Sept. 7, 1961.
[29] These plaintiffs were R. E. Farr, director of District 36 of the United Steel Workers; Marshall Meadows, president of Local 1013, USW; Jack Hopping, president of Local 1489, USW; Jack Ryan, president of Local 2176, USW; and Max Morgan, president of Local 2176, USW.

School, had been Supreme Court Justice Hugo Black's first law clerk when Black was appointed in 1937. Cooper had specialized in representing unions in Alabama as a Birmingham attorney. A liberal, "national Democrat," Cooper would aid considerably in the litigation of the Alabama case.[30]

While settling the problem of jurisdiction in apportionment cases, the Supreme Court's decision in *Baker* v. *Carr*[31] on March 26, 1962, shed little light upon the question of what standard the Fourteenth Amendment imposed upon state apportionment systems. On March 29, however, the plaintiffs in Alabama moved for a preliminary injunction in the district court, and the court ordered a hearing on this motion on April 14. At this hearing, Charles Morgan noted that the jurisdictional issue had been settled in the Tennessee case and argued against any delay in a judicial remedy for malapportionment in Alabama. He noted that "the Alabama Legislature had been apportioned as it presently is since the year 1901; that during the sixty-one years since the date of the last apportionment of our Legislature ... the Legislature of Alabama has grown constantly less responsive to the people and to their needs. We contend that this results in a denial of both due process of law ... and, secondly, it results in a deprivation of the equal protection of the laws for plaintiffs and others similarly situated." Because of this unresponsiveness of the legislature to the people of the state, Morgan declared, the government of the state had "come to a practice of States' wrongs rather than States' rights." The people of Alabama had constantly heard "the cries of the black belt of this State grow stronger and loud in our State legislative councils, so that it has come to the point where the voice of the boll weevil in Barbour, Lowndes, or Wilcox Counties is more strongly heard than that of the builders and bankers, the brokers and butchers, and all of the residents of the urban areas of our State."[32]

The plaintiffs therefore requested that the court order an election at large and issue an injunction to insure its administration. Unless such a "firm, forceful, vigorous assumption of jurisdiction" occurred, Morgan said, the Alabama legislature, with its record "through interposition, resolutions, and others, of disrespect, at least to a degree, of

[30] Interview with Jerome A. Cooper, June 21, 1965, Birmingham, Ala.

[31] 369 U.S. 186 (1962).

[32] Transcript of Hearing before Judges Richard T. Rives, Circuit Judge, Daniel H. Thomas, and Frank M. Johnson, Jr., District Judges, in Montgomery, Ala., April 14, 1962, pp. 4–7. Hereinafter cited as Arguments.

Federal law, will while away its time by a special session, if indeed one is called, and this court will be called upon at a later time to take action so far more drastic than that proposed by the plaintiffs that indeed we may be in this court trying this case a major portion of the next two years of our lives."[33]

Counsel for defendants appeared to accept that reapportionment of the legislature would now be necessary. Assistant Attorney General Gordon Madison limited his remarks to general observations and ended by saying that, although the federal court had rendered many decisions with which he disagreed, "in this case the combined legal knowledge of this court and the combined political experience of this court, in my opinion, makes this one of the best courts that we could have anywhere to consider this question."[34] E. C. Boswell, representing Harrell Hammonds, probate judge of Lowndes County, urged the court to allow the legislature time to reapportion, and noted that the Supreme Court "does not point to this court any way by which you can find to reapportion this State; you've got to work it out, yourselves, and if it comes to that, you have my sympathy."[35] And Roy D. McCord, representing the State Democratic Executive Committee, although arguing his clients had nothing to do with apportionment, assured the court that "we are ready to qualify the men and women that seek these offices after this court sees fit to reapportion it, if it does, or after the Legislature's reapportionment of it, or let them qualify as it is now constituted."[36]

Morgan, in rebuttal, declared that the plaintiffs believed that "we are involved . . . in man's age old struggle for freedom." He said, "We submit to you that in no field of the law is the phrase, 'Justice delayed is justice denied,' more important than when you discuss personal liberties."[37] The court, however, after a brief recess, announced that it would take no action until after the May legislative primaries and would hold its judgment in abeyance until further argument was heard on July 16. The court also indicated that, if the legislature failed to act before the July 16 hearing, it would follow the provisional

[33] *Ibid.*, pp. 7–8.
[34] *Ibid.*, p. 11.
[35] *Ibid.*, p. 15.
[36] *Ibid.*, p. 16. The Democratic primary election for the legislature was scheduled to be held in May. The district court's order requiring a partial reapportionment of the legislature therefore necessitated a special primary election.
[37] Arguments, p. 18.

remedy suggested in Justice Clark's concurring opinion in *Baker* v. *Carr*[38]—to consolidate grossly overrepresented districts, releasing representatives to be assigned to underrepresented areas, thus breaking the "stranglehold" of the less populous areas on the legislature and allowing it to reapportion more fully.[39] The next move was therefore up to the Alabama legislature.

Both before and after this first hearing in the district court, the plaintiffs received increased support from two new intervening groups of plaintiffs. Before the hearing, on April 9, a motion for leave to intervene as plaintiffs was filed by the Jefferson County Democratic Campaign Committee on behalf of its officers, David J. Vann, Robert S. Vance, and Richard P. Humphrey. The Jefferson County Democratic Campaign Committee had been established to support the candidacy of John F. Kennedy in 1960 and had remained as a vehicle for activities of the national party. The chairman of the committee, David Vann, a graduate of the University of Alabama, University of Alabama Law School, and George Washington Law School, and a former law clerk of Justice Black, had become particularly interested in the nature of the remedy for apportionment the court might grant. Vann felt that the most commonly proposed remedy in apportionment cases, an election at large, would disrupt a state's political process and require more judicial intervention in elections than was desirable. Vann and Vance therefore suggested in their intervening complaint that the more conservative remedy of consolidating some districts or counties, thus releasing representatives to be assigned to the more populous areas, would be most appropriate.[40]

In Mobile, John W. McConnell, Jr., had also become interested in the apportionment litigation and the promise it held for increased representation for Mobile, the most underrepresented county in South Alabama. McConnell, a graduate of the University of Alabama and Yale Law School, was convinced that the standard imposed by the Fourteenth Amendment upon state apportionment systems required equal population districts for both houses of the legislature. Joined by Joseph Langan, a Mobile city commissioner, William M. Williams,

---

[38] 369 U.S. 186, at 250.

[39] Arguments, pp. 19–21; the court's opinion subsequently filed is reported in 205 F. Supp. 245.

[40] Motion for Leave to Amend Complaint in Intervention, on behalf of David J. Vann, Robert S. Vance, and Richard P. Humphrey; interview with David J. Vann, June 18, 1965, Birmingham, Ala.

the southeastern representative of the Marine and Shipbuilding Workers of America, and fellow attorney Garet Von Antwerp, McConnell organized the Citizens Committee for Representative Government on a Fair Basis, an organization that, they hoped, would raise funds to meet the expenses of an intervention in the apportionment case and also indicate sufficient interest to support a motion to intervene before the district court. The committee, however, failed to raise any money and was allowed to die a quiet death during the litigation.[41]

On April 25, McConnell wrote the other plaintiffs stating his belief "that it might give strength to the arguments of the complainant if areas of the State, other than Jefferson County, were represented in the proceeding."[42] Charles Morgan replied, "I do indeed believe that a Mobile intervention would be most helpful."[43] And on July 2 the court granted McConnell's motion for leave to intervene.

With McConnell's intervention, the array of plaintiffs in the Alabama case was complete. The attorneys taking the lead had much in common. Charles Morgan, Jerome Cooper, David Vann, Robert Vance, and John McConnell were each generally liberal, loyal Democrats, and, with the exception of Cooper, all had been variously active in politics. Morgan had been active since his college days as a loyalist Democrat and a supporter of James ("Kissin' Jim") Folsom.[44] Vann served as organization chairman of the 1960 Democratic Presidential Campaign Committee, member of the Democratic State Steering Committee from 1960 to 1962, and chairman of the Jefferson County Democratic Campaign Committee, and in 1964 ran without success for Congress. Vance was vice chairman of the Jefferson County Democratic Campaign Committee, and McConnell in 1962 was elected to the Democratic State Executive Committee. All, with the exception of Cooper, were young men, and all appear to have shared a disillusionment with the course of public affairs in the state. The Alabama case was, therefore, a revolt of young loyalist Democrats, or as one of the leading attorneys said later, an example of "young people striking out against the old order in the only effective way we could."[45]

There were, however, important differences among the various

[41] Interview with John McConnell, Jr., June 12, 1965, Mobile, Ala.
[42] Letter, McConnell to David Vann and Charles Morgan, April 25, 1962.
[43] Letter, Morgan to McConnell, April 26, 1962.
[44] Morgan, *A Time to Speak*, pp. 25–99.
[45] This paragraph is based upon my interviews with John McConnell, David Vann, and Jerome Cooper during June, 1965, which are cited above.

plaintiffs' attorneys about what degree of reapportionment should be the goal in the district court. Morgan believed that the objective of the suit should be a reapportionment of the legislature based on the provisions of the Alabama Constitution. Under these provisions the apportionment of the house of representatives would still favor the less populous counties, since the assignment of at least one of the 106 representatives to each of the sixty-seven counties was required. The apportionment of the senate, however, would be roughly based upon population, taking into consideration the fact that the constitution prohibited the division of a county between two districts and required that counties composing a senate district be contiguous. Such a senate apportionment would increase Jefferson County's senate representation from one to seven, Mobile County's to three, and Montgomery County's to two, and the counties of Madison, Etowah, Calhoun, and Tuscaloosa would each compose a senate district electing one senator. But of course the total objective would be substantially less than equal population apportionment. "The result will be a Legislature in which the large counties can at least block Constitutional amendments in the Senate," Morgan said, "and a Legislature in which the small counties, by reason of the guarantee of one representative for each county, will always have a working majority in the House of Representatives." This would be, he continued, "not fair reapportionment, but reapportionment under the fair provisions of the Alabama Constitution which we believe, if applied in this manner, will not be so arbitrary as to violate the provisions of the Fourteenth Amendment."[46]

David Vann, who prepared the statistical data submitted to the court, generally agreed with Morgan. Although believing the one representative per county provision of the Alabama Constitution was perhaps questionable under the Fourteenth Amendment, Vann thought that an attack on this provision "would be better left to a subsequent attack after similar questions have been decided in other states where their decision is essential. For example, in several states there are more counties than there are members in the most numerous House." Vann acknowledged that "a substantial number of people" in Alabama "believe that, like the Federal Congress, one House of the Legislature should be based on population and one should be based on area. While I realize that a great deal of selling must be done, I have found that people in this group can be persuaded that the present Con-

[46] Letter, Morgan to McConnell, April 26, 1962.

stitution already provides for a House of Representatives based primarily on geography, with some weighting for population factors; and, because of the geographical considerations in the House of Representatives apportionment formula, the small counties will always have a working majority in that House." But if the large counties could obtain representation in the senate by population, Vann continued, "this would give the counties having the greatest interest in the future growth of this state sufficient votes in the Senate to guarantee that no Constitutional amendment would take away from them their right to proportional representation in either House of the Legislature. . . ."[47]

Baker v. *Carr* had of course failed to shed much light upon the Fourteenth Amendment's standard for state apportionment systems, but the Birmingham attorneys generally agreed that the apportionment provisions of the Alabama Constitution would meet the Fourteenth Amendment standard. "The Court is bound to follow the provisions of Alabama law concerning political rights," one of them said, "just as it would if the question were one of property rights—as long as Alabama law meets the requirements of the Federal Constitution." He continued, "We believe that the standard there is invidiousness. While in application at some other time with a different distribution of population the Alabama Constitution as applied might be invidious in its results, we do not believe the result is invidious now."[48]

The position that the Fourteenth Amendment prohibited "invidious discrimination" was supported by several of the Supreme Court's opinions interpreting the equal protection clause. In two of the leading cases involving the clause, *Skinner* v. *Oklahoma*[49] and *Williamson* v. *Lee Optical Co.*,[50] the Court had given support to the "invidious discrimination" formula as the standard imposed upon state legislative classifications by the equal protection clause. In the *Skinner* case the Court had held that the Oklahoma Habitual Criminal Sterilization Act involved "invidious discrimination," since some persons committing certain kinds of felonies could be sterilized under the terms of the Act while persons committing other types of felonies were not subject to the Act's provisions. In so classifying, the Court had said, the state had made "as invidious a discrimination as if it had selected a particular

[47] Letter, Vann to McConnell, May 9, 1962.
[48] Letter, Vann to McConnell, n.d.
[49] 316 U.S. 535 (1942).
[50] 348 U.S. 483 (1955).

race or nationality for oppressive treatment."[51] The Court had recognized, however, the need for flexibility in legislation and particularly the need for classification. As it said in the *Williamson* case, "the problem of legislative classification is a perennial one, admitting of no doctrinaire definition. Evils in the same field may be of different dimensions and proportions, requiring different remedies. . . . The prohibition of the Equal Protection Clause goes no further than the invidious discrimination."[52]

Justices Douglas and Clark, concurring in *Baker v. Carr*, had both alluded to the "invidious discrimination" formula under the equal protection clause as being applicable to state apportionment systems, with Douglas saying, "Universal equality is not the test; there is room for weighting," and Clark stating that only where, as in Tennessee, "the total picture reveals incommensurables of both magnitude and frequency can it be said that there is present invidious discrimination."[53] The problem was, of course, that the phrase "invidious discrimination" was hardly less vague than "equal protection of the laws," but until the Court itself clarified the degree of equality in population among legislative districts demanded by the Fourteenth Amendment, the position of the Birmingham attorneys was supported by the Court's limited expressions on the question.

John McConnell, who had first become interested in the subject of apportionment in a course taught by Professor Thomas I. Emerson at Yale Law School, ultimately became convinced that equality of representation in both houses of a state legislature was necessary. He was, therefore, the only attorney in the Alabama case who insisted from the beginning that this was the standard imposed by the equal protection clause of the Fourteenth Amendment. "Equal protection means equal voice in legislation and not equal voice in only a portion of the legislative process," he said in his brief filed with the federal court. "Having equality in one house would insure to the majority only a negative control or a veto over unfair legislation. However, as this case indicates, inaction may be as unfair as action. The purpose of government is to govern, and this requires action."[54]

Governor John Patterson responded to the federal district court's

[51] 316 U.S., at 541.
[52] 348 U.S., at 489.
[53] 369 U.S. 186, at 368–69, 260.
[54] Supplemental Brief and Argument, p. 12; interview with John McConnell, June 12, 1965, Mobile, Ala.

deadline of July 16 by calling a special session of the legislature, and on June 12 he urged the legislators to reapportion the state, reminding them that he had previously called upon them to do so because of the "dictates of good government, a decent respect for the principles of the democratic process, and the fond hopes of the people for half a century" and because the apportionment of the legislature no longer bore any reasonable relationship to population. "It remains the constitutional duty of the Alabama legislature to reapportion your seats in fairness and in faith to the people of Alabama," the governor said. "I beseech you to obey our law and do your duty."

Patterson, however, denounced the federal court order as a "shotgun ultimatum" which was "dictatorial, unwarranted and without any semblance of legal basis under the constitutions of both the United States and the State of Alabama." In addition, he denounced the Supreme Court's decision in *Baker* v. *Carr*, declaring that once again "the Supreme Court swept aside all precedents, including a unanimous decision only four years ago. Nowhere in the Constitution of our country is there one single word or phrase to justify or validate any such Federal seizure of power or authority." The legislature should reapportion, however, the governor said. "Let's beat the Federals to the draw," he declared. "Let's be masters of our own household."[55]

The legislature reluctantly began to consider various reapportionment proposals,[56] but immediately discovered that any proposal to consolidate smaller counties into senatorial districts posed serious problems, particularly when counties with heavy Negro populations were to be combined with counties having fewer Negroes. Representative Val Hain of Selma, for example, protested the placing of his county, Dallas, in a senatorial district with Lowndes County, with its heavy Negro population. "Our position might be likened to one who has been caught in a flood but who had desperately come close to reaching shore, only to be kicked back again," Hain said. "This is Anglo-Saxon blood calling from Anglo-Saxon blood. Do you have it in your heart to deny the white people of Dallas County the right to be ruled by white people?"[57] Legislators especially avoided having

[55] Message to the Legislature by John Patterson, Governor, special session, 1962, Tuesday, June 12, 1962, pp. 4–7, 11.

[56] For the suggestions of the Alabama Legislative Reference Service, see "Reapportionment in Alabama under Threat of Federal Action," Report to the Members of the Legislature of Alabama, May, 1962.

[57] Birmingham *Post-Herald*, July 11, 1962, p. 5.

176

their counties grouped with either Macon or Bullock counties where federal court orders requiring registration of Negro voters without discrimination were in effect. Indeed, Representative Walter Perry of Jefferson County urged the legislators from the heavily Negro-populated counties to surrender power to the urban areas of the state because the cities were the "last depositories of conservatism" in Alabama and their own counties would soon see Negroes voting in large numbers.[58]

The legislators finally produced two contingent reapportionment plans. The first, the "67 Senator Amendment," proposed amending the constitution to allow one senator from each county and apportioned the house according to the existing provisions of the Alabama Constitution, assigning one representative to each county and distributing the remaining seats among the counties on a population basis. Since similar amendments had been rejected by the people on three occasions in the past, the legislature also passed the "Crawford-Webb Act," which changed the existing thirty-five senate districts very little and failed even to approach compliance with the Alabama Constitution in its apportionment of the house. The Crawford-Webb Act, which received strong backing from the Patterson administration, was to go into effect in 1966 if the 67 Senator Amendment were rejected either by the voters or by the federal court.[59]

David Vann and Robert Vance telegraphed the governor urging him to use his power of veto and return the Crawford-Webb Act to the legislature with an executive amendment providing for reapportionment under the Alabama Constitution. "We urge you to use this power in the name of all citizens of Alabama," they said, "and to the honor of the great constitutional office which you hold." Governor Patterson refused the request, however, and on signing the bills said, "This is making history. We have done something no other administration has accomplished."[60]

On July 16 the federal district court heard arguments in Montgomery on the validity of the legislature's efforts. Judge Rives stated to counsel that the court desired all the light it could get on the case, but admonished them that the court wanted "light not heat; there is no use

[58] Birmingham *Post-Herald*, July 4, 1962, p. 9.
[59] Both the 67 Senator Amendment and the Crawford-Webb Act may be found in 208 F. Supp., at 443–44, 445–46, Appendix B and C.
[60] Birmingham *Post-Herald*, July 13, 1962, p. 1; July 11, 1962, p. 5.

in making a Fourth of July oratorical argument on this matter; but as much light as you can give us in this case."[61] Charles Morgan, opening for the plaintiffs, declared that the two plans passed by the legislature "meet the requirements of nothing but a fight for self-preservation on behalf of the men who sit in those legislative halls."[62] The 67 Senator Amendment, Morgan argued, violated section 284 of the Alabama Constitution, which prohibited changing the population basis of legis-lative apportionment by constitutional amendment, and also violated, in regard to the Senate, the Fourteenth Amendment of the federal Constitution.[63]

Under the Crawford-Webb Act, Morgan contended, the appor-tionment of the senate failed to meet any rational test. "In the first place," he said, "it is not based on square miles, so you can't call it geography, it is not based on population, so it can't be population, it is not based on even political units, so it can't be termed that.... There is just no rational explanation for [the Senate apportionment] of this bill that we can conceive of, other than the fact that the Legislature got it passed."[64] The apportionment of the house under the Crawford-Webb Act was equally irrational, Morgan asserted, and the plaintiffs therefore "accuse this Legislature of deliberately flying in the face of this Court and refusing to do its constitutional duty and to afford plaintiffs their rights under both the State Constitution and the Con-stitution of the United States. . . ."[65]

The Birmingham attorneys accepted the apportionment of the house under the proposed constitutional amendment, wherein each of the sixty-seven counties was assigned one representative and the re-maining thirty-nine representatives were assigned to the counties on the basis of the method of equal proportions. This apportionment fol-lowed the provisions of the Alabama Constitution, and, as Robert Vance stated to the court, "We start out with the premise that the Constitution of the State of Alabama is constitutional."[66] The re-mainder of the legislature's work, however, was unacceptable to the

[61] Transcript of Arguments before Three-Judge Court, District Court, Middle District of Alabama, Northern Division, July 16, 1962, Montgomery, Ala., Civil Action No. 1744–N, *Sims* v. *Frink*, pp. 21–22.

[62] *Ibid.*, p. 25.

[63] *Ibid.*, pp. 26–29.

[64] *Ibid.*, p. 32.

[65] *Ibid.*, p. 34.

[66] *Ibid.*, p. 39; see also the exchange between Jerome Cooper and Judge Rives, at p. 39.

Birmingham counsel and constituted, as Vance said, a "bald-faced defiance of the requirements of the Constitution of Alabama and the
previous order of this Court." By comparison, Vance continued, "the
situation recently treated on remand in Baker versus Carr was strictly
bush-league discrimination. . . ."[67]

John McConnell, however, insisted that the Fourteenth Amendment required apportionment on the basis of population. He argued
that the contention that "we have equal protection, if we have equal
representation in one house without having it in the other . . . is inapposite and not consistent, and we think that both houses, and we
earnestly contend this view, both houses have to be on population."[68]

The burden of the argument on behalf of the defendants fell upon
state Senator Douglas S. Webb, who appeared as a representative of
the legislature to explain its actions. The legislature, Webb said, had
found itself "confronted with a Gordian Knot with truly no quick or
efficient solution at hand, despite the suggestions from the daily press
as to how the job should be done." The legislature had found, he said,
that the problem was not one simply of mathematics or geography,
"but that there exists in our State today a very real and very serious
personality conflict, if I may, between a number of counties, the contiguous counties that we must combine of this great State."[69] At this
point Webb was interrupted by Judge Johnson, and the two engaged
in an extended colloquy:

> JUDGE JOHNSON: Does that grow out of the fact, Mr. Webb, that
> there hasn't been any reapportionment for fifty years, approximately,
> at least?
>
> MR. WEBB: Your Honor, I—it may be; I don't know what the rea-
> soning could be there, but I wanted to point out to the Court the actu-
> al factual problem we were faced with; due to this wholly unforeseen
> problem in order to obtain votes vital in order that any legislation
> be passed, an attempt had to be made to avoid, if possible, as many
> of these personality conflicts between counties as possible. As an
> example, we soon discovered that Bibb County was extremely re-
> luctant to be connected with Shelby County in a Senatorial District.
>
> JUDGE JOHNSON: What you are saying then, the Legislature couldn't
> achieve any effective reapportionment because it hadn't been re-
> apportioned for a long time, isn't it?

[67] *Ibid.*, pp. 44–45.
[68] *Ibid.*, p. 49.
[69] *Ibid.*, pp. 58–59.

MR. WEBB: Within set mathematical formulas without regard for the feelings of the people in the Districts, Your Honor. Conflicts developed between Lowndes County and adjoining counties. Every county contiguous to Macon County protested a Senatorial District with that county. Like conflicts developed between Winston and Cullman and Walker Counties and other counties of the State. It soon became very evident to many members of the Legislature that while statistical methods and trite mathematical formulas work nicely with inert substances or in chemical solution, it is quite another matter when the material to be mixed consists of people with firm minds of their own, unruly passions, and the general disposition in some instances of one member of the animal kingdom noted for his unusually long ears and stubborn traits.[70]

Webb asserted that while the legislation before the court was "not perfect, it is the product of a deliberative body elected by the people of this State with the welfare of the people at heart."[71] Charles Morgan, however, in rebuttal said the plaintiffs would "offer most of Mr. Webb's comments in evidence that this Legislature cannot reapportion itself. . . . We have received an explanation from the Legislature, and we are quite certain that they do have very severe problems with respect to the apportionment of themselves on a proper basis. . . . We are further certain that those problems were created by a Legislature through their century of inactivity. They are no faults of plaintiffs. We contend we are entitled to relief now under the Constitution of the United States and under the Constitution of the State of Alabama, and that the argument of defendants stands as authority therefor."[72]

Upon invitation by Judge Rives, Professor C. D. Sands of the University of Alabama Law School appeared as *amicus curiae*. Sands proposed that one solution the court might adopt would be a weighted voting plan in which there would be no changes in the legislative districts, but each legislator would cast the number of votes in the legislature to which the population of his county or district entitled him. One major difficulty with the proposal, as Sands admitted, was that the individuals to whom a court order effectuating such a plan would be directed—the presiding officers of the houses of the legislature—were not parties to the suit.[73]

[70] *Ibid.*, pp. 59–60.
[71] *Ibid.*, p. 64.
[72] *Ibid.*, pp. 73, 75–76.
[73] *Ibid.*, pp. 94–98; see also the Brief of C. D. Sands as *Amicus Curiae*.

Assistant Attorney General Gordon Madison followed Sands in argument and was told by Judge Rives that the court would be "extremely happy if those bills had been so worded that everybody could come in and say the Legislature performed what they thought was the proper task and the Court could step aside, but unfortunately we are not in that shape."[74] Madison explained to the court the difficulties he had encountered in attempting to advise the legislature, particularly when he himself was not aware of the standard imposed on apportionment by the Fourteenth Amendment. "I don't know right now standing in this Court after all this studying whether reapportionment of one house is sufficient or you have got to have two houses," Madison said.[75] "I think your Court could spell out what it requires to be done. . . . I don't believe out of this present Legislature that anything more could be accomplished by calling them back or anything else; I think they have done the ultimate that they can do with what they had."[76] In his brief filed with the court, Madison contended, however, that the argument made by Senator Webb "completely refutes any arbitrary or capricious action on the part of the Legislature. It demonstrated beyond doubt the rationality of the acts in question and the efforts made to pass reasonable legislation."[77]

In their brief, the Birmingham attorneys proposed three methods of relief by the court. The court could either reapportion the legislature under the provisions of the Alabama Constitution by court order; adopt the proposal of David Vann and Robert Vance to consolidate some districts and assign the representatives thus released to the more populous counties; or order weighted voting into effect as proposed by Professor Sands.[78] The decision of the court, announced on July 21, adopted the second of these choices.

"It has been generally conceded throughout this litigation by all parties," the court said, "that the present apportionment of both Houses of the Legislature of the State of Alabama constitutes 'in-

---

[74] *Ibid.,* p. 101.

[75] *Ibid.,* p. 117.

[76] *Ibid.,* p. 112; in his Amended Answer on behalf of Attorney General Gallion, July 15, 1962, Madison argued that the acts of the legislature were valid, and, defending the proposed constitutional amendment, argued that Section 284 of the Alabama Constitution, which prohibited the amendment of the population basis of legislative apportionment, was itself invalid.

[77] Brief and Argument of Defendants Gallion and Frink, p. 2.

[78] Brief of Plaintiffs, pp. 26–28.

vidious discrimination' in violation of the Equal Protection Clause of the Fourteenth Amendment."[79] The legislature had not changed this situation by its passage of either the Crawford-Webb Act or the 67 Senator Amendment, since neither, the court said, "meets the necessary constitutional requirements." They were, the court declared, "obviously discriminatory, arbitrary and irrational." The 67 Senator Amendment, in its apportionment of the senate, would reduce the percentage of people theoretically able to control that body from 25.1 percent to 19.4 percent and allow the representatives from the state's thirty-four smallest counties to form a majority of the senate. Since the Alabama Constitution assigned one representative in the house to each county, thus basing the lower house somewhat on geography, the court concluded that the additional abandonment of the population standard in the senate proposed by the amendment would be "invidious discrimination." The argument that the senate based on geography would merely be similar to the United States Senate, the court said, "cannot survive the most superficial examination into the history of the requirement of the Federal Constitution and the diametrically opposing history of the requirement of the Alabama Constitution that representation shall be based on population."[80] The court equally condemned the Crawford-Webb Act on the ground that its apportionment of the senate only raised from 25.1 percent to 27.6 percent the portion of the population theoretically able to control that body; the act's apportionment of the house, the court said, was also "totally unacceptable."[81]

The court noted, however, that the apportionment of the house under the 67 Senator Amendment was in accordance with the Alabama Constitution and therefore acceptable as a part of the court's order reapportioning that body. Under this plan, Jefferson County's representation in the house was increased from seven to seventeen seats and Mobile's representation increased from three to eight seats. Although believing the senate apportionment under the Crawford-Webb Act to be invalid, the court nevertheless accepted the plan as a temporary expedient and embodied it also, somewhat reluctantly, in its order.[82] "The Court hopes that the moderate steps taken by

[79] *Sims* v. *Frink*, 208 F. Supp. 431, at 435 (M.D. Ala. 1962).
[80] *Ibid.*, at 438.
[81] *Ibid.*, at 440.
[82] *Ibid.*, at 441–42. Under the house apportionment ordered into effect by the

this order may be enough to break the strangle hold," the opinion concluded. "They certainly will not suffice as any permanent reapportionment." The court warned, "If they should prove insufficient to break the strangle hold, the Court remains under the solemn duty to relieve the plaintiffs and other citizens like situated from further denial of the equal protection of the laws."[83]

The court's order was certainly a "moderate step" in relation to the senate, since although Jefferson and Mobile counties gained a total of fifteen seats in the house, they still elected only one senator each under the court's order. The court's order was therefore the opposite to the principal objective of the Birmingham attorneys, who had concentrated on winning a senate apportioned primarily on a population basis. But in many respects the order of the court was revolutionary, since it was the first occasion upon which a court had acted affirmatively to order into effect a reapportionment of a state legislature. Although the court had not given the plaintiffs the senate apportionment they desired, Charles Morgan and George Peach Taylor announced that they were pleased with the decision. "We have come a long way," they said, "but still have a long way to go. This represents an important step in the march for democratic government. As we read the ruling, this court has once again deferred to the Alabama Legislature and is affording it another opportunity to perform its duty—true reapportionment."[84]

David Vann, Robert Vance, and John McConnell, on the other hand, were not satisfied with the court's order, and a few days after the court announced its decision, they filed a motion requesting a rehearing and a modification of the decree "because of the conviction that this Court's provisional remedy should give assurance that the reapportionment problem can be fully resolved by the Legislature of Alabama without further resort to this Court, and because of the conviction that the plan proposed by the Court with reference to the

---

court, the following counties were increased as indicated: Jefferson from 7 to 17; Mobile, from 3 to 8; Calhoun, Etowah, Madison, and Tuscaloosa, from 2 to 3 each. Montgomery remained at 4; Lauderdale, Morgan, Talladega, and Walker counties remained at 2 each. Dallas was reduced from 3 to 2. The following were reduced from 2 to 1: Jackson, Chambers, Tallapoosa, Hale, Perry, Sumter, Marengo, Wilcox, Lowndes, Elmore, Butler, Pike, Lee, Russell, Barbour, Henry, Clark, and Bullock. All other counties, of course, remained at 1 each.

[83] *Ibid.*, at 442.
[84] Birmingham *News*, July 22, 1962, pp. 1, 6.

Senate will prevent this much desired result."[85] The court, however, denied this motion, and the machinery for implementing the court's decree, which entailed a special primary election to fill the seats opened up in the more populous counties, was set in motion.[86]

As in Alabama, across the nation similar suits had been filed in the wake of *Baker* v. *Carr*, and many of these suits were slowly edging toward review by the United States Supreme Court, which would soon be called upon to define the standard imposed upon legislative apportionments by the Fourteenth Amendment. But the Alabama case seemed destined not to join the other apportionment cases at the Supreme Court level, since the attorney general of Alabama advised the defendants in the case that the district court's decision should not be appealed, and at least publicly there were no indications that there would be an appeal by the plaintiffs. In mid-summer, 1962, therefore, it appeared that the litigation in the Alabama case had come to an end, at least until the next legislative session, and that the answer to the important question of what apportionment standard was embraced by the Fourteenth Amendment would be provided by the cases moving up the appellate ladder in other states.[87]

Out of the mass of litigation set off by *Baker* v. *Carr*,[88] which was called "the most spectacular rash of litigation involving state government in modern times,"[89] there ultimately emerged several cases presenting the issue of the standard imposed upon state apportionment systems by the Fourteenth Amendment. Two cases raising this issue and pending before the Supreme Court at approximately the same

[85] Motion for a Rehearing and Modification of Proposed Decree, July 25, 1962, p. 4.

[86] Most of the seats for which the special primary was held to nominate candidates were in the house. The Crawford-Webb Act's senate apportionment, which the court accepted and embodied in its decree, in addition to making very few changes in the 1901 districts was tailored to fit the candidates for the senate who had already been nominated in a primary election in the spring of 1962. Thirty-three of the Crawford-Webb Act's districts contained only one nominee who had been selected in the spring primary, one district contained no nominee, thus requiring a nominee to be selected in the special primary following the court's decree, one district contained two nominees, who engaged in a runoff in the special primary with new candidates prohibited. The net result of the court's order as it affected the senate was therefore minimal.

[87] Interviews with John McConnell, June 12, 1965, Mobile, Ala.; David Vann, June 18, 1965, Birmingham, Ala.; and McLean Pitts, June 16, 1965, Selma, Ala.

[88] 369 U.S. 186 (1962).

[89] *NCR*, Vol. 51 (Sept., 1962), p. 476.

time as *Baker* v. *Carr* were *Scholle* v. *Hare*,[90] challenging the apportionment of the state senate in Michigan, and *W.M.C.A.* v. *Simon*,[91] challenging the apportionment provisions of the New York Constitution. Both cases were remanded by the Court to the lower courts to be reconsidered in light of *Baker* v. *Carr* over the dissent of Justice Harlan, who felt that the Court should decide the Fourteenth Amendment issue tendered in the cases.

On reconsidering the *Scholle* case on remand, a majority of the Michigan Supreme Court in July, 1962, declared the apportionment of the Michigan Senate invalid under the equal protection clause of the Fourteenth Amendment.[92] Despite what the court called "an arrogant and amply headlined threat of impeachment 'if the senate districts are declared illegal,' "[93] the majority held that "plaintiff's vote for the office of State senator is invidiously unequal to the votes cast for State senator by other citizens of the State, the classification of citizens in the senatorial districts being arbitrary, discriminatory, and without reasonable or just relation or relevance to the electoral process."[94] Another appeal to the Supreme Court was expected, and it therefore appeared that the Court would soon be faced again with the Michigan case and the question of what apportionment standard the equal protection clause embraced.[95]

The New York case, *W.M.C.A.* v. *Simon*, was also reargued on remand before the Federal District Court for the Southern District of New York, but upon consideration of the merits of the case the court held in August, 1962, that the plaintiffs had failed to demonstrate that New York's apportionment provisions allowed "invidious discrimination." The New York apportionment provisions, the court held, "are rational, not arbitrary, are of substantially historical origin, contain no geographical discrimination, permit an electoral majority to alter

90 360 Mich. 1 (1960); remanded 369 U.S. 429 (1962).
91 202 F. Supp. 74 (S.D. N.Y. 1960); remanded 370 U.S. 190 (1962).
92 *Scholle* v. *Secretary of State*, 367 Mich. 176 (1962).
93 *Ibid.*, at 180.
94 *Ibid.*, at 186.
95 *NCR*, Vol. 51 (Sept., 1962), p. 444; for the impact of this decision on the Michigan constitutional convention which was meeting at the time and which ultimately changed the senate apportionment formula, see Karl A. Lamb, William J. Pierce, and John P. White, *Apportionment and Representative Institutions: The Michigan Experience* (Washington, D.C.: Institute for Social Science Research, 1963).

or change the same and are not unconstitutional under the relevant decisions of the United States Supreme Court."[96] The plaintiffs immediately served notice that the decision would be appealed, and, as *The
New York Times* said, the Supreme Court would be asked in the New
York case "whether it agrees that constitutional guarantees of equal
protection are satisfied by rules under which one vote for assemblymen in Schuyler County has the same weight as fourteen in Suffolk
or one vote for state senator in Monroe is equal to two in Man-
hattan."[97]

Rapidly joining the Michigan and New York cases on the road
to the Court were *Maryland Committee for Fair Representation* v.
Tawes[98] from Maryland, *Davis* v. *Mann*[99] from Virginia, *Roman* v.
Sincock[100] from Delaware, and *Lucas* v. *Colorado General Assembly*[101] from Colorado. The Court would obviously not want for a vehicle if it chose to enunciate the Fourteenth Amendment apportionment standard.

In Alabama, despite the apparent acceptance of the district court's
decision, the loose coalition of plaintiffs in the apportionment case was
debating internally whether or not to appeal the district court's decision. The coalition had always been much less than completely co-
hesive. There had been no real attempt to organize before filing the
complaint in the federal court; instead there had been only an *ad hoc*
attempt to consult and coordinate efforts among the various attorneys
once all the intervenors had made known their interest in the suit. The
unplanned nature of the coalition was perhaps best indicated by the
lack of adequate finances available to any of the plaintiffs, except the
Steel Workers represented by Jerome Cooper. Since litigation is an
activity not designed for the poor, lack of finances may be a fatal flaw
in organized litigation, as it almost proved to be for some of the plaintiffs in the Alabama case.

Disagreements over the objective in the litigation could reasonably
be expected in the Alabama case. With the standard imposed by the
Fourteenth Amendment upon state apportionments undefined, the

[96] 208 F. Supp. 368, at 379.
[97] Quoted in the *NCR*, Vol. 51 (Oct., 1962), p. 502.
[98] 229 Md. 406 (July 23, 1962).
[99] 213 F. Supp. 577 (E.D. Va. Nov. 28, 1962).
[100] Decided *sub nom Sincock* v. *Duffy*, 215 F. Supp. 169 (D. Del. April 17, 1963).
[101] Decided *sub nom Lisco* v. *Love*, 219 F. Supp. 922 (D. Col. July 16, 1963).

range of possible objectives in the litigation was rather broad and the possibilities of disagreement among reasonable men were therefore likely. With the exception of John McConnell, who insisted that the equal protection clause required both houses of a legislature to be based on population, the attorneys in the Alabama case had agreed on a roughly population-apportioned senate as their primary objective in the federal district court. And they failed to achieve this objective in the district court.

After losing their primary objective, the Alabama attorneys had to decide whether to appeal the district court's decision or to accept it and await the action of the Alabama legislature and initiate further litigation in the district court if the legislature's action proved unsatisfactory. One argument against an appeal emphasized the district court's decision to retain jurisdiction. The apportionment to be implemented under its order was only temporary, and if the legislature failed to apportion satisfactorily, the court would grant more extensive relief at a later time. An appeal to the Supreme Court might therefore be superfluous, since the likely result would be an affirmation of the district court's acceptance of jurisdiction and grant of temporary relief in the case. In addition, this was the first time a federal court had reapportioned by court order, and some of the attorneys felt that they should therefore support the district court and that an appeal would indicate a lack of support and faith in the court.

Another argument against an appeal was the considerable doubt that any decision of the Supreme Court in the case would be more favorable to the plaintiffs than the ultimate relief they would receive at the hands of the district court. It was argued that if the justices of the Supreme Court had been in agreement on a standard, such as population, imposed upon state apportionments by the equal protection clause, they would have enunciated it in *Baker* v. *Carr*. An appeal of the Alabama case might therefore jeopardize what had already been won. Also, the Court might well have decided to leave the working out of the Fourteenth Amendment standard to the district courts, and, if so, again an appeal would be useless.

Finally, as a result of the district court's order, a special primary election was to be held to select the nominees to fill the newly created seats in the more populous counties, and an appeal might result in a stay order delaying the special primary. This could bring about a great deal of public criticism, especially from the Birmingham press, if the appeal did indeed result in a disruption of the special primary process. In view of these considerations, the most appropriate action for the plaintiffs would be to file an *amicus curiae* brief in the *Scholle* case, which, it appeared, would be the first case to reach the Supreme Court raising questions similar to those raised in the Alabama case.

There was general concurrence in all of these arguments against an appeal among Charles Morgan, George Peach Taylor, Jerome Cooper, and, to an extent, David Vann.[102] Robert Vance, however, felt very strongly that an appeal should be taken from the district court's decision. Vance believed that the Supreme Court would decide the question of the apportionment standard during its October, 1962, term, probably in *Scholle* v. *Hare*. The decision of the Court in the *Scholle* case would therefore govern future decisions in the Alabama case, but the *Scholle* case, Vance felt, did not present a set of facts as favorable to the plaintiffs as did the Alabama case. Therefore, he argued, an appeal should be taken, since it was "just a matter of common sense that you want to have the issue decided on the most favorable facts possible."

From reading the district court's opinion, Vance had also concluded that the district court was not prepared to grant the plaintiffs full relief as far as the senate was concerned, and that therefore an appeal to the Supreme Court should be taken with the objective of securing from the Court a declaration of the relief to which they were ultimately entitled. Vance recognized that the Court would not likely reverse the district court and order it to grant immediate further relief, but by an appeal securing a declaration of the relief to which the plaintiffs were ultimately entitled, future proceedings in the district court would be simplified and any future relief granted would be more satisfactory.

Finally, Vance argued, the legislature was not likely to reapportion in any satisfactory manner. This meant that for perhaps four years the more populous counties would continue to be underrepresented, particularly in the senate. The smaller counties would still possess majorities, with their representatives in perhaps not the best of moods because of the large counties' attempts to force reapportionment in the

---

[102] I have not exhausted all of the arguments or factors which influenced the decision not to appeal, but those listed above are the most important ones. I have not discussed more personal factors, which are not necessary for an understanding of the litigation in the Alabama case.

federal courts. An appeal, Vance argued, would reduce this rather dangerous interim period for the large counties in the legislature.

All factors considered, it seemed to Vance that an appeal was necessary. The Supreme Court would have to meet the question of geographical representation since this was the "key issue in most of the pending reapportionment cases, and unless some reasonably definitive guidelines are set down by the Supreme Court, continued litigation is probably going to be interminable." Vance argued, therefore, "that the court will not be able to sidestep this key issue and that since we have the most favorable facts which could be presented to it, that we should be the ones to go all-out for immediate relief with respect to the Senate."[103]

This internal debate among the plaintiffs' attorneys continued during July and early August following the decision of the district court. Since Charles Morgan opposed an appeal, along with Jerome Cooper, representing the Steel Workers, any appeal would have to be pursued by either David Vann and Robert Vance, representing the Jefferson County Democratic Campaign Committee, or John McConnell, representing the Mobile plaintiffs. By mid-August, however, all the plaintiffs had decided not to appeal the case. McConnell, Vann, and Vance were unable to appeal because they lacked the necessary finances.[104]

As this decision was reached or imposed upon the plaintiffs, however, the probate judges of Dallas and Marion counties, B. A. Reynolds and Frank Pearce, filed notices of appeal in the case. The attorney general had advised the defendants that, while he was opposed to the district court's decision, an appeal by the defendants might result in a worse order from the defendants' standpoint from the Supreme Court, and therefore he recommended against an appeal. Although Marion County's previous legislative representation was unaffected by the district court's order, Dallas County was reduced from three representatives in the house to two, and, having previously composed a senate district by itself, the county was combined under the court's order with Lowndes County to form the thirtieth senatorial district. Counsel for the probate judges, McLean Pitts, Joseph Wilkinson, Jr.,

[103] Letter, Vance to McConnell, Aug. 10, 1962. In this letter Vance set forth the thoughts of all the Birmingham attorneys on the question of an appeal, and I have based the paragraphs above dealing with the positions of the various attorneys to a great extent upon this letter, supplemented by my interviews with the attorneys during the summer of 1965.

[104] Letter, Vance to the author, July 1, 1965.

and Thomas G. Gayle, all of Selma, were also in touch with Governor Wallace, who favored an appeal in the case. Upon receiving assurances of financial support from Montgomery sources, the notice of appeal was filed.[105] On appeal to the Supreme Court, the Alabama case would thus be known as *Reynolds* v. *Sims*.

Upon learning of the probate judges' appeal, John McConnell wrote Robert Vance and pointed out that "it looks now as if we have all the advantages of the appeal without any of the onus on us of having taken the appeal."[106] In addition, since most of the costs would be borne by the probate judges, the plaintiffs could now have a relatively "free appeal." Vance replied in early September that he and David Vann would file a cross-appeal in the case and asked McConnell to join them. "I think the main thrust of our argument will be connected with the seeking of declaratory relief as to the ultimate Senate apportionment to which we are entitled," Vance said. "I think that a good argument could be made that this is the proper vehicle for such a determination by the Supreme Court rather than *Scholle* v. *Hare*."[107] Charles Morgan and Jerome Cooper, on the other hand, adhered to their judgment that an appeal was unnecessary. "We have no thought that the District Court in Montgomery will not grant full and complete relief in the event that the Alabama Legislature does not (and most of us are reasonably certain that it will not)," Morgan said. "It is for this reason that we do not desire to either appeal or cross-appeal. In short we are at least as confident of the three-judge court in Montgomery as we would be of the United States Supreme Court when viewing these questions."[108]

David Vann and Robert Vance, therefore, filed notice of a cross-appeal in the case, and John McConnell also filed a cross-appeal.[109] It was agreed among the cross-appellants that Vann and Vance

---

[105] Interview with McLean Pitts, June 16, 1965, Selma, Ala.; this paragraph is also based upon information derived from the files of McLean Pitts and Thomas Gayle.

[106] Letter, McConnell to Vance, Sept. 4, 1962.

[107] Letter, Vance to McConnell, Sept. 10, 1962.

[108] Letter, Morgan to McConnell, Sept. 22, 1962.

[109] Thus one appeal and two cross-appeals were filed in the Alabama case. The appeal by the probate judges was *Reynolds* v. *Sims*; the cross-appeal by Vann and Vance was *Vann* v. *Baggett*; and McConnell's cross-appeal was *McConnell* v. *Baggett*. Since the Supreme Court consolidated the cases and decided them under the title *Reynolds* v. *Sims*, the latter will be used to designate all three cases herein.

would primarily seek a declaration by the Supreme Court that the senate should be based upon population, while McConnell would pursue his argument that both houses of the legislature must be based on population under the Fourteenth Amendment, which would entail McConnell's attacking the district court's order as it related to the house of representatives as well as the senate.[110]

The Birmingham *News* was editorially critical of the appeals of the probate judges and the plaintiffs. The plaintiffs who were appealing were a "rump segment," the *News* said, and it was "unfortunate that confusion has been proposed by any of the Jefferson group which had won so much." The three-judge court had only ordered into effect a temporary apportionment and was retaining jurisdiction, the editorial noted, and an appeal was therefore useless. The appeal, the *News* concluded, was "a well-intentioned goof."[111] This "well-intentioned goof," however, was ultimately to become the vehicle for one of the Supreme Court's farthest-reaching decisions in a generation.

[110] Letter, Vance to author, July 1, 1965; interviews with John McConnell, June 12, 1965, Mobile, Ala.; and David Vann, June 18, 1965, Birmingham, Ala.
[111] Birmingham *News,* Aug. 25, 1962, editorial, "Well-Intentioned Goof."

CHAPTER VIII

EQUAL PROTECTION AND REPRESENTATION:

THE CLASH OF ARGUMENT

THE ALABAMA CASE, *Reynolds* v. *Sims*, was joined before the Supreme Court by apportionment cases from New York, Maryland, Colorado, Delaware, and Virginia. These cases were argued sporadically before the Court throughout the 1963 term—during November, December, March, and April—and the Court's decisions were finally announced on June 15, 1964.[1] The solicitor general, having intervened in *Baker* v. *Carr* as *amicus curiae*, continued to participate in the cases spawned in the wake of the Tennessee case. He now found it necessary to formulate the government's position on the ultimate issue under the Fourteenth Amendment which the Court, as he had urged, had avoided in the Tennessee case.

While the apportionment cases were being appealed, however, the Court was confronted with similar Fourteenth Amendment issues in the Georgia county unit case, *Gray* v. *Sanders*.[2] The three-judge district court in Georgia had invalidated the unit system under the equal protection clause, but had held that such a system was constitutionally permissible if the weighting of votes did not exceed that permitted in the federal electoral college.[3] The case thus presented issues close-

---

[1] There were nine other cases before the Court involving challenges to state apportionment cases during this period, but they were not argued, and were later disposed of by the Court in *per curiam* opinions upon the basis of its opinions in these six cases. These additional cases involved challenges of the apportionment systems in Florida, *Swann* v. *Adams*, 378 U.S. 553; Ohio, *Nolan* v. *Rhodes* and *Sive* v. *Ellis*, 378 U.S. 556; Illinois, *Germano* v. *Kerner*, 378 U.S. 560; Michigan, *Marshall* v. *Hare*, 378 U.S. 561; Idaho, *Hearne* v. *Smylie*, 378 U.S. 563; Connecticut, *Pinney* v. *Butterworth*, 378 U.S. 564; Iowa, *Hill* v. *Davis*, 378 U.S. 565; Oklahoma, *Baldwin* v. *Moss*, *Oklahoma Farm Bureau* v. *Moss*, and *Williams* v. *Moss*, 378 U.S. 558; and Washington, *Meyers* v. *Thigpen*, 378 U.S. 554.

[2] 372 U.S. 368 (March 18, 1963).

[3] *Sanders* v. *Gray*, 203 F. Supp. 158 (N.D. Ga. 1962).

192

ly related to those in legislative apportionment cases. The issues were not identical, however, and Solicitor General Cox, participating in the county unit case as *amicus curiae*, urged the Court to keep in mind the difference between legislative apportionment and the election of a governor, senator, or other state officials. "Since a legislature is representative," the government's brief said, "there may be room for choice among theories of representation . . . so long as there is no more than modest departure from *per capita* equality. Within whatever unit of representation is established, however, each citizen casts an equal vote for his representative."[4] Thus he emphasized the distinction between the unequal weighting of votes in an election within a given constituency and the weighting of the representation of a given constituency within a system of legislative representation. The equal protection clause required strict *per capita* equality in the former, the government argued, but might allow some deviation from *per capita* equality in the latter. The solicitor general thus avoided in the Georgia county unit case the problem of the relation between the equal protection clause and legislative apportionment systems.[5]

In its decision in *Gray v. Sanders*, announced on March 18, 1963, the Court also distinguished the issues raised under the equal protection clause by the unit system from those presented by legislative apportionment. In the majority opinion written by Justice Douglas, expressing the views of eight of the justices (Justice Harlan alone dissented), the Court noted that the case "does not involve a question of the degree to which the Equal Protection Clause of the Fourteenth Amendment limits the authority of a State Legislature in designing the geographical districts from which representatives are chosen either for the State Legislature or for the Federal House of Representatives. . . . Nor does it present the question, inherent in the bicameral form of our Federal Government, whether a State may have one house chosen without regard to population."[6]

Reaching the issue thus distinguished, the Court declared that "once the geographical unit for which a representative is to be chosen is designated, all who participate in the election are to have an equal vote —whatever their race, whatever their sex, whatever their occupation,

---

[4] Brief of the United States as *Amicus Curiae, Gray v. Sanders*, p. 32.

[5] For a discussion of the unit system and this litigation, see Emmet J. Bondurant, "A Stream Polluted at Its Source: The Georgia County Unit System," *Journal of Public Law*, Vol. 12, No. 1 (1963).

[6] 372 U.S., at 377.

whatever their income, and wherever their home may be in that geographical unit. This is required by the Equal Protection Clause of the Fourteenth Amendment."[7] The concept of political equality, the Court said, "from the Declaration of Independence to Lincoln's Gettysburg Address, to the Fifteenth, Seventeenth, and Nineteenth Amendments can mean only one thing—one person, one vote."[8]

The Georgia county unit case thus shed little light on the Court's attitude toward the issues in the legislative apportionment cases, except on one significant point. The lower court had ordered that a unit system could exist if the weighting of votes was no greater than the weighting of votes by the federal electoral college, but the Supreme Court specifically rejected this form of "federal analogy" as a measure of the equality required by the equal protection clause. "We think the analogies to the electoral college, to districting and redistricting, and to other phases of the problems of representation in state or federal legislatures," it said, "are inapposite."[9] Although the Court expressly denied that "the question here [has] anything to do with the composition of the state or federal legislature," the Court's rejection of a federal analogy argument cast doubt upon the argument that the geographic apportionment of the U. S. Senate justified the geographic apportionment of one house of a state legislature. The latter was the form of federal analogy argument that had been most often advanced by those wishing to apportion at least one house of state legislatures on a basis other than population in the period after *Baker* v. *Carr*, and the Georgia county unit case would be cited against such arguments in the apportionment cases that followed.

The Georgia county unit case also demonstrated that the two justices who had joined the Court since *Baker* v. *Carr*, White and Goldberg, accepted the Court's decision in that case and were willing to utilize the jurisdiction thus established and the "one person, one vote" doctrine at least to the extent of striking down the unit system. How they would react to the rather different issues in the apportionment cases was, of course, yet to be seen.

With the arrival of the legislative apportionment cases before the Court, the solicitor general finally had to formulate the government's position on the meaning of the equal protection clause for legislative

7 *Ibid.*, at 379.
8 *Ibid.*, at 381.
9 *Ibid.*, at 378.

apportionment. The solicitor general in these cases did not urge the Court to define the ultimate test of legislative apportionments under the Fourteenth Amendment, but instead spelled out in the government's main brief, filed in *Maryland Committee for Fair Representation* v. *Tawes*, certain standards that such a test must include—standards, the government argued, met by none of the apportionment systems in the cases before the Court. The solicitor general urged the Court to approach the standard embraced by the Fourteenth Amendment cautiously on a case by case basis.

The government's position in the 1964 cases was therefore based on the argument that state apportionments must meet certain tests of rationality while not repudiating the "one man, one vote" standard if such a standard were enunciated by the Court in some future case. The Fourteenth Amendment required first, the government argued, that the starting point for legislative apportionment be *"per capita equality of representation."* Where deviations from this principle existed, "the apportionment stands condemned unless the differentiation has a relevant and substantial justification."[10] Second, the government contended that an apportionment was invalid if it created gross inequalities "without rhyme or reason"; that is, any deviation from *per capita* equality must have "a rational basis in the objectives the apportionment law is designed to achieve."[11] Third, an apportionment violated the equal protection clause if it contained discrimination based upon constitutionally proscribed criteria, such as race, sex, religion, national origin, or political philosophy, or if it contained discrimination based upon criteria of an invidious or irrelevant nature, such as giving greater representation to some economic groups than to others. There was no reason, the government argued, "to attribute extra virtue or great added power to voters of a particular occupation, economic status or place of residence in the apportionment of a State legislature. A rural voter is not entitled, by reason of that fact alone, to have greater or less representation than an urban resident."[12]

Finally, the government contended that the equal protection clause was violated if an apportionment subordinated the principle of *per*

[10] Brief of the United States as *Amicus Curiae, Maryland Committee* v. *Tawes*, pp. 29–33.
[11] *Ibid.*, p. 34.
[12] *Ibid.*, p. 41.

capita equality to the representation of political subdivisions so as to allow small minorities to control the legislature, although it was assumed that political subdivisions could be recognized in the apportionment of representation.[13] "When one house of a bicameral legislature is apportioned substantially according to population, the Fourteenth Amendment may leave considerable room in the other house for recognition of conflicting objectives," the government's brief concluded. "We assume as much *arguendo*, reserving judgment until the questions are presented." But an apportionment was invalid if it was found to be "virtually submerging the principles of voter equality and majority rule by excluding them from all consideration in one house and subordinating them in the other."[14]

In arguing that population must be the primary consideration in representation, the government relied heavily upon the debates in the Philadelphia convention in 1787 and especially upon later remarks of Jefferson and Madison. The founding fathers, the government argued, were "virtually unanimous" in the belief that "all voters [should] be represented equally in the legislature." The Court should therefore "look to the basic concepts of democracy of Jefferson, Madison, and the other founding fathers, not to the use of power of those living on the seacoast and then later by those living in rural areas to protect their own interests. For it is the basic notions of democracy which are incorporated into the equal protection and due process clauses of the Fourteenth Amendment."[15] The government also cited the theory suggested by Justice Stone in the *Carolene Products* case[16] in support of its contention that discrimination affecting "the right to equal representation, even more than restrictions upon freedom of communication, destroys the essential preconditions of an alert democracy." The Court should therefore vigilantly protect equal representation, it was argued, since those "whose voice is greatly diluted by malapportionment have almost no protection by exercise of their franchise."[17] The Court's vigilance in protecting equal representation

[13] *Ibid.*, p. 46.

[14] *Ibid.*, p. 47.

[15] *Ibid.*, pp. 61, 65. See also the Appendix to the Brief of the United States as *Amicus Curiae, Maryland Committee* v. *Tawes*, which contains the government's evidence on this point.

[16] *United States* v. *Carolene Products Co.*, 304 U.S. 144 (1938).

[17] Brief of the United States as *Amicus Curiae, Maryland Committee* v. *Tawes*, p. 69.

was therefore as necessary to the maintenance of an open political process as the protection of freedom of expression.

After the government had spelled out the principles which it argued the Fourteenth Amendment embraced in regard to apportionment, it proceeded to measure the Alabama, Colorado, Delaware, Maryland, New York, and Virginia apportionment systems by those principles. The apportionment of Alabama under the 67 Senator Amendment, the government argued, was invalid because it subordinated the principle of *per capita* equality to the principle of representation of political subdivisions to such a degree as to give small minorities control of both houses of the legislature.[18] The apportionment under the Crawford-Webb Act was also invalid because it created a "crazy quilt" and subordinated population too much to the representation of political subdivisions.[19] "Thus, both branches of the legislature are deliberately constituted by rules that discriminate against voters who live in the more populous counties," the government's brief said. "The equal protection clause forbids a State to create favored political classes on the basis of race, religion, occupation, or economic status. Where a man lives, like the number of his neighbors, is irrelevant to any permissible purpose of electoral policy."[20]

The government conceded, however, that although the lower court's order in the Alabama case had not accorded the plaintiffs the full measure of relief to which they were entitled under the Fourteenth Amendment, the lower court had acted within permissible limits of discretion. The court could afford full relief if the legislature once again had an opportunity to reapportion and failed to enact valid legislation. The government thus urged the Supreme Court to affirm the decision of the court below in *Reynolds* v. *Sims*.[21]

In the oral argument in the Alabama case, Solicitor General Cox stated that if one assumed, as the government did in these cases, that the Fourteenth Amendment standard was not "one man, one vote," then one house of a legislature could deviate from a population basis if the other house did not. Justice Goldberg interrupted to ask whether one did not have to judge the whole result, and if both houses had to approve legislation, then either could block majority rule. Cox replied

[18] Brief of the United States as *Amicus Curiae, Reynolds* v. *Sims*, p. 30.
[19] *Ibid.,* p. 37.
[20] *Ibid.,* p. 42.
[21] *Ibid.,* pp. 43–47.

that he was not "arguing for absolute majority rule," only that a state "could not depart too far from it." Goldberg then asked, "How far is too far?" Cox replied that the answer to that question should be determined by the Court on a case by case basis, but the test was whether in looking at an apportionment "does one get the conviction that the legislature has struck a balance, or has it weighted some areas or interests as more important than others." Justice White then wanted to know whether, if one house were allowed to deviate from population, would there "have to be a reason other than preferring rural to urban?" The solicitor general responded in the affirmative, saying, "That is absolutely out. That is class legislation." White continued, "So if a state says we want to keep nine cities from taking control, that is not an adequate reason?" No, Cox replied. "Your Honor put it well yesterday. If you take control from the majority, you give it to the minority; and that is not our constitutional system."[22]

The plaintiffs in *Reynolds* v. *Sims* continued to be divided in their arguments before the Court as they had been on the question of an appeal. David Vann and Robert Vance urged the Court to reverse the lower court's reapportionment of the Alabama Senate because it contained invidious discrimination. The lower court had accepted the Alabama Constitution's provisions allowing one representative per county in the house. This exhausted the latitude allowed for deviation from population under the Fourteenth Amendment, they argued, and therefore the senate should be based on population. The lower court's order put the more populous areas of Alabama "adrift on the same turbulent seas where their Constitutional rights to equal and fair representation have been washed away for over 62 years. The decision of the District Court provided neither chart nor compass nor sail."[23] And in the oral argument Vann argued that the district court had left in

[22] *U. S. Law Week,* Vol. 32, No. 20 (Nov. 26, 1963), p. 3195 (hereinafter cited as *LW*). Extensive excerpts from the oral arguments in the 1964 apportionment cases were reported in *LW*, Vol. 32, No. 20 (Nov. 26, 1963), pp. 3189–93; No. 39 (April 7, 1964), pp. 3345–47; excerpts from the arguments were also reported in *The New York Times,* Nov. 13, 1963, pp. 1, 30; Nov. 14, 1963, p. 29; Nov. 15, 1963, p. 23; Nov. 19, 1963, p. 25; Dec. 10, 1953, p. 39; April 2, 1964, p. 16. I have in some instances combined the excerpts from both of these sources, and to avoid excessive footnoting, I cite both sources on the occasions where this has been done without designating which parts of a series of quotations come from each source.

[23] Brief of Appellants David Vann, Robert Vance, and C. H. Erskine Smith, *Vann* v. *Baggett,* p. 21.

control of the legislature "the same people who don't want to give up power." He said, "I think we're entitled to equal protection in the formation of the permanent plan."[24]

John McConnell continued to argue before the Court, as he had argued throughout the litigation, that the equal protection clause required both houses of a legislature to be based on population. The "representative voice of the constituent citizens in the legislature must not only be equal in electing the members of each house," he said in his brief, "but must be equal in the voice of each representative in *each* house."[25] McConnell therefore attacked the district court's order reapportioning both the Alabama house and senate, and urged the Court during oral argument to establish population as the required basis for representation in both houses. Whatever the Court said was "the minimum," he declared, "is the maximum we'll get from the Alabama legislature."[26]

Charles Morgan, George Peach Taylor, and Jerome Cooper, who had opposed an appeal of the district court's order, argued before the Court that the decision of the lower court should be affirmed. As Cooper said in his brief, the district court had acted to "release the stranglehold" on the legislature and the "path leading to equality at the ballot box has been cleared."[27] The district court, as Morgan suggested in his brief, had thus proceeded with all "deliberate speed" in vindicating the rights of the plaintiffs.[28] While thus supporting the decision of the district court, Morgan contended during the oral argument that the "one standard that is measurable, leaving less room for doubt, is population." A standard based on land or political units to the exclusion of population would result in an unrepresentative system, he said. "Farms will always have more area than cities. . . . This country's dream says the people should govern themselves. The courts are there to protect the minority from the majority, but surely the majority should have power in both branches of the legislature."[29]

The Alabama attorney general, Richmond Flowers, also supported the action of the district court as "reasonable, rational and fair as to the guide lines stated." While arguing that the equal protection clause

[24] 32 *LW* 3190.
[25] Brief for the Appellants, *McConnell v. Baggett*, p. 27.
[26] 32 *LW* 3190.
[27] Brief for Appellees, R. E. Farr et al., *Reynolds v. Sims*, pp. 5–6.
[28] Brief for Appellees, M. O. Sims et al., *Reynolds v. Sims*, pp. 10–11.
[29] 32 *LW* 3190.

did not require "mathematical equality or rigid equality," he conceded that both houses of a legislature must to some extent be based on population. If population were the only consideration, he pointed out in his brief, then state constitutional provisions in many states would fall.[30] In his oral argument Flowers assured the Court, as a former state senator, that it would have been "politically impossible" to have obtained reapportionment in Alabama without judicial intervention. "A handful of men had gained power, and you can't expect people to vote themselves out of office," he concluded. "I do not think there is a citizen of Alabama who could say that the 1901 apportionment was anything but unfair, unjust, and ridiculous [in 1962]. Even the Supreme Court of Alabama has occasionally recognized that fact."[31]

McLean Pitts and the other attorneys for B. A. Reynolds and Frank Pearce, probate judges of Dallas and Lowndes counties, not only attacked the order of the district court but also pursued the rather futile argument before the Court that *Baker* v. *Carr* had been wrongly decided and ought to be reversed.[32] Assuming the Court would refuse to reverse the Tennessee case, however, they argued that both the 67 Senator Amendment and the Webb-Crawford Act were valid under the Fourteenth Amendment. The 67 Senator Amendment was valid because it was similar to the United States Senate apportionment and thus "rational." The Webb-Crawford Act's apportionment provisions were similarly rational and did not embrace invidious discrimination. The Fourteenth Amendment only prohibited state action that was based on "no policy," it was argued, and both the 67 Senator Amendment and the Webb-Crawford Act had been based upon rational policy considerations. The district court should therefore be reversed.[33]

In oral argument, McLean Pitts continued to urge the Court to reverse *Baker* v. *Carr*, which was, he said, "an invitation to the courts to

[30] Brief for the Appellee Richmond Flowers, as Attorney General, State of Alabama, *Reynolds* v. *Sims*, pp. 4–6.

[31] 32 *LW* 3190. In order for the reader to fully understand Attorney General Flowers' position in this case, it should be noted that the attorney general in Alabama is an independently elected official, and is thus not controlled by the governor through appointment. Flowers, a racial moderate, was, and continued to be, the highest state official in Alabama who was outspoken in his opposition to the adamantly segregationist policies of Governor George Wallace. While Governor Wallace favored an appeal in *Reynolds* v. *Sims*, it is therefore not incongruous that Flowers defended the district court's order.

[32] Brief for Appellants, B. A. Reynolds et al., *Reynolds* v. *Sims*, pp. 30–34.

[33] *Ibid.*, pp. 34–41.

sit in judgment on political power." Quoting extensively from Justice Harlan's dissent in *Baker*, Pitts was interrupted by Harlan, who wryly noted that it "would have been better if you had found something that would give comfort to the majority." Harlan also stated that Pitts should be arguing whether or not the Alabama apportionment violated the Fourteenth Amendment, since if it did it was "the duty of the federal courts to vindicate the constitutional right." Pitts conceded that there had been "malapportionment" in Alabama, but contended that the district court should have allowed the legislature more time to remedy the situation. "How long do we have to wait?" Chief Justice Warren asked. Pitts replied that the district court should have only declared the old districts invalid and gone no further. "In other words," Warren said, "it would be a right without a remedy." Yes, Pitts responded, "I don't think they had a right to legislate for the people of Alabama." Opposing population as the basis of representation in both houses of a legislature, Pitts argued that if population were the basis required by the Fourteenth Amendment, "you will have areas in Alabama with no representation, under the thumbs of those living in the dense[ly populated] areas. That would be just as bad as having the minority rule the majority." Attacking also the district court's injunction against a referendum on the 67 Senator Amendment, Pitts concluded that if a "federal court can sit over a state and say it may not submit a constitutional amendment to its own people, state sovereignty is at an end."[34]

As in the Alabama case, the solicitor general argued that the apportionment systems being challenged in the Delaware, New York, Maryland, and Virginia cases could be invalidated without necessitating a ruling from the Court on the ultimate standard under the equal protection clause.[35] In the New York case, *W.M.C.A., Inc.* v. *Lomenzo*, the somewhat complex apportionment provisions of the New York Constitution of 1894 were challenged. These provisions required the more populous counties to meet a larger population ratio to have a senator than the less populous counties. In addition, increases in senate representation for the more populous counties resulted in an increase to more than fifty senators, although losses in senate representation by

[34] *The New York Times*, Nov. 14, 1963, p. 29; 32 *LW* 3190, 3191.
[35] The Colorado case is not discussed at this point because of the unique issues it raised; it is considered in detail following this discussion of the other five cases.

the more populous counties did not result in reducing the total number of senators. Since the number of senators allocated to the more populous counties was subtracted from the total number of senators and the remainder distributed to the less populous counties, this provision obviously favored the less populous counties. The apportionment provision relating to the lower house required that each of the fifty-two counties be assigned one representative, with the exception of two small counties, which were combined for purposes of house representation with the remaining 99 of the 150 representatives assigned roughly on a population basis.[36]

In the government's brief *amicus curiae*, the solicitor general contended that the New York apportionment provisions relating to the senate created inequities "without rhyme or reason." The discrimination against *per capita* representation involved in these provisions, the government's brief said, "is based upon irrelevant, even invidious criteria." The government also contended that even if the apportionment of the New York Senate were based on a permissible criterion, its deviation from *per capita* representation was so great and the discrimination so gross as to be unreasonable. "Stripped to its essentials, therefore," the brief said, "the challenge to the apportionment of the New York Senate raises an issue as clear cut as it is fundamental—may a State discriminate in *per capita* representation against the voters in populous areas and in favor of voters in less populous areas when the only function of the discrimination is to increase the political power of the latter beyond their numerical weight. We submit that the Fourteenth Amendment does not tolerate discrimination based upon such irrelevant criteria."[37] Even if the senate apportionment were based on permissible criteria, however, the government further argued that the discrimination in both houses of the New York legislature was so gross as to be unreasonable. "In short," the government's brief said, "both houses of the New York legislature substantially discriminate against citizens living in populous areas. New York offers no reasons justifying such substantial discrimination. The apportionment therefore violates the Fourteenth Amendment."[38]

In the oral argument of the New York case, Solicitor General Cox

[36] The New York apportionment provisions are analyzed in detail in *W.M.C.A., Inc.* v. *Lomenzo,* 377 U.S. 633, at 641–53.

[37] Brief of the United States as *Amicus Curiae, W.M.C.A., Inc.* v. *Lomenzo,* p. 29.

[38] *Ibid.,* pp. 33, 37.

relied heavily on the Georgia county unit case, pointing out to the Court that if "it violates our fundamental precepts to give one class of voters more weight in an election for governor, it does the same in an election of representatives." Abandoning the distinction between a state-wide election and an election of representatives which the government itself had made in the county unit case, Cox argued such a distinction "is as irrelevant as the fact that the Attorney General argued that case and I am arguing this. We say the 14th Amendment in matters of representation requires blindness to classes of people." Justice Harlan inquired how it could be said that the Fourteenth Amendment applied to apportionment at all, and Cox replied that *Baker* v. *Carr* had so held "implicitly." An apparently surprised Justice Brennan asked, "Only implicitly?" "I was speaking conservatively," Cox replied. "Very conservatively," Brennan shot back.[39]

Applying its criteria to the Maryland apportionment challenged in *Maryland Committee for Fair Representation* v. *Tawes*, the government contended that Maryland discriminated unreasonably and subordinated *per capita* representation to representation of political subdivisions to an extent that small minorities could control its legislature.[40] Maryland's legislature, reacting to a state court challenge of the existing apportionment, had enacted in 1962 temporary reapportionment legislation affecting the lower house. The Maryland Constitution fixed the number of members in the house at 123, but the 1962 legislation raised this number to 142, and the additional 19 seats were distributed to the more populous counties. There still remained, however, six times as many persons per representative in the most populous county as in the least populous county. The Maryland Constitution guaranteed a senator to each of the twenty-three counties and one to each of the six legislative districts in the city of Baltimore, allowing fifteen counties with less than 15 percent of the state's population to elect a majority of the senators.[41] The Maryland Court of Appeals, however, sustained the senate apportionment against a challenge under the equal protection clause.[42]

The government argued in its brief that the apportionment of the

[39] 32 *LW* 3190.
[40] Brief of the United States as *Amicus Curiae, Maryland Committee* v. *Tawes,* pp. 48–49, 57.
[41] For a detailed discussion of Maryland's provisions and the litigation challenging them, see *Maryland Committee* v. *Tawes,* 377 U.S. 656, at 658–73 (1964).
[42] *Maryland Committee* v. *Tawes,* 229 Md. 406 (1962).

Maryland Senate discriminated without "rhyme or reason" by assigning one senator to each county but one senator also to each of Baltimore city's legislative districts. "Even if rural voters possessed their fabled superiority," the brief said, "the voters of Baltimore, Prince George's and Montgomery Counties would come closer to possessing that enviable virtue than the people of Baltimore City, for surely even those who credit the fable do not believe that the supposed virtue resides in the country and the large city but not in the small city or suburbs."[43] The apportionment of both the Maryland house and senate was invalid, the government also argued, because of the subordination of the principle of *per capita* equality to representation of political subdivisions to the extent that small minorities could control both houses. The government's brief thus concluded that the "resulting inequalities are so great and the departure from the principle of majority rule is so excessive as to constitute a denial of equal protection of the laws."[44]

The apportionment of the Maryland Senate had been defended successfully in the Maryland Court of Appeals on the basis of the federal analogy argument. The government, however, contended that the system of equal state representation in the United States Senate was not analogous to state apportionment because the system of representation in the United States Senate was the product of historic compromise in the constitutional convention involving issues not valid in relation to state apportionment systems. The states were not federations of counties or local units of government, as the government of the United States was a federation of states, and the framers of the Constitution had agreed generally that both houses of the legislatures of the states should be based on population. The government also pointed out that neither house of Maryland's legislature was based on population, and, citing the Georgia county unit case, argued that the "electoral college is just as analogous to the Georgia county unit system as the United States Senate is to the upper house of the State legislatures."[45]

The Virginia case, *Davis* v. *Mann*, presented a challenge by residents of Arlington and Fairfax counties and the City of Norfolk to the 1962

[43] Brief of the United States as *Amicus Curiae, Maryland Committee* v. *Tawes*, p. 53.
[44] *Ibid*, p. 57.
[45] *Ibid.*, p. 82.

apportionment of both houses of the Virginia legislature. The apportionment of the Virginia Senate involved population variations between the most and the least populous districts of 2.65 to 1; the house apportionment permitted population variations between the least and most populous districts of 4.36 to 1.[46] While Virginia's apportionment system raised much less serious issues of discrimination than did other cases, the government contended that the *per capita* discrimination against Fairfax and Arlington counties and the City of Norfolk was without rhyme or reason and therefore violated equal protection. "We believe," the government's brief said, "that a State may not apportion its legislature so as to discriminate significantly against a substantial number of voters when it can suggest no rational basis for the discrimination, even though a large minority is needed to elect a majority of the legislature."[47]

The Delaware case, *Roman* v. *Sincock*, involved a challenge by residents of New Castle County and the City of Wilmington of the apportionment of the Delaware legislature. Delaware has but three counties, and the state constitution allocated five senators and ten representatives each to Kent and Sussex counties and to "rural" New Castle County (that part of New Castle County outside the City of Wilmington). The City of Wilmington was allocated two senators and five representatives. Senate districts ranged from 4,177 to 64,820, with a population variation from the most to the least populous districts being approximately 35 to 1. A constitutional amendment, adopted in 1963 in response to the litigation challenging this apportionment system, allocated to each of the three counties seven senators, keeping the population variation at about 15 to 1, and allocated more house representation to the more populous areas, changing the house districts' population variation to approximately 12 to 1. The amendment thus established area as the basis of representation in the senate, adhering to the "federal plan" of representation, but representation in the house still was not based on equal population.[48]

Rejecting the federal analogy argument advanced to support the Delaware apportionment system, the government contended that the Delaware apportionment of both its house and senate was invalid be-

[46] For a fuller discussion see *Davis* v. *Mann*, 377 U.S. 678, at 680–90.
[47] Brief of the United States as *Amicus Curiae*, *Davis* v. *Mann*, p. 47.
[48] For a more detailed discussion, see *Roman* v. *Sincock*, 377 U.S. 695, at 697–707.

cause it was based upon "*no* policy" and, again, because it subordinated *per capita* representation to the representation of political subdivisions to the extent that small minorities could control the legislature. "This is by far the easiest of the reapportionment cases now before the Court on the merits," the government's brief declared. "The apportionment of the Delaware legislature plainly violates any standard of equal protection."[49]

In the Alabama, New York, Maryland, Virginia, and Delaware cases, therefore, the solicitor general was able to urge the Court to invalidate apportionment systems on the basis of the standards enunciated by the government in its main brief without adopting a position on the ultimate standard embraced by the Fourteenth Amendment. The argument that the equal protection clause embraced a "one man, one vote" standard, requiring both houses of a state legislature to be based solely on population, was urged upon the Court by some of the primary parties in the apportionment cases and by some of the *amici curiae*, but not by the solicitor general.

The "one man, one vote" standard had been advanced, in the months following the 1962 decision in *Baker* v. *Carr*, in a report by a conference of research scholars and political scientists sponsored by the Twentieth Century Fund and in a report of the Advisory Commission on Intergovernmental Relations. These reports, *One Man—One Vote* and *Apportionment of State Legislatures*,[50] respectively, were extensively cited in the briefs filed in the 1964 cases by those attacking apportionment systems. Indeed, forty copies of the Twentieth Century Fund report, *One Man—One Vote*, were filed with the Court along with the jurisdictional statement in the New York case.[51] This report was written by Anthony Lewis, the *New York Times* reporter specializing at the time in covering the Supreme Court. In 1958, Lewis had written an article that had been cited extensively in the briefs filed in *Baker* v. *Carr*.[52] In addition, his coverage of the apportionment problem and apportionment litigation in the *Times* was consistently

[49] Brief of the United States as *Amicus Curiae, Roman* v. *Sincock*, p. 13.

[50] Conference of Research Scholars and Political Scientists, *One Man—One Vote* (New York: Twentieth Century Fund, 1962); and *Apportionment of State Legislatures* (Washington, D. C.: Advisory Commission on Intergovernmental Relations, 1962).

[51] See the Brief for Appellants, *W.M.C.A., Inc.* v. *Simon*, p. 40.

[52] "Legislative Apportionment and the Federal Courts," 71 *Harvard Law Review* 1057 (1958).

accurate and perceptive. If one person were to be singled out whose writing was most influential in the apportionment litigation, and perhaps influential in its impact upon the Court itself, Anthony Lewis would be that person.

The "one man, one vote" argument was typically expressed in the brief for the appellants in the New York case, where it was contended that the equal protection clause "is broad enough to invalidate all invidious discriminations which deprive groups—be they urban residents, redheads or left-handed persons—of the full and free exercise of their basic civil liberties, including the right to vote and the right to have one's vote fully and fairly counted." The brief submitted that "any apportionment, such as New York's, which has the effect of giving greater weight to the votes cast by persons residing in a particular area of the state than that given to votes cast elsewhere embodies an implicit value judgment that some persons are entitled to a greater influence in government than is proportionate to their numbers."[53]

A similar stand was expressed in the joint brief of the American Civil Liberties Union, American Jewish Congress, and National Association for the Advancement of Colored People—perhaps the most important *amicus* brief filed with the Court supporting the invalidation of apportionments not based on population. These groups, being interested in the protection of minorities which "tend to concentrate in the more populous areas,"[54] argued nonetheless that there was no justification "for allowing any minority interest group, whether rural voters or any other, to gain absolute control of a state legislature with concomitant power to enact legislation which is unacceptable to the majority." Checks upon majority rule through the executive veto, bills of rights, and the requirement of special majorities for change in the organic law were acceptable, the brief said, but "it is quite another matter, and utterly indefensible, to place in the hands of a minority the power to enact positive legislation along with the power to prevent diminution of its own dominant role in the legislative process."[55]

---

[53] Brief for Appellants, *W.M.C.A., Inc.* v. *Simon*, p. 40.

[54] Brief *Amici Curiae* for the American Jewish Congress, American Civil Liberties Union, and National Association for the Advancement of Colored People, Legal Defense and Education Fund, Inc., p. 4. Other *amicus* briefs were filed by Montgomery County, Maryland, in *Maryland Committee* v. *Tawes*, and by Kenneth Schmied, president of the Board of Aldermen of the City of Louisville, Kentucky, in all six cases.

[55] *Ibid.*, pp. 45–46.

Arguing along "one man, one vote" lines before the Court, Leonard B. Sand, representing the appellants in the New York case, was asked by Justice Harlan where he "found that in the Constitution." Sand replied that "one man, one vote" was the meaning of the equal protection clause. Harlan also wanted to know if it was irrelevant legally that a majority of the people of New York had approved the constitutional provisions being attacked in the New York case. "We're dealing with the rights of individuals," Sand replied. "Certainly if a state majority chose to deny Negroes the vote, this court would not hestitate to strike it down." Justice Stewart suggested that a state might adopt proportional representation or a tricameral legislature, and said that he was "only suggesting that the problems before us in these cases are somewhat more complicated and subtle than the briefs suggest, and cannot be solved by eighth grade arithmetic." What if the cities in a state traded some of their representation in the legislature for home rule? Stewart asked. "No," Sand replied, "these are individual rights that cannot be traded away."[56]

Pursuing a similar "one man, one vote" argument in the Maryland case, Alfred L. Scanlan, counsel for appellants, was also interrupted by Justice Stewart, who suggested that the people in suburban Maryland, where Scanlan himself lived, might have "their social and economic interests in the District of Columbia," whereas the people in rural Maryland were tied to the state. Would it be irrational, therefore, Stewart asked, "for Maryland to realize that people in the rural areas are completely tied to the State of Maryland, are more committed to it than those who go to Washington to work every morning?" Scanlan replied, "Within the framework of American representative government, it would be irrational." Justice Harlan again asked whether *Baker* v. *Carr* had held that the Fourteenth Amendment applied to apportionment at all. "It was implicit," Scanlan answered. And again Justice Brennan seemed surprised by such a response, and said, "It was explicit." "I stand corrected by a more knowledgeable source," Scanlan replied. "He speaks for himself," Harlan retorted. "I hope he still speaks for the majority he spoke for in Baker v. Carr," Scanlan shot back.[57]

Not all the parties challenging apportionment systems before the Court urged the Court to adopt a strict "one man, one vote" stand-

[56] 32 *LW* 3189; *The New York Times*, Nov. 13, 1963, pp. 1, 30.
[57] 32 *LW* 3191; *The New York Times*, Nov. 15, 1963, p. 23.

ard.[58] The group challenging the Delaware apportionment and one of the groups challenging the Virginia apportionment, for example, followed the solicitor general's contention that the test was rationality; population might be the dominant, but it was not the only factor to be considered in apportionment.[59] The Virginia group thus contended that "equality is reasonable equality" and that mathematical equality was not possible "unless Virginia is redistricted without regard to county and city lines—something which the appellees have not contended should be done."[60]

Those defending the apportionment systems before the Court relied upon two principal arguments on the merits. First, the federal analogy was used, especially in the Maryland and Delaware cases, to defend the apportionment of one house of a legislature on the basis of area rather than population.[61] This argument was presented most thoroughly in a brief *amici curiae* filed on behalf of the attorneys general of fifteen states, which asserted that the federal analogy could apply to the states. The apportionment of a state legislature with one house representing population and the other representing area was, they contended, a rational plan of representation. It was inaccurate to argue that local units of government were not sovereignties analogous to the states, the brief said, since the states had surrendered much of their sovereignty to the federal government, and, "although local subdivisions of a State are not entirely sovereign units, they have been granted considerable autonomy by the higher government. Thus in both relationships [that between the federal government and the states and the states and their local subdivisions] neither unit of government has the exclusive sovereignty."[62]

[58] It should be noted that the Maryland group, discussed above, generally favored the "one man, one vote" standard, although admitting that if one house of a legislature were based exclusively on population, the second house could deviate somewhat from population, but such deviation should not allow a population variance ratio among districts of more than 1½ to 1; see Brief for Appellants, *Maryland Committee* v. *Tawes*, p. 26.

[59] Brief for Appellees, Mann, Stone, Webb, and Donovan, *Davis* v. *Mann*, p. 9; and Brief of Appellees, *Roman* v. *Sincock*.

[60] Brief for Appellees, Mann, Stone, Webb, and Donovan, *Davis* v. *Mann*, p. 9.

[61] See Brief for the Appellants, *Roman* v. *Sincock*; Brief on behalf of Appellees, *Maryland Committee* v. *Tawes*.

[62] Brief for the Attorneys General of the States as *Amici Curiae*, pp. 24–26. The states were Arizona, Colorado, Georgia, Hawaii, Idaho, Indiana, Kansas, Louisiana, New Jersey, North Carolina, North Dakota, Pennsylvania, Rhode

The brief also attempted to demonstrate, contrary to the government's brief, that the framers of the Constitution had supported and favored the apportionment of state legislatures along federal lines, believing that houses not based on population in state legislatures would protect minorities and provide balanced representation. The brief contained a thirty-two-page appendix containing extensive quotations from the framers to support this contention. The attorneys general also rejected the notion that area representation in the United States Senate was the result of historic compromise, not applicable to the states. "The fact that the system finally evolved for the National government to some extent as a matter of compromise does not deprive that system of its rational, sensible characteristics," they argued. "It does not matter if these characteristics were contemporaneously recognized, which was the case, or whether these characteristics were later used to encourage acceptance of the system or later described to explain the rightness or the success of the system. That a plan is evolved as a means of compromise does not mean that it is arbitrary, that it is without sense or reason. . . . An engine and a brake serve seemingly inconsistent purposes, but it is not irrational to put both in an automobile, or in [a] legislative system." Basing one house on area or other non-population factors thus protected minorities and prevented the tyranny of the majority.[63]

The federal analogy was particularly used to defend the apportionment of the Delaware Senate, as well as in the Maryland case. The Delaware attorney general noted in his brief that the three Delaware counties had existed as sovereign entities before the formation of the state, just as the thirteen states had existed prior to the adoption of the Constitution, and therefore the equal representation of these counties in the state's senate was just as appropriate as the representation of the states equally in the United States Senate. "Consequently," the attorney general argued, "if there is any one State that is now completely free to follow the Federal arrangement for its legislature, Delaware is the State."[64] The attorney general also pointed out that, following the Civil War, the Congress had readmitted southern states with legislatures based on factors other than population, at least in one house,

Island, South Dakota, and Vermont. The brief was written by Theodore I. Botter, first assistant attorney general of New Jersey.
[63] *Ibid.*, pp. 38–39.
[64] Brief for the Appellants, *Roman* v. *Sincock,* p. 29.

and that this contemporaneous construction of the equal protection clause of the Fourteenth Amendment by Congress denied that it required equal *per capita* representation in both houses of state legislatures.[65]

In the Virginia and New York cases, the second major argument advanced by the defenders of the apportionment systems in those states was that a rationality standard allowed an apportionment to be based on many factors, including population, which did not necessarily have to be the dominant factor. Representation of political subdivisions, a desire to reduce the size of constituencies, and protection of the interests of less populous areas were among factors that might reasonably justify deviation from equal *per capita* representation. The New York attorney general thus argued that New York's apportionment provisions were rational because they "established a systematic plan for apportioning legislative seats which gives heavy emphasis to per capita representation, while relying also on other perfectly rational factors which tend to promote equal access by all citizens to the legislative process."[66]

During oral argument, the defending attorneys were subjected to heavy bombardments of questions from the bench. New York's Assistant Solicitor General Irving Galt argued that "there should be equality of representation, but we don't regard per capita representation as the only test." Counties and other political subdivisions should be represented, he said, and the size of districts as well as "accessibility of representation" and the "diffusion of political power" should be considered.[67] Justice Black interrupted to ask whether, if New York City were given only one assemblyman and one senator, and the rest of the state given one hundred representatives, the Constitution would be violated. Galt replied that "in any constitutional area there comes a point of absurdity where this Court steps in," but that New York's apportionment system "presents no such problem." Chief Justice Warren then asked how important population was in apportionment. "Who is to say?" replied Galt. "No particular weight can be ascribed to population or any other factor."

[65] *Ibid.*, pp. 55–71.

[66] Brief for Appellees, *W.M.C.A., Inc.* v. *Simon*, pp. 19–20; for a similar argument see the Brief on behalf of Appellants, *Davis* v. *Mann*.

[67] This was a reference to *MacDougall* v. *Green*, 335 U.S. 281 (1948), a case heavily relied on by the defenders of the apportionment systems under attack in the 1964 cases. *The New York Times*, Nov. 13, 1963, pp. 1, 30.

Justice White also asked why New York treated the less populous counties differently than the more populous counties in its apportionment. Galt answered that this was to insure that "a few counties will not dominate . . . counties with an institutional weight, a concentrated power." Justice White then asked, "What about the concentrated power of the areas with a minority of the population? Which do you prefer, the tyranny of the minority or the tyranny of the majority?" Galt replied that he preferred no tyranny at all, getting a laugh, and added that "this isn't a question of entrenching minorities, it's a question of giving the smaller counties a voice." Justice Goldberg then remarked, "You keep saying, 'Give the less populous counties a voice.' Aren't you really saying they should be given a dominant voice? Don't you have to say that it is not unreasonable for a state to give the less populous areas a dominant voice in order to insure that great economic concentrations such as New York do not dominate?" Galt answered yes, the smaller interests should be heard. "What about Justice White's suggestion that the majority of the voters be given a majority in the Legislature?" Goldberg continued. "The minority could still be heard." Justice Clark also asked if Galt thought "accessibility [of representatives] is sufficient?" Galt replied that the New York system tried to "secure that accessibility to the greatest degree," but Justice Harlan noted that New York did not do so in its senate. "You've got to recognize," Harlan said, "that if your case stands or falls on numbers, you've got a very difficult time." Galt undoubtedly agreed with this sentiment.[68]

Assistant Attorney General Robert S. Bourbon of Maryland also was subjected to extensive questioning by the justices. Arguing that Maryland had "a deep historical tradition of counties," Bourbon contended that a state could give weight to geographically diverse political subdivisions in its apportionment system. "Suppose Maryland should decide that Baltimore has a lot of compensatory advantages and needed no representation," Justice Black asked. "Would that violate any provision of the Constitution?" Bourbon responded, "It might, as Mr. Galt said—when you reach the point of absurdity." But Justice Black retorted, "There is no provision in the Constitution against absurd legislation." Justice Stewart interjected, "Why not say that it would violate the Equal Protection Clause under Baker v. Carr? Just admit it." But Black continued to press his point. "You are arguing,"

[68] 32 *LW* 3190.

he said, "that you have a right to deprive people in a concentrated area of their full right of suffrage so that their power can be held down." Bourbon insisted, however, that the "State may look at the whole system in context."

Bourbon argued that the federal analogy justified the apportionment of the Maryland Senate on an area basis, but Black again challenged him. The basis of representation in the United States Senate, he said, was the result of a compromise among the sovereign states in the 1787 convention in order to make the Union possible. "I do not see," Black continued, "how you can possibly say the counties in a state are in the same situation as the original 13 colonies and must be given a seat to protect their sovereignty." Chief Justice Warren asked if the people of Maryland could force reapportionment through any political remedies, and Bourbon answered in the negative, but he pointed out that even where the initiative and referendum were available the people sometimes rejected reapportionment, as had been the case in California. Warren, however, emphasized the contrast between California and Maryland, saying that in California at least "the people did have a remedy."

Bourbon's federal analogy argument was supported by First Assistant Attorney General Theodore I. Botter of New Jersey, who argued on behalf of the fifteen attorneys general as *amici curiae*. "Our view is that an intentional check on majority rule of both houses of a bicameral legislature is a rational objective for a state," he said. "Majority rule in both houses does not provide adequate protection for minorities. The minority should have bargaining power in one house."[69] And Frederick Bernays Wiener, defending the Delaware apportionment system, also pursued the same argument, objecting to the "simple nose-count principle" which would give equal weight to all votes. There was nothing in the equal protection clause, Wiener said, "that forever subjects the few and the poor to the rich and the many." He also warned that if the Court imposed a strict population standard upon the states under the equal protection clause it would repeat the "tragic history" of the period when the Court read the principles of laissez faire into the Constitution. The imposition of such a standard, he said, "would really be amending the Constitution with a cleaver" and would "make the states mere geographic entities."

[69] 32 *LW* 3191.

Assistant Attorney General Robert D. McIlwaine of Virginia, on the other hand, pointed out to the Court that the apportionment of his state's legislature was based on population to the extent that Virginia ranked eighth in the nation in terms of the percentage of its population theoretically required to elect a majority of the legislature. Justice Goldberg inquired, however, what it was "that stands in the way of perfect equality." McIlwaine replied that what stood in the way was the "importance the General Assembly places on not having less populous counties overborne by the more populous." Citing *MacDougall* v. *Green*, he contended that a state had the right to provide for the "proper diffusion of political power." He also argued that Norfolk was not really seriously underrepresented when one discounted the military personnel residing there temporarily, but Justice White asked, "But your proposition necessarily is that a state may rest legislative power in a minority of the population?" Yes, as a check, McIlwaine replied.[70]

The sixth of the 1964 apportionment cases, the Colorado case, was appealed late to the Court and was not argued until March 31 and April 1, 1964. In this case, *Lucas* v. *Colorado General Assembly*, an apportionment system was challenged which had neither been enacted by a legislature nor been the product of legislative inaction, but was adopted by the Colorado electorate by an overwhelming majority in 1962 through the initiative and referendum process, while at the same time the voters had rejected a proposal to base both houses of the legislature on population. Although, theoretically, political remedies for reapportionment were available in two of the other states whose apportionments were being challenged before the Court,[71] the Colorado apportionment case raised the question of whether an apportionment system so recently approved overwhelmingly in every county of a state would be invalidated by the Court, especially when the very enactment of the system demonstrated the viability of an alternative political remedy. Certainly one of the major arguments of many of those

---

[70] 32 *LW* 3192.

[71] Maryland provided for a vote of the people every twenty years on the question of calling a constitutional convention, but when a favorable vote on the question was cast by the voters in 1950, the legislature refused to authorize the convention; in New York the question of calling a convention is also submitted to the people every twenty years, beginning in 1957, but such a convention would be based on the apportionment of the senate; no realistic political remedies existed in Alabama, Delaware, or Virginia.

who had urged federal court intervention had been the lack of any alternative relief for malapportionment, an argument that had been pressed especially, for example, in the Tennessee case. But in the Colorado case a majority of a state's electorate had used a political remedy to enact an apportionment system. The Court had to determine whether this in any way affected the constitutional validity of that system or the propriety of the federal judiciary's invalidating such a system.

The Colorado system did involve substantial deviation from equal *per capita* representation in the senate, allowing a theoretical minority of 33.2 percent of the population to elect a majority of that body and establishing districts with a maximum population variance ratio of 3.6 to 1. The lower house of the legislature, however, was based substantially on population.[72] The system was defended in the brief of the appellees with the argument that "a majority of voters in every county in Colorado, including the counties wherein Appellants reside and which they claim are discriminated against, has voted to impose restraints upon its own rule. . . . In point of fact, it should be regarded as a voluntary relaxing of the power of the majority over the minority, and this is by no means unreasonable."[73]

The appellants challenging the system, however, argued that the right "under the Fourteenth Amendment of any individual, in any state, is a right guaranteed by the Constitution of the United States and the institutions of the United States, and cannot be put aside by any state by popular vote, no matter how heavy." The appellants argued that it was possible "to assert that racial segregation would almost undoubtedly be approved by popular vote in many areas, were it submitted to that process, but its validity under the Fourteenth Amendment would be no whit strengthened by that approval. In like manner, no popular vote may take from any citizen his constitutional right of equal suffrage."[74]

The position of the government as *amicus curiae* in the Colorado case was rather ambiguous. The government's brief admitted that an apportionment adopted through the initiative and referendum gave such a system "a distinctive aspect." It was also impossible to treat voters in the same district differently in terms of representation, and

---

[72] See *Lucas* v. *Colorado General Assembly*, 377 U.S. 713, at 715–29 (1964).
[73] Brief of Appellees, *Lucas* v. *Colorado General Assembly*, pp. 29–30.
[74] Brief of Appellants, *Lucas* v. *Colorado General Assembly*, p. 57.

thus any "relief granted to those who request it in the courts will un-avoidably be forced upon those who rejected it at the polls." Under such circumstances, the government's brief said, "the will of those similarly situated and necessarily affected would seem to be a factor that equity should take into account in deciding whether to intervene or stay its hand."[75]

The government did not reject the rule of *per capita* equality, the brief continued, but such an interpretation "would press the Equal Protection Clause to an extreme and, as applied to State legislative ap-portionment, would require radical changes in three-quarters of the State governments, and would eliminate the opportunities for local variation." On the other hand, the government argued, for the Court to reject the rule of one man, one vote at "this early stage of the devel-opment under *Baker* v. *Carr*, would prematurely close an important line of constitutional evolution."[76] Although the Colorado Senate's apportionment was arbitrary and capricious in its discrimination, the government concluded that the "wrong, if any, is not very great" in the case. The constitutional question in the Colorado case was "much closer than those which preceded it." And the government's brief closed by noting that the Court could affirm the lower court's decision upholding the Colorado apportionment without approving the appor-tionments challenged in the other five cases.[77]

In his oral argument, Solicitor General Cox admitted that the issues in the Colorado case were "more closely balanced" than those in the other cases, but he rejected the argument that the Colorado appor-tionment system was rational because it balanced economic interests. Justice White asked if Colorado could grant representation to farmers as farmers, for example, and Cox replied that this could be done only if every economic group was accorded such representation on the basis of its *per capita* weight. A man "because he is a farmer cannot be given twice or five times the vote of another man," he said. There was some-thing to be said for keeping a legislative house small enough to be de-liberative and also allowing representatives to be familiar with their districts as justifications for weighting representation, Cox conceded, as was the principle of following county lines. But the problem was

---

[75] Brief of the United States as *Amicus Curiae, Lucas* v. *Colorado General Assembly*, p. 27.
[76] *Ibid.*, p. 32.
[77] *Ibid.*, pp. 33–57.

that Colorado's reasons for deviation from population in its senate were not sufficient to justify the severe deviation from *per capita* representation.

Because the case was so close, it might be dismissed for want of equity, Cox suggested. The issue of equal protection in apportionment was different from the right to vote, he said, because the right to representation was a "shared right" in a sense. The appellants in the Colorado case were attempting to force the majority even in their classification to accept what they had explicitly rejected. Cox therefore suggested that if the appellants could not win without breaking new ground and forcing the Court to rule upon the question of whether both houses of a legislature had to be based on population, it might be best for the Court to dismiss the case for want of equity.

When Anthony F. Zarlengo, the special assistant attorney general of Colorado, argued in defense of the Colorado apportionment system, he encountered a flurry of questions from the bench, making it obvious that the Court had made up its mind, even though the solicitor general had not assumed a strong position. The other apportionment cases, having been argued in the fall and winter, had perhaps already been voted on in conference. As Anthony Lewis noted in his report on the Colorado case arguments in *The New York Times*, although questions from the bench are not "a sure clue to the Justices' thinking," it appeared to observers that their questions indicated the justices were "leaning toward population as the only proper basis for apportioning both houses of state legislatures."[78]

Zarlengo defended the Colorado system as one in which everyone was represented and argued that "if you apportion both houses on a strict population basis, the interests of certain areas will not be represented at all." But Justice White suggested that Zarlengo's "real point is not representation, but effective representation." Zarlengo replied, "Those are better words." The people of Colorado had always reserved their sovereignty under the state bill of rights, he continued, but Justice Black interrupted to note that the "question here is whether they passed a law against the Federal Constitution." Zarlengo admitted that the popular enactment of a measure through the initiative and referendum did not mean it was unaffected by federal constitutional limitations, but he argued that the approval of the Colorado system by

[78] *The New York Times*, April 2, 1964, p. 16.

a majority of the people indicated the conviction on their part that a senate composed of senators familiar with the diversities of the state was desirable.

Justice Goldberg, however, stated that he could not follow "the argument that the need to safeguard the interest of the rural areas, but not urban, justifies discrimination in weighting votes." Zarlengo replied that Goldberg's objection would be pertinent if the Colorado system gave rural areas control, but that actually urban areas elected 72 percent of the lower house and 59 percent of the senate. Justice Black asked specifically if "a majority of your Senate [is] elected by a minority of the voters." Zarlengo replied that it was not, but Justice Brennan disputed his statement, saying that "33.2 percent of your population can elect a majority of your Senate." Zarlengo argued that the percentage quoted by Brennan contained "some urban area people." There followed a somewhat heated exchange between Zarlengo and the Court and among the justices themselves:

> CHIEF JUSTICE WARREN: Isn't the basic issue whether these appellants and all other people in the state of Colorado have proper representation, whether they are city people or farmers, liberals or conservatives, or whatever?
>
> MR. ZARLENGO: That is the issue, but does that mean that there must be strict per capita apportionment?
>
> CHIEF JUSTICE WARREN: If that is not the result, who has the power to say one should have more representation than another?
>
> MR. ZARLENGO: I say the people have the right.
>
> CHIEF JUSTICE WARREN: If the Constitution is interpreted to mean that representation must be equal, who has the power to weight votes?
>
> JUSTICE STEWART: But this Court has never held that.
>
> JUSTICE GOLDBERG: Strauder v. West Virginia, 100 U.S. 303, held that the object of the Fourteenth Amendment was to insure perfect equality of civil rights.
>
> JUSTICE HARLAN: That was a racial case.
>
> JUSTICE GOLDBERG: Civil rights is more than racial matters.

Justice Harlan then observed that if the Fourteenth Amendment required apportionment systems to be based solely on population, Zarlengo's argument was "all over." The real issue, he continued, was what the Fourteenth Amendment standards should be, and no one on either side had really argued the question. Zarlengo answered sarcastically that the standards under the Fourteenth Amendment were "the well-known and familiar standards of the Equal Protection Clause." Justice Stewart then observed that to speak of rural-urban conflict oversimplified the issues and that the real question was providing in the Colorado legislature for representation of the diverse areas of the state. Stephen H. Hart, representing a Denver citizens' group defending the Colorado system, emphasized that his state's system was the product of prolonged public debate, university research, and testimony of political scientists. The Chief Justice asked if there was "any constitutional difference between a referendum vote and a vote by the Legislature." Hart replied that the system had been approved in every county, and the urban minority it discriminated against had also approved it. "Isn't the question," Goldberg then asked, "whether it invidiously discriminates against the appellants?"

Perhaps the most graphic indication of the ultimate decision of the Court came when Justice Stewart pointed out to Hart that if "the Equal Protection Clause requires equal representation in both houses," Hart's argument would go "down the drain." Hart replied that the Court had never held the equal protection clause required mathematically exact representation. Justice Black observed that mathematical exactitude was not required by the Fourteenth Amendment, only as "nearly as practicable" equality, whereupon Justice Stewart said to Hart, "It requires that you lose."[79]

The briefs and arguments in the apportionment cases contrasted with those in the school desegregation cases[80] a decade earlier. When the Court had ordered reargument of the desegregation cases, it had specifically asked the attorneys involved to present materials and arguments upon the intent of the framers of the Fourteenth Amendment as it related to school segregation,[81] and both sides in those cases had recruited their historians and marshaled evidence to support their positions. As one of the historians who participated in this process on behalf of the NAACP commented later, the evidence thus produced resulted in a "draw" but satisfied the NAACP's strategy, which was based on the belief that the Court only wanted assurance that an invalidation of segregation under the Fourteenth Amendment had some

[79] 32 *LW* 3346–47.
[80] *Brown* v. *Board of Education*, 347 U.S. 485 (1954).
[81] 345 U. S. 972.

evidence to support it historically.[82] But in its opinion in the school desegregation cases the Court said that the historical evidence was, at best, "inconclusive," and largely dismissed the historical argument.[83]

In the apportionment cases, however, the Court did not request argument on the intent of the framers of the Fourteenth Amendment as it related to apportionment. And those attacking apportionment systems did not rely on the intent of the framers of the Fourteenth Amendment, undoubtedly because there was little evidence on this point supportive of their position. Also, any argument that the framers of the Fourteenth Amendment intended in the equal protection clause to require equal *per capita* apportionments would have been vulnerable to attack. In fact, Justice Frankfurter had vigorously and convincingly attacked such a proposition in his dissenting opinion in *Baker v. Carr*.[84] The government in its brief *amicus curiae* thus limited itself to an attempt to demonstrate that the framers of the Constitution in 1787 had favored population as the principal basis of apportionment in the states,[85] and the state attorneys general answered by citing contrary expressions of the framers.[86] The only extensive citation of evidence relating to the intent of the framers of the Fourteenth Amendment was presented in the brief of the Delaware attorney general.[87]

The Court of course has never adhered to the intent of the framers as the only controlling element in judicial construction of the Constitution; rather, as Justice Stone once said, the Constitution is read "not as we read legislative codes which are subject to continuous revision with the changing course of events, but as the revelation of the great purposes which were intended to be achieved by the Constitution as a continuing instrument of government."[88] The Court was being asked to decide whether one of the "great purposes" of the Constitution was

---

[82] Alfred Kelley, address presented to the Mississippi Valley Historical Association Annual Dinner, American Historical Association Convention, December 28, 1961, Washington, D. C.; reprinted in H. Malcolm MacDonald, Wilfred D. Webb, Edward G. Lewis, and William L. Strauss, *Readings in American National Government* (New York: Thomas Y. Crowell, 1964), pp. 109–28.

[83] 347 U.S., at 486–90.

[84] 369 U.S. 186, at 266–330.

[85] Appendix to the Brief of the United States as *Amicus Curiae, Maryland Committee* v. *Tawes*.

[86] Brief and Appendix for the Attorneys General of the States as *Amici Curiae*.

[87] Brief of the Appellants, *Roman* v. *Sincock*, pp. 55–71.

[88] *United States* v. *Classic*, 313 U.S. 299, at 316 (1941).

to impose standards upon the apportionment systems of the several states and, if so, whether such constitutional standards required equal *per capita* apportionments or allowed other factors to be considered as well. Anthony Lewis reported that on the opening day of the arguments in the 1964 apportionment cases, there was "the feeling of a great occasion" in the courtroom,[89] and well there should have been. In these cases the Court would choose among competing theories of representation and render decisions that would affect all, and revolutionize many, of the political systems in the states of the Union.

[89] *The New York Times,* Nov. 13, 1963, p. 30.

CHAPTER IX

ONE MAN, ONE VOTE

As the Supreme Court considered the apportionment cases, conflict over its decisions in several fields was widespread. Reapportionment under federal and state judicial supervision which followed the Court's decision in *Baker* v. *Carr* had gone surprisingly smoothly from 1962 to 1964, but opposition soon appeared when the General Assembly of the States, a group of state legislators affiliated with the Council of State Governments, proposed in December, 1962, that state legislatures petition Congress to call a constitutional convention to consider three amendments to the federal Constitution. The three amendments sought to allow two-thirds of the state legislatures to propose constitutional amendments, thus bypassing Congress in the amending process; to create a "Court of the Union" composed of the chief justices of the state supreme courts to review decisions of the United States Supreme Court "relating to the rights reserved to the states or the people"; and to repeal the jurisdiction of the federal courts, including the Supreme Court, in any case "relating to apportionment of representation in a state legislature." The National Legislative Conference, another organization affiliated with the Council of State Governments and composed of state legislators, conducted the campaign for the amendments, arguing that their adoption was essential to the preservation of the powers of the states. The Tenth Amendment, as one of the legislators said, has been "raped twice a day for ten years."[1]

Several state legislatures passed resolutions petitioning Congress to

---

[1] 21 *Congressional Quarterly* 662–63 (1963); see also Charles L. Black, "The Proposed Amendment of Article V: A Threatened Disaster," 72 *Yale Law Journal* 957–66 (1963); "Amending the Constitution to Strengthen the States in the Federal System," 36 *State Government* 10 (1963); and Alexander M. Bickel, *Politics and the Warren Court* (New York: Harper & Row, 1965), chap. 11, "Curbing the Union."

call a constitutional convention to consider some or all of the proposed amendments. These actions aroused little publicity until the Supreme Court justices themselves called attention to the amendments in a series of speeches in the spring of 1963. Justice Goldberg warned that the amendments would make the Constitution "quite different from that intended by the founding fathers,"[2] and Chief Justice Warren called for a "great national debate" on the amendments, since they would "radically change the character of our institutions" and had not received much public mention. "If proposals of this magnitude had been made in the early days of the Republic," Warren said, "the great debate would be resounding in every legislative hall and every place where lawyers, scholars and statesmen gather." Warning that the amending process could be used by an "uninformed public" to "destroy the foundations of the Constitution," the chief justice chided the legal profession for ignoring the proposed amendments and asked, "If lawyers are not to be the watchmen for the Constitution, on whom can we rely?"[3] These somewhat unusual out-of-court comments by the justices were soon seconded by President Kennedy and other national figures, and the resulting publicity appeared to slow the approval of amendments by state legislatures.[4]

Opposition to the Court's decisions in regard to prayer and Bible-reading in the public schools also increased the number of the Court's critics. It is ironic that while the Tennessee case was undoubtedly the most significant case decided by the Court during the 1961 term, it did not receive the attention or arouse the public reaction caused by the Regents' prayer case,[5] decided by the Court June 25, 1962. While the press reaction to the decision in the Tennessee case had been generally favorable, the press reaction to the Regents' prayer case was unfavorable, with many newspapers featuring rather irresponsible comments from obviously uninformed individuals. The latter was perhaps contributed to by the sadly uncraftsmanlike concurring opinion filed in the case by Justice Douglas. Also, the Court made adequate press cov-

---

[2] *Newsweek*, Vol. 61, No. 20 (May 20, 1963), pp. 35–36.

[3] *The New York Times*, May 23, 1963, pp. 1, 23; see also Kenneth Crawford, "Reaction's Refuge," *Newsweek*, Vol. 61, No. 22 (June 3, 1963), p. 31; Walter Lippmann, "The Assault on the Union," *Newsweek*, Vol. 61, No. 23 (June 10, 1963), p. 25.

[4] Anthony Lewis, "Opposition Slows Amendment Push," *The New York Times*, May 19, 1963, pp. 1, 81.

[5] *Engel* v. *Vitale*, 370 U.S. 421 (1962).

erage difficult at best by announcing the decision along with a mass of other decisions on the last day of the term.[6]

The Regents' prayer case and the Court's decisions the following year, in which Bible-reading and prayer in the public schools were prohibited,[7] appear to have been more intensely felt by the general public than any decision since the school desegregation cases. Pressure for a constitutional amendment to overturn these decisions was great, and for a time during 1963–64 it seemed likely that the Congress would respond. Congressman Emanuel Celler, who opposed the proposed prayer amendments as chairman of the House Judiciary Committee, was finally forced to begin hearings on the subject when 167 members of the House signed a petition to discharge the Judiciary Committee of the proposed amendments. These hearings continued throughout the spring of 1964.[8]

The prayer and Bible-reading decisions also subjected the Court to such minor harassments as South Carolina Congressman Robert Ashmore's proposal that Congress require that the inscription "In God We Trust" be placed in the courtroom in the Supreme Court building. As the 1964 apportionment cases were being argued before the Court, Chief Justice Warren was constrained to write the capitol architect, in response to an inquiry regarding Ashmore's proposal, that it had "always been the view of the members of the Court then sitting that no changes in the decor of the Courtroom should be made. This has been true regardless of the significance of the language or its relevance to patriotic or religious sentiment." Ashmore, however, had declared that the tone of Warren's letter indicated that the "Supreme Court [should] be made painfully aware of the fact that there is an Authority higher than that of the Supreme Court of these United States."[9]

In addition to its decisions on prayer and apportionment, the Court's decisions in the area of censorship, particularly in relation to allegedly obscene literature and films, and in the area of the procedural rights of criminal defendants also increased the ranks of its critics. That the jus-

---

[6] Chester A. Newland, "Press Coverage of the United States Supreme Court," *Western Political Quarterly*, Vol. 17 (March, 1964), pp. 15–36.

[7] *Murray* v. *Curlett* and *Abington School District* v. *Schempp*, 374 U.S. 203 (1963).

[8] 22 *Congressional Quarterly* 881–85; see also School Prayers, Hearings before the Committee on the Judiciary, House of Representatives, 88th Cong., 2d sess. (1964).

[9] *The New York Times*, Nov. 13, 1963, p. 30.

tices recognized the strength and perhaps the danger of the Court's opponents was indicated by the extent to which they were resorting to public speeches to criticize their opponents and call for support of the Court. Justice Brennan, for example, probably reflected the fears of the justices in a speech delivered in August, 1963, in which he declared that it was presupposed that "a mature people will judge the judges rationally and, unless maturity exists, the whole system is in danger of breaking down." The Court was not and should not be exempt from criticism, Brennan said. "People don't have to agree with the decisions if they are successfully able to refute them." The Court was threatened, he thought, by criticism based on lack of understanding, as exemplified by the criticism of the prayer decisions. The opinions in these decisions were over one hundred pages long, but "within two hours the critics were in print saying the Court was wrong. It is obvious they could not have read the explanations." As a result of its recent decisions, Brennan continued, the Court was under attack by a strong coalition of interests. "There is sectional opposition because of the desegregation cases; state opposition because of recent decisions involving state powers as they relate to aspects of criminal law; rural opposition because of the reapportionment cases, and church opposition because of the prayer case." The Court's supporters, the Justice said, were in contrast weak and scattered.[10]

As Brennan indicated, the Court was threatened by the possibility that disaffected groups might form a coalition of opposition sufficiently powerful in the Congress to strike at the Court either through a repeal of a part of its appellate jurisdiction or through the amending process. A similar threat to its appellate jurisdiction in 1957–58 had, in the opinion of some observers, caused the Court to retreat from its decisions relating to internal security.[11] In the apportionment cases, the justices had the opportunity to choose courses of action which might neutralize opposition. If the Court accepted the federal analogy argument and ruled that the equal protection clause allowed one house of a state legislature to be based on factors other than or in addition to population, it could neutralize most opposition to its reapportionment decisions. Even if the federal analogy argument was unaccept-

---

[10] *Ibid.*, Aug. 30, 1963, p. 13.

[11] Walter Murphy, *Congress and the Court* (Chicago: University of Chicago Press, 1962), pp. 224–46; see also Glendon Schubert, *The Judicial Mind* (Evanston: Northwestern University Press, 1965), p. 280.

able, the Court could still accept the solicitor general's suggestion that it adopt for the moment a rationality test and decide apportionment cases on a case by case basis, avoiding any commitment on the ultimate Fourteenth Amendment standard. This course might at least delay the intensification of opposition which the enunciation of a "one man, one vote" standard would surely arouse.[12]

The pressure on the Court, however, was easing temporarily by the late spring of 1964. The hearings before the House Judiciary Committee on the prayer amendments had become a vehicle for public expressions of support for the Court's decisions on prayer and Bible-reading by the leaders of most of the larger denominational groups in the country. When the hearings were suspended on June 3, therefore, the extreme hostility of the initial reaction to the decisions had been counteracted to a degree, and the pressure on the Congress for action had been somewhat eased. Chairman Celler's tactics of delay seemed, at least for the moment, to have saved the Court from a reversal by constitutional amendment.[13]

The enactment of the Civil Rights Act of 1964 on July 2, a decade after the Court's desegregation decisions, was also a major victory for the Court.[14] Presidential endorsement of the desegregation policy had first been given by President Kennedy, and the Congress, with its passage of the Civil Rights Act, not only indicated its support for the Court's policy but also provided legislative means for effective enforcement of the Court's decisions for the first time. After ten years, both the President and the Congress had thus been converted to the Court's policy.

Within this mixed climate of powerful opposition and significant support, the Court reached its decisions in the 1964 apportionment cases. Pending before the Court at the same time was the congressional districting case, *Wesberry* v. *Sanders*, which had been argued along with the Alabama, New York, Delaware, and Virginia apportionment cases in the fall of 1963. The Georgia appellants in *Wesberry* argued

---

[12] Another alternative would have been an order for the reargument of the cases. For an excellent analysis of the lines of action open to the justices in the formation of judicial policy, see Walter Murphy, *Elements of Judicial Strategy* (Chicago: University of Chicago Press, 1964).

[13] 22 *Congressional Quarterly* 2386 (1964); see also School Prayers, Hearings before the Committee on the Judiciary, House of Representatives, 88th Cong., 2d sess. (1964).

[14] 78 Stat. 241.

that their state's congressional districts, varying in population from 823,680 to 272,154, were invalid under the equal protection clause of the Fourteenth Amendment and Article I of the Constitution, which provides that the members of the House of Representatives be elected "by the People of the several States."[15] The government had proposed as *amicus curiae* that the Court should reverse the lower court's dismissal of the suit and remand the case for trial, without ruling on the merits.[16] During oral argument, however, the justices bombarded the government counsel with questions about the value of simply remanding the case; it was clear that they desired to reach the merits. Even Justice Harlan, while expressing his views that the Court should not decide cases involving such matters, conceded that the Court was "in it as much as we are, and I cannot see any reason for not deciding this aspect of the matter now."[17]

The Court's decision in *Wesberry* v. *Sanders*[18] was announced on February 17, 1964. In the majority opinion, Justice Black held that gross population disparities among congressional districts violated Article I of the Constitution, which required that "as nearly as is practicable one man's vote in a congressional election is to be worth as much as another's."[19] The *Wesberry* case, resting as it did on an interpretation of Article I, thus shed little light on the standard required of state apportionments by the Fourteenth Amendment. As in the Georgia county unit case, however, Justices Goldberg and White voted with the majority, reaffirming their support for the burial of the *Colegrove* doctrine.[20]

On June 12, four months after its decision in the *Wesberry* case, the Court announced its decisions in the state legislative apportionment cases, holding that the equal protection clause of the Fourteenth Amendment required both houses of state legislatures to be based on population. The Court selected the Alabama case, *Reynolds* v. *Sims*,

[15] Brief for Appellants, *Wesberry* v. *Sanders*, pp. 16, 27.
[16] Brief of the United States as *Amicus Curiae*, *Wesberry* v. *Sanders*.
[17] *The New York Times*, Nov. 19, 1963, p. 25.
[18] 376 U.S. 1 (1964).
[19] *Ibid.*, at 8.
[20] Justice Harlan dissented, arguing that the case involved nonjusticiable issues and that Article I did not require equal population-based congressional districts; Justice Stewart also dissented, agreeing with Harlan's Article I contentions; Justice Clark dissented in part and concurred in part, agreeing the issues were justiciable but believing the equal protection clause governed the case and that the Court should have remanded the case for trial on the merits.

227

as the vehicle for setting forth the "one man, one vote" standard.[21] Writing for the majority of six justices, Chief Justice Warren reviewed the course of the litigation in the Alabama case and, citing decisions of the Court involving voting rights, including the white primary cases, declared that the "right to vote freely for the candidate of one's choice is of the essence of a democratic society, and any restrictions on that right strike at the heart of representative government. And the right of suffrage can be denied by a debasement or dilution of the weight of a citizen's vote just as effectively as by wholly prohibiting the free exercise of the franchise."[22] The problem for the Court, the chief justice said, was "to ascertain, in the instant cases, whether there are any constitutionally cognizable principles which would justify departures from the basic standard of equality among voters in the apportionment of seats in state legislatures."[23]

"Legislators," Warren declared, "represent people, not trees or acres. Legislators are elected by voters, not farms or cities or economic interests. As long as ours is a representative form of government, and our legislatures are those instruments of government elected directly by and directly representative of the people, the right to elect legislators in a free and unimpaired fashion is a bedrock of our political system." Certainly, he continued, a state could not allow certain voters to vote two, five, or ten times while allowing other voters to vote only once; nor could a state provide that the votes of certain of its citizens be multiplied two, five, or ten times while counting at face value the votes of other citizens. Yet the effect of "state legislative districting schemes which give the same number of representatives to unequal numbers of constituents is identical."[24]

State legislatures, Warren said, are, "historically, the fountainhead of representative government in this country," and representative government required "full and effective participation" of all voters in the political processes of the state legislatures. "Most citizens can achieve this participation only as qualified voters through the election of legislators to represent them. Full and effective participation by all citizens

[21] 377 U.S. 533 (1964).
[22] Ibid., at 555. Voting with the chief justice were Justices Black, Douglas, Brennan, White, and Goldberg.
[23] Ibid., at 560.
[24] Ibid., at 562–63.

in state government requires, therefore, that each citizen have an equally effective voice in the election of members of his state legislature. Modern and viable state government needs, and the Constitution demands, no less." A majority of the people of a state must be able to elect a majority of the state legislature, for otherwise, the Court held, a minority would control and this would "deny majority rights in a way that far surpasses any possible denial of minority rights that might otherwise be thought to result." There were no criteria sufficient "to justify any discrimination, as to the weight of their votes, unless relevant to the permissible purposes of legislative apportionment. Since the achieving of fair and effective representation for all citizens is concededly the basic aim of legislative apportionment, we conclude that the Equal Protection Clause guarantees the opportunity for equal participation by all voters in the election of state legislators. . . . Our constitutional system amply provides for the protection of minorities by means other than giving them majority control of state legislatures. And the democratic ideals of equality and majority rule, which have served this Nation so well in the past, are hardly of any less significance for the present and the future."[25]

The Court had been warned, the chief justice noted, that apportionment was "complex and many-faceted," that factors other than population could be rationally considered, that the Court should not restrict the power of the states to choose among different theories of representation, and that the whole problem was a political thicket. The Court's answer, Warren said, was that "a denial of constitutionally protected rights demands judicial protection; our oath and our office require no less of us."[26] Despite the changing nature of society, he continued, the

basic principle of representative government remains, and must remain, unchanged—the weight of a citizen's vote cannot be made to depend on where he lives. Population is, of necessity, the starting point for consideration and the controlling criterion for judgment in legislative apportionment controversies. A citizen, a qualified voter, is no more nor no less so because he lives in the city or on the farm. This is the clear command of our Constitution's Equal Protection Clause. This is an essential part of the concept of a government of laws and not men. This is at the heart of Lincoln's vision of "govern-

[25] *Ibid.*, at 564–66.
[26] *Ibid.*, at 566.

ment of the people, by the people, [and] for the people." The Equal Protection Clause demands no less than substantially equal state legislative representation for all citizens, of all places as well as of all races. . . . We hold that, as a basic constitutional standard, the Equal Protection Clause requires that the seats in both houses of a bicameral state legislature must be apportioned on a population basis.[27]

Turning to the merits in the Alabama case, the Court held that neither the 1901 apportionment of the Alabama legislature, nor the Crawford-Webb Act, nor the 67 Senator Amendment met the requirements of the equal protection clause. The 1901 apportionment act and the Crawford-Webb Act, the Court held, "presented little more than crazy quilts, completely lacking in rationality, and could be found invalid on that basis alone."[28] In answer to the federal analogy argument advanced in support of the 67 Senator Amendment, the Court observed that such arguments were often "little more than an after-the-fact rationalization offered in defense of maladjusted state apportionment arrangements." The original constitutions of a majority of the states, the Court said, had based apportionment primarily on population, and the "Founding Fathers clearly had no intention of establishing a pattern or model for the apportionment of seats in state legislatures when the system of representation in the Federal Congress was adopted." The system of representation in the Congress was the outcome of a historic compromise involving considerations not applicable to the states. Local units of government have never been sovereign entities as were the original states which formed the Union and received equal representation in the Senate. The federal plan of representation, the Court concluded, was thus "impermissible for the States under the Equal Protection Clause, since perforce resulting, in virtually every case, in submergence of the equal-population principle in at least one house of a state legislature."[29]

The Court recognized, however, that mathematical exactness was not required by the equal protection clause, and that so "long as the divergencies from a strict population standard are based on legitimate considerations incident to the effectuation of a rational state policy, some deviations from the equal-population principle are constitution-

[27] *Ibid.*, at 567–68.
[28] *Ibid.*, at 568–69.
[29] *Ibid.*, at 573–75.

ally permissible with respect to the apportionment of seats in either or both of the two houses of a bicameral state legislature." But historical considerations alone, or economic or other group interests, were not legitimate considerations that would justify deviation from the population standard, the Court observed, nor was the desire to represent sparsely populated areas and to prevent overly large legislative districts. The only legitimate reason for deviation from the population standard was the desire to represent political subdivisions, and even where such representation occurred, the Court warned that if "population is submerged as the controlling consideration in the apportionment of seats in the particular legislative body, then the right of all of the State's citizens to cast an effective and adequately weighted vote would be unconstitutionally impaired."[30] The Court also noted that the equal protection clause did not require "daily, monthly, annual or biennial reapportionment" to reflect population changes among districts, but suggested that decennial reapportionment would meet the minimal requirements of the equal protection clause and that less frequent reapportionment would be "constitutionally suspect."[31]

The Court next answered the contention that Congress had approved state apportionment systems deviating from the population standard because it had voted that the state constitutions met the requirements of a "republican form of government" when admitting states to the Union. The equal protection clause, the Court said, required a higher standard of state apportionment systems than the guaranty clause, and the Congress undoubtedly did not pass on all constitutional questions relating to state governmental organization when admitting new states to the Union. But in any case, Congress could not validate an unconstitutional state apportionment system because it "simply lacks the constitutional power to insulate States from attack with respect to alleged deprivations of individual constitutional rights."[32]

The Court suggested that the federal district courts, in enforcing the equal population standard under the Fourteenth Amendment, should avoid the disruption of a state's electoral process as far as possible. In the Alabama case, the Court thought, the district court had

[30] *Ibid.*, at 580–81.
[31] *Ibid.*, at 583–84.
[32] *Ibid.*, at 582.

proceeded in a "most proper and commendable manner" in adopting a temporary apportionment plan and allowing the legislature time to adopt an acceptable permanent plan, while retaining jurisdiction in case further relief was necessary. The Court therefore affirmed the lower court's decision in *Reynolds* v. *Sims*.[33]

Having enunciated the controlling constitutional standard in *Reynolds* v. *Sims*, the Court proceeded to invalidate the apportionment systems challenged in the New York, Maryland, Virginia, Delaware, and Colorado cases.[34] The Court, however, distinguished the Colorado case, *Lucas* v. *Colorado General Assembly*, from the other cases involving state legislative apportionment.[35] First, the apportionment system under challenge had been adopted in 1962 by a majority of the voters in every county of Colorado through the initiative and referendum process, and, under the plan, the lower house of the legislature was based on population. The Court thus recognized that the "initiative device provided a practicable political remedy to obtain relief against alleged legislative malapportionment in Colorado"[36] and admitted that it might justify "a court in staying its hand temporarily." But, the Court said, "An individual's constitutionally protected right to cast an equally weighted vote cannot be denied even by a vote of a majority of a State's electorate if the apportionment scheme adopted by the voters fails to measure up to the requirements of the Equal Protection Clause. A citizen's constitutional rights can hardly be infringed simply because a majority of the people choose that it [*sic*] be." The Court concluded, "We hold that the fact that a challenged legislative apportionment plan was approved by the electorate is without federal constitutional significance, if the scheme adopted fails to satisfy the basic requirements of the Equal Protection Clause, as delineated in our opinion in Reynolds v. Sims."[37] Since the Colorado apportionment system failed to meet these "basic requirements," it also was invalidated.

Justices Stewart and Clark, while willing to accept a "rationality" standard under the equal protection clause, were unwilling to accept

---

[33] *Ibid.*, at 585–87.
[34] *W.M.C.A., Inc.* v. *Lomenzo*, 377 U.S. 633; *Maryland Committee* v. *Tawes*, 377 U.S. 656; *Davis* v. *Mann*, 377 U.S. 678; *Roman* v. *Sincock*, 377 U.S. 695; *Lucas* v. *Colorado General Assembly*, 377 U.S. 713.
[35] 377 U.S. 713, at 730.
[36] *Ibid.*, at 732.
[37] *Ibid.*, at 736–37.

the equal population standard enunciated by the majority of the Court.[38] Justice Stewart, dissenting from the majority's "draconian pronouncement,"[39] declared that the population standard for state legislative apportionment "finds no support in the words of the Constitution, in any prior decision of this Court, or in the 175-year political history of our Federal Union." The decisions, he said, "mark a long step backward into that unhappy era when a majority of the members of this Court were thought by many to have convinced themselves and each other that the demands of the Constitution were to be measured not by what it says, but by their own notions of wise political theory." The Court had converted "a particular political philosophy into a constitutional rule, binding upon each of the 50 States, from Maine to Hawaii, from Alaska to Texas, without regard and without respect for the many individualized and differentiated characteristics of each State, characteristics stemming from each State's distinct history, distinct geography, distinct distribution of population, and distinct political heritage."[40] The standard embraced by the majority, Stewart declared, "can be met by any State only by the uncritical, simplistic, and heavy-handed application of sixth-grade arithmetic."[41]

The proper standard under the equal protection clause, Stewart felt, should allow the apportionment systems of the states to reflect their diverse historical, political, population, and geographic characteristics. He thought that, "in the light of the State's own characteristics and needs, the plan must be a rational one," which did not "permit the systematic frustration of the will of a majority of the electorate of the State."[42] By this test, the apportionment systems of New York and Colorado were valid under the equal protection

---

[38] Stewart and Clark, applying a rationality test, concurred in the invalidation of the apportionment systems challenged in the Alabama, Virginia and Delaware cases; *Reynolds* v. *Sims*, 377 U.S. 533, at 587–89; *Davis* v. *Mann*, 377 U.S. 678, at 693; *Roman* v. *Sincock*, 377 U.S. 695, at 712. They dissented, however, in the Colorado and New York cases; *Lucas* v. *Colorado General Assembly*, 377 U.S. 713, at 741; *W.M.C.A., Inc.* v. *Lomenzo*, 377 U.S. 633, at 744. Clark concurred in *Maryland Committee* v. *Tawes*, 377 U.S. 656, at 676, while Stewart voted to remand this case to the Maryland Court of Appeals for reconsideration, 377 U.S. 656, at 676.
[39] *Ibid.*, at 746.
[40] *Ibid.*
[41] *Ibid.*, at 747–48.
[42] *Ibid.*, at 750.

clause. Each of these states, he concluded, "while clearly ensuring that in its legislative councils the will of the majority of the electorate shall rule, has sought to provide that no identifiable minority shall be completely silenced or engulfed."[43]

Justice Clark agreed with Stewart that the Colorado and New York apportionment systems were valid and expressed the view that if one house of a state legislature were based on population, "the other house might include some departure from it . . . in order to afford some representation to the various elements of the State."[44] Dissenting in the Colorado case, he also reaffirmed his position, advanced in *Baker* v. *Carr*, that the availability of the initiative and referendum in a state should prevent a federal court from entertaining a challenge to the apportionment system of that state. He repeated his view that the equal protection clause required only a rational basis for apportionment systems, since it was not an "algebraic formula." The Court's invalidation of the Colorado apportionment system was thus to Clark a "grievous error which will do irreparable damage to our federal-state relationship."[45]

Justice Harlan, dissenting from the Court's decisions in all six cases, continued his opposition, begun in *Baker* v. *Carr*, to the application of federal judicial power to apportionment. In announcing his dissent orally from the bench, Harlan declared that the Court's decision "in every accurate sense of the term . . . involves . . . amending the Constitution. . . . If the time comes when this Court is looked upon by well-meaning people—or worse yet by the Court itself . . . as the repository of all reforms, I think the seeds of trouble are being sown for this institution."[46] Reviewing in his opinion much of the same historical evidence that had been presented by Justice Frankfurter in *Baker* v. *Carr*, Harlan concluded that the Court's interpretation of the equal protection clause was not sustained by the intent of the framers of the Fourteenth Amendment or the legislatures that ratified the amendment, nor by the practice of the states in apportioning their legislatures since the amendment had been ratified in 1868. The equal protection clause, he said,

43 *Ibid.*, at 765.
44 *Ibid.*, at 588.
45 *Ibid.*, at 741–43.
46 22 *Congressional Quarterly* 2537 (1964).

was never intended to inhibit the States in choosing any democratic method they pleased for the apportionment of their legislatures. This is shown by the language of the Fourteenth Amendment taken as a whole, by the understanding of those who proposed and ratified it, and by the political practices of the States at the time the Amendment was adopted. It is confirmed by numerous state and congressional actions since the adoption of the Fourteenth Amendment, and by subsequent constitutional amendments and decisions of this Court before *Baker* v. *Carr* . . . made an abrupt break with the past in 1962.[47]

In both his oral and written opinions, Harlan warned against the view, which he thought was given support by the Court's decisions, that "every major social ill in this country can find its cure in some constitutional 'principle,'" and that the Court should 'take the lead' in promoting reform when other branches of the government fail to act." The Constitution was not, he said, a "panacea for every blot upon the public welfare," and the Court should not be "thought of as a general haven for reform movements." The Constitution, Harlan concluded, is "an instrument of government, fundamental to which is the premise that in a diffusion of governmental authority lies the greatest promise that this Nation will realize liberty for all its citizens." *Baker* v. *Carr*, he thought, should therefore be recognized as an "experiment in venturesome constitutionalism," and the cases decided by the Court disposed of on the grounds that the plaintiffs had failed to state a cause of action under the Fourteenth Amendment.[48]

A week following the announcement of its decisions in the Alabama, New York, Maryland, Colorado, Delaware, and Virginia cases, in a series of *per curiam* opinions the Court remanded cases involving challenges to the apportionment systems in Florida, Ohio, Illinois, Michigan, Idaho, Iowa, Connecticut, Oklahoma, and Washington.[49] Within a one-week period, therefore, the Court had rendered decisions directly affecting the apportionment systems of almost one-third of the states. The Court's ruling that the apportionment of both houses

[47] 377 U.S., at 590–91.
[48] *Ibid.*, at 624–25.
[49] Florida: *Swann* v. *Adams*, 378 U.S. 553. Ohio: *Nolan* v. *Rhodes* and *Sive* v. *Ellis*, 378 U.S. 556. Illinois: *Germano* v. *Kerner*, 378 U.S. 560. Michigan: *Marshall* v. *Hare*, 378 U.S. 561. Idaho: *Hearne* v. *Smylie*, 378 U.S. 563. Connecticut: *Pinney* v. *Butterworth*, 378 U.S. 564. Iowa: *Hill* v. *Davis*, 378 U.S. 565. Oklahoma: *Baldwin* v. *Moss*, *Oklahoma Farm Bureau* v. *Moss*, and *Williams* v. *Moss*, 378 U.S. 558. Washington: *Meyers* v. *Thigpen*, 378 U.S. 554.

of state legislatures must be based on population was the farthest-reaching, *The New York Times* said, "since Marbury v. Madison established its power of judicial review in 1803." The *Times* editorial further suggested that "when the history of the Court under Chief Justice Warren is written, these decisions may outweigh even the school integration decision of 1954 in importance."[50] The chief justice apparently agreed with the *Times'* estimate of the importance of the decisions; asked later what was the most important opinion he had written for the Court, Warren replied without hesitation, "*Reynolds v. Sims*, of course."[51]

Few of the Court's decisions, Anthony Lewis reported from Washington, had "stunned this hardened capital city" as had the apportionment decisions.[52] The initial reaction of the spokesmen for both the Democratic and Republican parties, however, was favorable. John M. Bailey, the Democratic National Committee chairman, lauded the decisions as the beginning of the end of "archaic" apportionment systems, and added that "this is something the Democratic party had long advocated and fought for and certainly welcomes." William E. Miller, the chairman of the Republican National Committee, also praised the decisions as being "in the national interest and in the Republican party's interest."[53]

This initial enthusiasm from both parties was short-lived, however. On June 22 it was reported that the Republican minority leader in the Senate, Senator Everett Dirksen of Illinois, had begun preparing a constitutional amendment to partially overrule the Court's decisions.[54] Within a month the Republican national convention also adopted as part of its platform a plank pledging support for a "constitutional amendment, as well as legislation, enabling states having bicameral legislatures to apportion one house on bases of their choosing including factors other than population."[55] The Democratic national convention was obviously divided on the issue, and, in response to the wishes of President Johnson, failed to include any statement

[50] *The New York Times*, June 16, 1964, p. 38; June 21, 1964, p. 8E.
[51] Fred Rodell, "It is the Earl Warren Court," *The New York Times Magazine*, March 13, 1966, pp. 30, 94.
[52] *The New York Times*, June 17, 1964, p. 29.
[53] *Ibid.*
[54] *The New York Times*, June 22, 1964, p. 37.
[55] *The New York Times*, July 13, 1964, p. 16.

on reapportionment in its platform.[56] It was thus soon apparent that the Court's 1964 apportionment decisions were not to receive the support of the broad consensus that had responded favorably to its decision in *Baker* v. *Carr*.[57]

Perhaps indicative of the attitude of Congress toward the Court was the action of the Senate during July reducing by five thousand dollars a pay increase for Supreme Court justices provided for in a House-passed bill. Although Senator Allott of Colorado, who introduced the amendment to the House bill, stated that the reduction in the proposed pay increase should not be taken "in the spirit of criticism of the decisions of the Supreme Court," the Senate amendment was denounced in the House as an "act of vengeance" which in effect said "to the members of the Court, 'If you do not decide cases the way we believe, we will engage in reprisals against you.' " Although the conference committee restored part of the amount which had been reduced by the Senate, the justices did not receive the amount originally provided for in the House bill, nor did they receive an increase equal to the salary increases of the lower federal judges.[58]

Senator Dirksen, striking more directly at the Court's apportionment decisions, offered as a rider to the foreign-aid appropriations bill a resolution providing for at least a two-year delay in the enforce-

[56] According to Professor Royce Hanson, those seeking an endorsement of the Court's decisions agreed that the platform would say nothing on the subject of apportionment in exchange for an administration pledge of aid in defeating the Dirksen rider in the Senate, which would have postponed the enforcement of the Court's decisions for at least two years. See Royce Hanson, *The Political Thicket* (Englewood Cliffs, N.J.: Prentice-Hall, 1966), p. 87.

[57] The Gallup poll reported in Aug., 1964, however, that 47 percent of the public approved the Court's decisions, 30 percent disapproved, and 23 percent expressed no opinion. Nashville *Tennessean*, Aug. 19, 1964, p. 13. That there was broad and general support for federal court assumption of jurisdiction in the apportionment cases, but much less support for the proposition that both houses of state legislatures be based on population, is best illustrated in the testimony before the Senate Subcommittee on Constitutional Amendments during 1965 on possible apportionment amendments. Even the proponents of the partial reversal of *Reynolds* v. *Sims* by constitutional amendment generally indicated in their testimony that the availability of federal judicial relief in apportionment cases under *Baker* v. *Carr* was unobjectionable. See Reapportionment of State Legislatures, Hearings before the Subcommittee on Constitutional Amendments, Committee on the Judiciary, U.S. Senate, 89th Cong., 1st sess. (1965).

[58] 110 Cong. Rec. 15843–46, 17912–13; *Congress and the Nation* (Washington, D. C.: Congressional Quarterly, Inc., 1965), p. 1454.

ment of the Court's decisions by the lower federal courts. By delaying the enforcement of the Court's decisions, Dirksen hoped to allow time for the Congress to propose, and the states to ratify, a constitutional amendment allowing one house of state legislatures to be based on factors other than population.[59] The House Judiciary Committee was holding hearings on various proposed amendments, but it was generally assumed that the committee would not report out any proposal hostile to the Court's decisions since Chairman Emanuel Celler supported the Court's action. In an unusual but not unprecedented action, however, the House Rules Committee on August 13 removed from the Judiciary Committee's jurisdiction a bill sponsored by Representative William Tuck of Virginia which would deny to the federal courts jurisdiction over apportionment suits, and reported a resolution bringing the bill directly to the floor of the House.

Celler denounced the bill as "a rather vicious attack upon the Supreme Court" and a product of the "deliberations of angry men, irate men" which would make "a shambles of the 14th Amendment."[60] During the often vituperative and angry debate on August 19, however, Representative Tuck defended the bill as necessary in order to "preserve the Constitution of the United States, already bleeding from assaults made upon it by the Supreme Court. . . . If Congress foregoes the duty to restrain the unbridled powers asserted by the Supreme Court," he said, "then I say, 'God save the United States of America.' "[61] Representative Howard Smith of Virginia, the chairman of the Rules Committee, also warned the House that it must think "about what this Court can do to you. You can come to live under just as much a dictatorship—and I hate to say this—as any European country which has gone through the regimes of Hitler and Khrushchev."[62] The passage of the Tuck bill, another of its supporters declared, was a necessary first step in "curbing a power-mad, rampaging Supreme Court running roughshod over the Congress, over the States, the communities and the people of this country."[63] The bill was passed by the House on August 19 by a vote of 218 to 175.

The passage of the Tuck bill in the House immediately put a great

[59] Royce Hanson, *The Political Thicket*, pp. 83–84.
[60] 110 Cong. Rec. 20236–37.
[61] *Ibid.*, pp. 20223–25.
[62] *Ibid.*, p. 20220.
[63] *Ibid.*, p. 20295.

deal of pressure on the senators who supported the Court's decisions to accept the Dirksen proposal as the lesser of two evils. As Representative Celler was reported to have said, "I don't relish the idea of the Senate proposal, but it is sometimes better to yield than to break when faced with an inordinate danger."[64] Reference of the Tuck bill to the Senate Judiciary Committee was blocked on August 21 by Senator Strom Thurmond of South Carolina, who announced his intention of bringing the bill directly to the Senate floor. In the angry debate that ensued, Senator Russell Long of Louisiana shouted that the Supreme Court had never tried to "usurp the President's power," because if it did, he "might send a squad of Marines down there and put those screwballs in jail." Thurmond agreed, saying that "the country might welcome such a step."[65]

Reconvening after the Democratic convention, however, the Senate refused to invoke cloture against a filibuster being conducted by the opponents of the Dirksen rider. A compromise "sense of Congress" resolution suggesting to the federal courts that they allow the state legislatures "reasonable" time to comply with reapportionment orders and also that they take into consideration any constitutional amendment proposed in the meantime was also defeated, as was Thurmond's attempt to substitute the Tuck bill for this resolution. Finally, however, the Senate adopted a nonbinding "sense of Congress" resolution, sponsored by the majority leader, Senator Mike Mansfield of Montana, which directed the courts to allow legislatures one legislative session plus thirty days in which to obey court orders; the resolution permitted the 1964 elections to proceed under existing apportionment systems where no court orders were in effect, but it did not affect court orders rendered before September 20; if the legislatures failed to act in the time specified by the resolution, the courts themselves were to reapportion.

The Mansfield resolution was adopted by a vote of 44 to 38 on September 24, and the foreign aid bill of which it was a rider was later sent to conference. The House opponents of the Court's decisions were so angered by the mild Senate resolution that the House members of the conference committee considering the aid bill were instructed to vote against the Senate resolution. The Senate resolution was thus eliminated from the foreign aid bill by the conference com-

[64] Nashville *Tennessean*, Aug. 14, 1964, pp. 1, 8.
[65] 110 Cong. Rec. 20908.

mittee, with the result that no congressional action on the Court's decisions emerged, despite weeks of bitter debate and the obvious fact that a majority of the Congress desired some action to be taken.[66]

The adjournment of Congress for the 1964 elections, however, did not end the assault on the Court's decisions, for the apportionment issue then became one of the moral-constitutional issues that formed the ideological core of Senator Goldwater's presidential campaign. In a real sense, the Goldwater campaign as it related to constitutional issues was a repudiation of, and an attempt to redirect, the path American constitutional development had taken since the Court had bowed to the New Deal in the spring of 1937.[67] The national power the Court had consistently sanctioned since 1937 seemed to Goldwater and his adherents to have been used to stifle the individual under an increasing burden of bureaucratic regulation and to undermine the moral fiber of the nation through the seductive use of federal largesse. Goldwater's vote against the Civil Rights Act of 1964 was thus in part a reiteration of this opposition to the expansion of federal power that had occurred for thirty years, since the act was based to a substantial degree upon a conception of the commerce clause that since 1937 had legitimized many of the programs to which he objected so strenuously.[68] Explaining to the Senate his vote against the act because of its public accommodations and fair employment sections, Goldwater thus stated that he could "find no constitutional basis for the exercise of federal authority in either of these areas; and I believe the attempted usurpation of such power to be a grave threat to the very essence of our basic system of government; namely, that of a constitutional republic in which 50 sovereign states have reserved to themselves and to the people those powers not specifically granted to the central or Federal Government."[69]

In addition, the Goldwater-led Republican campaign in 1964 at-

[66] Royce Hanson, *The Political Thicket*, pp. 84–89; *Congress and the Nation*, pp. 1526–27.

[67] Senator Goldwater's *The Conscience of a Conservative* (Shepherdsville, Ky.: Victor Publishing Co., 1960) indicates this rather clearly.

[68] For an analysis of the emergence of the post-1937 conception of the commerce power, see the author's *The Wagner Act Cases* (Knoxville: University of Tennessee Press, 1964).

[69] 22 *Congressional Quarterly* 2526 (1964). The Court predictably sustained the constitutionality of the public accommodations section of the act in *Heart of Atlanta Motel* v. *United States*, 379 U.S. 241, and *Katzenbach* v. *McClung*, 379 U.S. 294 (1964).

tacked most of the important constitutional initiatives taken by the Court since the 1930's, including to a degree the desegregation decisions,[70] decisions expanding the Fourteenth Amendment procedural protections of criminal defendants in state trials, decisions restricting censorship of allegedly obscene literature, decisions relating to subversion and internal security, the school prayer and Bible-reading decisions, and, finally, the 1964 apportionment decisions.[71] The Republican platform specifically called for a partial reversal of *Reynolds* v. *Sims* by a constitutional amendment allowing states to apportion one house of a bicameral legislature "on bases of their choosing, including factors other than population." The platform also called for an amendment "permitting those individuals and groups who choose to do so to exercise their religion freely in public places, provided religious exercises are not prepared or prescribed by the state or political subdivision thereof and no person's participation therein is coerced, thus preserving the traditional separation of church and state."[72] The platform also pledged Republican support for "legislation, despite Democratic opposition, to curb the flow through the mails of obscene material which has flourished into a multimillion dollar obscenity racket."[73]

The Republican campaign thus attempted to weld together a coalition of the Court's critics, a coalition such as Justice Brennan had feared a year earlier, and during the campaign the Court was as much the "enemy" as the Democratic party and President Johnson. Not since the liberal attacks on the Court during the 1930's had constitutional issues played such a prominent role in national electoral politics. Symbolic of the involvement of the Court in the campaign was the report that, although Chief Justice Warren had been a Republican governor of California and his party's vice presidential nominee in 1948, the mention of his name during the 1964 Republican

[70] I am aware that Senator Goldwater in *The Conscience of a Conservative*, p. 36, denied that the desegregation decisions were the "law of the land," and that in the 1964 campaign he generally repudiated this position (21 *Congressional Quarterly* 1639 [1963]), but his vote against the Civil Rights Act of 1964, the "southern strategy" of his campaign, and his use of the rhetoric of states' rights made him the segregationist candidate in the South, whatever may have been his personal views.

[71] For an excellent review of the constitutional issues in the 1964 campaign, see 22 *Congressional Quarterly* 2525–41, 2569.

[72] *Ibid.*, pp. 2538, 2534.

[73] *The New York Times*, July 13, 1964, p. 16.

convention produced a "chorus of boos."[74] Of all three branches of the government, Senator Goldwater declared during the campaign, "today's Supreme Court is least faithful to the constitutional tradition of limited government, and to the principle of legitimacy in the exercise of power," and the prayer and apportionment decisions were "two leading examples" of this fact.[75]

The Democrats, however, would not take up Goldwater's constitutional debate, and President Johnson would only say that there was "nothing to be gained by involving another independent branch of Government in a political campaign."[76] As one Goldwater aide said later, "We were punching a pillow."[77] The attacks on the Court were answered, however, by a group of fifty prominent lawyers, including twelve law school deans and five former presidents of the American Bar Association, who denounced Goldwater's attacks as exceeding "the limits of comment appropriate in a Presidential candidate." The group supported, it said, "responsible" criticism of the Court, but Goldwater's attacks were "not based on reasoned analysis of the Court's opinions. Instead they resort to catch phrases and slogans." All who support "our constitutional heritage," the group said, "whatever their party, must share our concern at this attack upon the ultimate guardian of American liberty."[78]

The avalanche of votes in November, 1964, which buried the hopes of Senator Goldwater and the Republican party for the presidency did not, however, bury the attack on the Court's apportionment decisions. On December 1, the Council of State Governments adopted a resolution urging the amendment of the Constitution to permit one house of state legislatures to be based on factors other than population, and two days later the General Assembly of the States called upon Congress to convene a national constitutional convention to adopt such an amendment.[79] By May 20, 1965, twenty-five state legislatures had adopted resolutions calling for a constitutional convention to consider amendments allowing one house of bicameral state legis-

[74] Anthony Lewis, "Convention Mood Reflects a Historic Change," *The New York Times,* July 19, 1964, p. 4E.

[75] 22 *Congressional Quarterly* 2534 (1964).

[76] *Ibid.*, p. 2525.

[77] Theodore H. White, *The Making of the President 1964* (New York: Atheneum Publishers, 1965), pp. 330–31.

[78] 22 *Congressional Quarterly* 2534 (1964).

[79] Robert B. McKay, *Reapportionment: The Law and Politics of Equal Representation* (New York: Twentieth Century Fund, 1965), p. 209.

latures to be based on factors other than population or to remove entirely the jurisdiction of the federal courts in apportionment cases.[80] The strategy of those supporting the proposal was to force the Congress to frame an apportionment amendment partly reversing *Reynolds* v. *Sims* in order to avoid a national convention; it was apparently believed that many congressmen shared the feelings of Senator Paul Douglas of Illinois, who said, "I shudder to think what would happen if it [the convention] were called."[81]

Responding to this pressure from the states and to widespread support for an apportionment amendment in the Senate, the Senate Judiciary Committee's Subcommittee on Constitutional Amendments held hearings on an amendment proposed by Senator Dirksen, as well as amendments proposed by Senators Church of Idaho and Javits of New York. The subcommittee's hearings, which continued from March 3 to May 21, gave both the opponents and proponents of the decision in *Reynolds* v. *Sims* a chance to reargue the merits of the case. Supporting the Dirksen amendment, or some variation of it, were most of the senators, representatives, and state legislators indicating their positions at the hearings. Most of the governors who recorded their opinions, however, were noncommittal, although ten governors favored the amendment. Most of the college professors and all but one of the mayors recording their views opposed the amendment, as did Burke Marshall, the former head of the Civil Rights Division of the Justice Department, and former Solicitor General J. Lee Rankin.

Support and opposition among interest groups followed predictable lines. The U. S. Chamber of Commerce, National Association of Manufacturers, National Association of Real Estate Boards, American Farm Bureau Federation, National Farmers Union, National Grange, National Cattlemen's Association, and many other farm organizations formed the core of the interest group support for the amendment. Joining these groups was the American Bar Association, which supported the amendment although it had opposed the reversal of *Baker* v. *Carr* through the withdrawal of federal court jurisdiction in apportionment cases.

[80] Article V of the Constitution provides that upon petition of two-thirds of the states (34) the Congress shall call a constitutional convention; amendments proposed by such a convention would be subject to ratification by three-fourths of the states. By the summer of 1969, the legislatures of 33 states had called for a constitutional convention.

[81] 23 *Congressional Quarterly* 972–73 (1965).

The opposition groups included the AFL-CIO and other member unions, the American Civil Liberties Union, the National Association for the Advancement of Colored People, Americans for Democratic Action, American Jewish Congress, the U. S. Conference of Mayors, and the American League of Cities (formerly the American Municipal Association).[82] The League of Cities, composed of representatives of state municipal leagues as well as representatives of member cities, added a resolution announcing opposition to the Dirksen amendment to the agenda of its convention meeting in July. The resolution carried by a vote of 429 to 166, with most of the opposition votes coming from delegates from Mississippi, Louisiana, New Mexico, Idaho, and California.[83]

The organized opposition to the Dirksen amendment was led by Senator Paul Douglas and a coalition of individuals and groups including the American Civil Liberties Union, the Maryland Committee for Fair Representation, the Conference of Mayors, and labor unions. A coordinating group, the National Committee for Fair Representation, was established to issue opposition publicity, to act as a clearinghouse for information, and to recruit witnesses for the hearings.[84] The Leadership Conference on Civil Rights, which had effectively lobbied for the Civil Rights Act of 1964 on behalf of over ninety national organizations, also joined the opposition and undertook the lobbying campaign against the amendment in Congress.[85]

The increasing number of state legislatures petitioning the Congress for a constitutional convention to consider an apportionment amendment, as well as the widespread opposition to the Court's decision in *Reynolds* v. *Sims*, appeared by June, 1965, to foretell victory for the Dirksen amendment; Lawrence Speiser, the Washington office director of the ACLU and chairman of the Committee for Fair Representation, characterized the chances for defeating the amendment in the Senate as "dim but not hopeless."[86] The opponents of

[82] Reapportionment of State Legislatures, Hearings before the Subcommittee on Constitutional Amendments, Committee on the Judiciary, U. S. Senate, 89th Cong., 1st sess. I have listed only the major groups which recorded opposition or support for the amendment.

[83] Nashville *Tennessean*, July 28, 1965, p. 3; July 29, 1965, p. 4.

[84] Hanson, *The Political Thicket*, pp. 91–99.

[85] *News Bulletin*, National Committee for Fair Representation, No. 2 (June 21, 1965), p. 2.

[86] *Civil Liberties*, Monthly Publication of the American Civil Liberties Union, No. 227 (June, 1965).

the amendment realized that time was their greatest ally, since, as more state legislatures were required to reapportion under judicial pressure, the chances lessened for their adoption of petitions for a constitutional convention or their acceptance of a constitutional amendment proposed by Congress.[87] The strategy of the opposition was thus to delay a Senate vote on the Dirksen amendment as long as possible.

The tide had turned by July, however, when Senator Dirksen was unable to obtain a majority on the full Judiciary Committee in favor of his amendment. He was forced to bring his proposal to the floor of the Senate by offering it as a substitute for a resolution designating a National American Legion Baseball Week.[88] And the vote on the amendment on August 4 was 57 to 39, seven votes short of the two-thirds majority necessary for the proposal of constitutional amendments.[89] The amendment as finally voted on would have permitted one house of a bicameral legislature to be apportioned on the basis of population, geography, or political subdivisions, but such a plan would have had to be approved by the voters of a state in a referendum offering an alternative population plan. Finally, the amendment would have required a referendum within two years following each decennial census in which the voters could have decided whether or not to retain the previously approved plan.[90]

Senator Dirksen vowed after his first defeat in the Senate that he would not allow the reapportionment matter to die, and threatened to block the administration's immigration bill in the Judiciary Committee unless a majority of the Committee agreed to report out his amendment. "I am not going to devote that much time, effort and sweat to the constitutional amendment," he said, "and then lose the psychological effect of having it on the calendar in January." Although Dirksen's tactic was denounced by Senator Tydings of Maryland as "blackmail," Senator Dodd of Connecticut broke the previous tie in the committee on the Dirksen amendment on September 8. "I am for the immigration bill and Dirksen is the key to it," Dodd said. "If I have to pay the price to get the immigration bill I am inclined to do

---

[87] *News Bulletin*, No. 1 (June 4, 1965), p. 3.

[88] For a description of the tactics of the Senate fight, see Hanson, *The Political Thicket*, pp. 96–101.

[89] 23 *Congressional Quarterly* 1541 (1965).

[90] McKay, *Reapportionment*, pp. 211–12.

so."[91] Dodd's vote thus allowed the amendment to be reported out of the Judiciary Committee for consideration in 1966. Time, however, was of no help to Senator Dirksen, and despite a reportedly well-financed public relations campaign for the amendment headed by the firm of Whittaker & Baxter, Dirksen's proposal was again defeated in the Senate on April 20, 1966, by a vote of 55 to 38.[92]

Although Senator Dirksen vowed to continue his efforts to partially reverse *Reynolds* v. *Sims*, this second defeat appeared to be fatal to the possibility that Congress would propose a constitutional amendment on the subject. And Dirksen's death in 1969 removed the leading congressional opponent of the one man, one vote principle. By 1969, on the other hand, it appeared that thirty-three of the required thirty-four state legislatures had petitioned for a constitutional convention to reverse the Court on the apportionment issue. The petitions adopted by the legislatures varied in their wording, and opponents of the proposed convention disputed the count of legislatures petitioning for a convention. It was also pointed out that many of the petitions had been adopted by legislatures before reapportionment had occurred. Even if a convention were called by Congress, and it proposed an amendment reversing *Reynolds* v. *Sims*, it appeared doubtful that such an amendment would be ratified by legislatures that by 1969 had been reapportioned on the principle of one man, one vote.[93]

In Tennessee, for example, where the reapportionment revolution had begun, the legislature was finally reapportioned on an equal population basis in 1965, after almost ten years of litigation.[94] The three-judge federal court in Tennessee had invalidated the reapportionment acts passed by the Tennessee legislature immediately after the Supreme Court's decision in *Baker* v. *Carr*, but allowed the legislature another chance to reapportion constitutionally. The 1963

[91] Birmingham *News*, Sept. 1, 1965, p. 33; Sept. 9, 1965, p. 37.

[92] 24 *Congressional Quarterly* 827–28 (1966). Sensitive to the charge that non-population apportionment in one house of a legislature could be used to discriminate against Negroes, Dirksen's 1966 amendment provided that non-population plans had to "insure effective representation in the state's legislature of the various groups and interests making up the electorate." The 1966 version was also amended before the final Senate vote to require legislatures to be apportioned on a population basis in both houses before the amendment could be considered by them for ratification.

[93] 28 *Congressional Quarterly* 1372–73 (1969).

[94] See *Baker* v. *Carr*, 247 F. Supp. 629 (M.D. Tenn. 1965).

session of the legislature produced another reapportionment that deviated substantially from a population basis in the lower house while also discriminating against the urban counties in the senate. In the fall of 1963, the three-judge court accepted the 1963 house apportionment, while invalidating the senate apportionment and accepting a plan submitted by the plaintiffs basing the senate substantially on population.[95] The court ultimately delayed entering a final order in the case, however, pending the Supreme Court's decisions in the 1964 apportionment cases.[96]

Thus, the court's decision in *Reynolds* v. *Sims* made possible for the first time in Tennessee an apportionment based on population for both houses of the legislature. As Hobart Atkins said upon hearing of the decision in *Reynolds*, "It sure has been a long fight, but this is what we've been waiting for."[97] The plaintiffs moved immediately for an order from the three-judge court requiring a population-based apportionment for both houses of the legislature. On June 27, 1964, the court accepted the plaintiffs' plans for such an apportionment, but again delayed an order implementing these plans to allow the 1965 legislature another, final, chance to reapportion.[98]

In a special session called in May, 1965, the legislature again struggled with reapportionment. "It's no wonder we've not reapportioned every 10 years," Representative James Cummings commented. "This is the most difficult thing you ever did."[99] On May 27, however, the legislature passed new apportionment acts, which were signed the following day by Governor Frank Clement, who observed that "the members of the General Assembly have made a sincere and honest effort to set their affairs in order. This required much courage, and I congratulate them for it."[100]

Although Hobart Atkins and Walter Chandler urged the three-judge federal court to invalidate the 1965 act, the court ruled on November 15, 1965, that the act was valid under the equal protection

[95] *Baker* v. *Carr*, 222 F. Supp. 684 (M.D. Tenn. 1963).

[96] *Baker* v. *Carr*, 247 F. Supp. 629, at 632. This final opinion in the case contains a good account of the steps in the litigation.

[97] Knoxville *Journal*, June 16, 1964, p. 1.

[98] 247 F. Supp., at 632.

[99] Knoxville *News-Sentinel*, May 2, 1965, p. A–6.

[100] Knoxville *News-Sentinel*, May 28, 1965, p. 1. The 1965 act gave Shelby County (Memphis) 16 house and 6 senate seats; Davidson County (Nashville) 11 house and 4 senate seats; Knox County (Knoxville) 8 house and 2 senate seats; and Hamilton County (Chattanooga) 7 house and 2 senate seats.

clause of the Fourteenth Amendment. Writing for the court, Judge William Miller noted the long history of *Baker* v. *Carr* and the importance of the case. "Not every citizen has heard of Baker v. Carr . . . but it is perhaps not fanciful to suggest that the impact of the Supreme Court's decision will be felt for many years to come," Miller said. "It has certainly been felt by the courts. Since that decision, there have been literally hundreds of published opinions dealing with apportionment. And published opinions do not tell the whole story. In this case alone, the single-spaced docket entries require more than 13 pages, and the file is measured not in pages but in feet."[101] Although admitting that the population of senate districts varied from 56,996 in the smallest district to 78,922 in the largest, and that there were similar variations in the house districts, the court held these variations to be within the limits of tolerance of the equal protection clause of the Fourteenth Amendment. Therefore the judgment to be entered, Judge Miller concluded, "will declare the 1965 Apportionment Act to be a federally constitutional apportionment of Tennessee's General Assembly. This being a final disposition of this protracted proceeding, it will be placed on the retired docket."[102]

Walter Chandler was disappointed with the court's ruling and urged an immediate appeal to the Supreme Court. But the litigating coalition that had sustained *Baker* v. *Carr* from the beginning was breaking up. The City of Nashville had not joined Chandler and Hobart Atkins in attacking the 1965 act,[103] and when the three-judge court's decision was announced, Atkins was so critically ill that he could not be informed of the decision, and he died one week later without knowing the final outcome of the litigation in *Baker* v. *Carr*.[104] Atkins' death, Chandler said, "throws the responsibility back on me," but, while still critical of the 1965 reapportionment, Chandler finally decided not to appeal the ruling of the three-judge court but instead to await the outcome of the reapportionment that would result from the 1970 census. The litigation in *Baker* v. *Carr* thus finally came to an end.[105]

[101] *Baker* v. *Carr*, 247 F. Supp. 629, at 631.
[102] *Ibid.*, at 641.
[103] Knoxville *News-Sentinel*, July 11, 1965, p. B–3.
[104] Knoxville *News-Sentinel*, Nov. 16, 1965, p. 2; Nov. 22, 1965, p. 1.
[105] Knoxville *News-Sentinel*, Nov. 22, 1965, p. A–2; Nov. 25, 1965, p. E–3. The 1965 apportionment act subdivided the large counties into districts for the pur-

The litigation in *Reynolds* v. *Sims* was also ultimately resolved in a similar manner. The Supreme Court's decision in *Reynolds* v. *Sims* was denounced by Alabama Governor George Wallace as "asinine, ridiculous and stupid," and the governor called for a national constitutional convention to remove such cases from the Court's jurisdiction. The federal courts, he said, "have taken over the nation," and in the *Reynolds* case he saw "nine non-elected members of an oligarchy who have spoken again."[106]

Undoubtedly reflecting the views of the plaintiffs in the Alabama case, however, was John McConnell's comment that while he deplored the trend toward governmental centralization, he believed such centralization had been "due to a vacuum at the State level." States' rights, he said, "without a recognition of the concomitant State responsibilities are a farce." The trend toward unrepresentative government was not of recent origin, McConnell continued, but began in "Alabama in 1911 when the Legislature meeting in that year failed to abide by the mandate of the Alabama Constitution in reapportioning [itself]. In that year, our State became a government of men not of laws. Oddly enough, the defender of the representative form of government is the Supreme Court in its reapportionment decision."[107]

Two of the plaintiffs' attorneys immediately petitioned the federal court to order into effect a reapportionment of the Alabama legislature, but the court delayed any action in order to give the legislature further time to act.[108] When more than a year passed and the legislature had given no indication that it would reapportion, the three-judge federal court set a pre-trial hearing on August 25, 1965, in preparation for a judicially ordered reapportionment. The court ordered the U. S. Justice Department to participate as *amicus curiae* and to submit, along with the other parties to the suit, proposals for

---

pose of senate representation, and this aspect of the act was later challenged in the state courts on the grounds that it violated the state constitution's provision, Art. II, sec. 6, that "no county shall be divided in forming a district." The subdistricting provision of the 1965 act was ultimately invalidated under the Tennessee Constitution by the state supreme court. See *Williams* v. *Carr*, opinion reprinted in the Nashville *Tennessean*, May 17, 1966, p. 8.

[106] Birmingham *Post-Herald*, June 23, 1964, p. 2; Birmingham *News*, June 15, 1964, p. 1.

[107] Letter, McConnell to Jack Edwards, n.d.

[108] Birmingham *Post-Herald*, June 23, 1964, p. 1.

a judicial remedy to eliminate the invidious discrimination resulting from the Alabama apportionment system.[109]

Although the legislature was in session when the court issued its order, it adjourned without acting on apportionment, and Governor Wallace was constrained to call the legislature back into special session in September. In an address to the legislators, televised state-wide, Wallace devoted most of his time to asking the people if they wanted him to run for re-election and to attacking the President, Congress, and the federal courts. The very "fabric of our American system is being torn to shreds," Wallace said; the Supreme Court had held that the "people do not have the power to determine how and in what manner their state governments shall be formed." Alabama was "compelled" to change its legislature "to meet the dictates" of a Supreme Court decision that was but "one example of steam roller tactics employed against the people." The Court, Wallace said, was the "most revolutionary force in the nation today," sanctioning the occupation of communities "by thousands of out-of-state riff-raff, Communists, and fellow travelers, kooks, beatniks, prostitutes and bums" and handcuffing "local law enforcement personnel who seek to prevent depredations against the peace and order."[110]

Following Wallace's address, the legislators struggled over reapportionment until September 23, when both houses finally passed reapportionment acts.[111] Two days later, when the federal court reviewed the legislation, Assistant Attorney General John Doar, head of the Civil Rights Division of the Justice Department, declared that the evidence "points overwhelmingly to the inference that the state of Alabama unconstitutionally discriminates against Negro citizens." The new apportionment acts were also attacked during the hearing by Alabama Attorney General Richmond Flowers, David Vann, and Jerome Cooper, but McLean Pitts urged the court to accept the acts as valid under the Fourteenth Amendment.[112]

In early October, the three-judge court held that the act reapportioning the senate was valid, but that the act reapportioning the house was invalid under the equal protection clause and the Fifteenth

109 Birmingham *News*, July 28, 1965, pp. 10, 24.
110 Birmingham *News*, Sept. 10, 1965, pp. 1, 6.
111 Birmingham *News*, Sept. 24, 1965, pp. 1, 8.
112 Birmingham *News*, Sept. 26, 1965, p. 1.

Amendment because of deviations from the population principle and because of the racial discrimination embodied in the act.[113] Besides deviations from the population standard in the house apportionment, the court found that the legislature had grouped several sets of counties into house districts in an attempt to prevent potential Negro majorities where federal registrars were registering Negro voters under the 1965 Voting Rights Act. "The House plan adopted by the all-white Alabama Legislature was not conceived in a vacuum," the court said. "If this court ignores the long history of racial discrimination in Alabama, it will prove that justice is both blind and deaf."[114] The court thus substituted its own plan for the apportionment of the house, which would take effect following the November, 1966, elections. Under the court's plan, six districts electing ten representatives contained Negro majorities.[115]

The fight for reapportionment in Alabama and Tennessee thus came to a close, but the effects of the Supreme Court's decisions in *Baker* v. *Carr* and *Reynolds* v. *Sims* would be felt in the politics of all the states. Those decisions marked a revolutionary shift of political power to the metropolitan areas which would redirect the course of American politics and change state political patterns that in some instances had existed for half a century. What was happening was perhaps best summed up by a legislator during debate on the 1965 reapportionment of the Alabama legislature. Noting that he represented a small county, he admitted that the state was moving rapidly from a rural to an urban economy, and that perhaps that was as it should be. "It is a sad time in a changing era, but we are going from one era to another," he said. "Old political ties of a half-century are being ignored here. . . . Never again will we have a senator from my district and I doubt that there will ever be a House member to sit

[113] *Sims* v. *Baggett*, 247 F. Supp. 96 (M.D. Ala. 1965).
[114] *Ibid.*, at 109.
[115] Birmingham *News*, Oct. 5, 1965, p. 2. These districts were Pickens and Greene counties, electing 1 representative; Sumter, Marengo and Perry counties, electing 2 representatives; Dallas County, electing 2 representatives; Autauga and Lowndes counties, electing 1 representative; Macon, Bullock and Barbour counties, electing 2 representatives; and Wilcox, Monroe and Conecuh counties, electing 2 representatives. Under the final apportionment, as modified by the court, the large counties received the following representation in the legislature: Jefferson County (Birmingham), 20 representatives and 7 senators; Mobile, 10 representatives and 3 senators; and Montgomery, 5 representatives and 2 senators.

from the county I represent." Nothing could change this, he concluded. "But I could not let this pass without telling you that you have witnessed the end of an era."[116]

[116] Birmingham *News*, Sept. 19, 1965, p. C–13.

CHAPTER X

APPORTIONMENT, THE COURT,

AND THE JUDICIAL PROCESS

THE SUPREME COURT'S DECISIONS in the apportionment cases involved
the most remarkable and far-reaching exercise of judicial power in
our history. Chief Justice Earl Warren has called them the most important decisions made during his tenure on the Court. By 1968,
legislatures in forty-nine of the states had been reapportioned. Only
Oregon's legislature, the upper house in Massachusetts, and the lower
houses in Alaska, Hawaii, and South Carolina remained untouched
by the reapportionment revolution that followed *Baker* v. *Carr* and
Reynolds v. *Sims.* And in twelve states, reapportionment of one or
both legislative houses had been by judicial decree.[1]

The apportionment cases illustrate with great clarity the dual, and
often conflicting, concepts of the legitimacy[2] of governmental power
in the American political system and the role of the Supreme Court
in mediating between them. On the one hand, possession of political
authority and the power to act in the name of the public is legitimized
through the electoral process. Indeed, the acceptance of the electoral
process as the appropriate method of legitimizing the possession of
political power in the United States is so widespread that only on
one occasion at the national level—the Civil War—has the electoral
method proven unacceptable to a substantial segment of the population. This acceptance of the electoral method of legitimization facili-
tates the nonviolent transfer of power from individual to individual
and group to group. Thus, even when at the presidential level the
successful candidate prevails by only a narrow margin of popular
votes, as in 1960 and 1968, the outcome is not violently contested
by the losing side. The strength of the electoral process as a means

[1] *The Christian Science Monitor*, Oct. 29, 1968, 2d sec., p. 1.
[2] I use the term "legitimacy" here as the willingness of one individual to accept the possession and exercise of political power by another as proper.

of legitimizing political power is symbolized by such phrases as "the majority rules," "popular sovereignty," and "government rests on the consent of the governed."

While recognizing and sanctioning the electoral process as the principal means of legitimizing political power, the American constitutional system also has always recognized limitations upon the exercise of political power, no matter how large a majority may be involved. This concept of course lies at the heart of American constitutionalism, and its widespread acceptance required the addition of the Bill of Rights to the Constitution. As Justice Robert Jackson said in 1943, "The very purpose of a Bill of Rights was to withdraw certain subjects from the vicissitudes of political controversy, to place them beyond the reach of majorities and officials and to establish them as legal principles to be applied by the courts. One's right to life, liberty, and property, to free speech, a free press, freedom of worship and assembly, and other fundamental rights may not be submitted to [a] vote; they depend on the outcome of no elections."[3] The concept of constitutional limitations thus denies legitimacy to those exercises of political power which exceed the powers delegated to government or which encroach upon the fundamental rights of the individual.

When John Marshall declared in *Marbury* v. *Madison*[4] that it was "the province and duty of the judicial department, to say what the law is," and asserted the power of judicial review, the Court became the mediator in conflicts between the dual concepts of legitimacy embodied in the American political system. Judicial review involves essentially the power of the Court to determine whether or not particular public policies may be finally resolved in the electoral process. As a result, exercises of judicial review—from *Marbury* v. *Madison* to the apportionment cases—have been characterized by attacks based upon one or the other of the dual concepts of legitimacy. A decision by the Court sustaining the constitutionality of a given public policy may thus be attacked by those who feel the Court has sanctioned an illegitimate exercise of governmental power which infringes upon the fundamental rights of the individual. A decision invalidating a particular policy, on the other hand, will be

[3] *West Virginia Board of Education* v. *Barnette*, 319 U.S. 624, at 638 (1943).
[4] Cranch 137 (1803).

denounced on the grounds that the Court has unjustifiably blocked the will of the majority.

There is no better example of the conflict between the dual principles of legitimacy than the Court's decisions in the apportionment cases, and especially in *Lucas* v. *Colorado General Assembly*.[5] The Colorado apportionment system under attack in the *Lucas* case had been adopted in 1962 by an overwhelming majority of the voters in every county in the state. At the same election, the voters had rejected an apportionment system that would have based both houses of the Colorado legislature substantially upon population. As an example of the electoral principle of legitimacy, the Colorado apportionment system was clearly a legitimate policy approved by the voters of the state. The Supreme Court, however, applying the principle of constitutional limitations, held that the Colorado apportionment system was invalid because it denied equality of representation in violation of the equal protection clause.

The Court's opinion in the *Lucas* case clearly asserted that the principle of constitutional limitations prevails whenever "fundamental rights" are infringed by any given policy, no matter how large the majority that authorizes it. The Court said in the *Lucas* case:

> An individual's constitutionally protected right to cast an equally weighted vote, cannot be denied even by a vote of a majority of a State's electorate, if the apportionment scheme adopted by the voters fails to measure up to the requirements of the Equal Protection Clause. Manifestly, the fact that an apportionment scheme is adopted in a popular referendum is insufficient to sustain its constitutionality. . . . A citizen's constitutional rights can hardly be infringed simply because a majority of the people choose that it [*sic*] be. We hold that the fact that a challenged legislative apportionment plan was approved by the electorate is without federal constitutional significance, if the scheme adopted fails to satisfy the basic requirements of the Equal Protection Clause, as delineated in our opinion in Reynolds v. Sims.[6]

In the apportionment cases, the Court was therefore performing in its role as mediator between the dual principles of legitimacy within the American system. By holding that both houses of state legislatures were required to be based substantially upon population, the Court

[5] 377 U.S. 713 (1964).
[6] *Ibid.*, at 736–37.

in essence determined that the degree of equality accorded the individual by a legislative apportionment system was not an issue that could be finally determined in the electoral process. Such an issue, the Court held, involved fundamental individual rights that were not subject to a majority vote.

Decisions such as those in the appointment cases point up the nature of the power the Court possesses in the American system, and they also graphically illustrate the policy discretion the Court exercises. When it holds that fundamental rights are infringed, or that more power than delegated is being exercised, the Court of course points to a particular provision of the Constitution as the source of its ruling; in the apportionment cases this constitutional source was the equal protection clause. Constitutional provisions, such as the equal protection clause, the due process clause, and the commerce clause, which form the constitutional bases of most of the Court's major decisions, are ambiguous. This ambiguity is one of the reasons for the continued viability of our constitutional system, but it also means that the Court must supply the policy content of such clauses.

In characterizing the discretionary power of the Court in constitutional interpretation, Charles Evans Hughes once remarked that the Constitution means what the Supreme Court says it means, and the apportionment cases would appear to support that conclusion. The relatively speedy and effective enforcement of the mandate in the apportionment cases, despite the opposition in Congress and in state legislatures, has been a remarkable exercise of judicial power. And in contrast to the reaction to *Reynolds* v. *Sims*, the Court's 1968 decision in *Avery* v. *Midland County*,[7] extending the equal population principle of apportionment to more than eighty thousand units of local government, has gone largely unquestioned. Although on the surface the apportionment cases seem to confirm the Hughes characterization of Supreme Court power, the cases in fact reveal the very conditional nature of the Court's policy-making power in constitutional interpretation.

This conditional power is best illustrated by a comparison of the apportionment cases and the desegregation decisions in 1954, the most important policy initiatives by the court since the 1930's. Both involved the use of judicial power to enforce mandates of broad social

[7] 390 U.S. 474 (1968).

and political significance, thus revealing a greater than usual number of factors conditioning compliance with judicial decisions. The factors having a significant impact upon compliance are (1) the nature of the Court's mandate, (2) the responsiveness of the lower courts and their ability to enforce the Court's mandate, (3) the availability of enforcement litigants willing and able to enforce the Court's mandate, (4) the technical ease of the enforcement process, (5) the degree to which enforcement of the mandate depends upon nonjudicial actors, and (6) the relative power of those adversely affected by the Court's action.[8]

The clarity of the Court's mandate concerning what is required, and when, will affect the degree of compliance.[9] The mandates in the desegregation and apportionment cases differed most crucially upon the question of timing. The "all deliberate speed" requirement in the desegregation mandate unquestionably permitted delaying tactics to frustrate the Court's policy. In the South, the emphasis has been upon deliberation and not upon speed. The absence of any such imprecise standard in *Reynolds* v. *Sims* cut short the time available for delaying tactics in reapportionment. The Court's instructions to the lower federal courts in *Reynolds* v. *Sims*—that they should "avoid a disruption of the election process which might result from requiring precipitate changes that could make unreasonable or embarrassing demands on a State" in adjusting to the requirements of the Court's decree—did allow room for some delay in the enforcement of the Court's mandate, but certainly not of the proportions permitted by the "all deliberate speed" mandate.[10]

Rapid and effective enforcement of its mandates may, of course, be only one among competing considerations in the Court's decision-making process. A vague mandate may be the result of the internal problem of mustering a majority among justices who are unable to

[8] The degree to which a Court decision is effectively and accurately communicated by the media or other means to those actors who will be wholly or in part responsible for compliance with the decision is not discussed here. This factor may be of considerable importance, but in both the desegregation and apportionment cases the message of the Court was well known. The relation between communication and compliance is discussed in Richard M. Johnson, *The Dynamics of Compliance* (Evanston: Northwestern University Press, 1967).

[9] Richard E. Neustadt, *Presidential Power* (New York: John Wiley & Sons, Science Ed., 1962), p. 19; cf. Walter Murphy, *Elements of Judicial Strategy* (Chicago: University of Chicago Press, 1964), pp. 92–93.

[10] 377 U.S. 533, at 585.

agree on a highly specific mandate, as was apparently the case in *Baker* v. *Carr* and may have been the case with the "all deliberate speed" mandate in the desegregation cases.[11] The Court may also intentionally frame a vague mandate in order to allow a problem to "ripen" and allow time in which to assess the consequences of a given policy. If a policy could result in the threat of severe sanctions against the Court, such as the repeal of part of its appellate jurisdiction, the Court may find the sacrifice in terms of compliance a small price to pay.

A second factor that affected compliance in the desegregation and apportionment cases was the degree of acceptance of those policies by the lower courts. Again the contrast between the two sets of cases is great, since the mandate of the apportionment cases seems to have been accepted and applied with alacrity by the lower federal courts, while the federal district courts in the South generally approached the enforcement of desegregation with reluctance.[12] Therefore, the Court's mandate must not only be delivered with clarity but must also be sufficiently persuasive to the lower courts so that their known powers of resistance are not invoked against the Court's policy.[13]

The lower courts must also have the means at hand to execute a Supreme Court mandate, and these means may not be available, despite the willingness of the courts to implement a mandate. Certainly the federal district court in Little Rock lacked the means to deal effectively with the mob in the desegregation crisis of 1957 and had to rely upon troops dispatched by the President. A more prosaic example would be unreasonable searches and seizures conducted by police in cases that do not come to trial in the courts. In such instances, the enforcement of the Court's decisions prohibiting unreasonable searches and seizures is beyond the reach of the local courts.[14]

Another contrasting feature between the desegregation and appor-

[11] Daniel M. Berman, *It Is So Ordered* (New York: W. W. Norton & Company, 1966), p. 114.

[12] Jack Peltason, *Fifty-Eight Lonely Men* (New York: Harcourt, Brace & World, 1961).

[13] Walter Murphy, "Lower Court Checks on Supreme Court Power," *American Political Science Review*, Vol. 53 (1959), p. 1017.

[14] Jerome H. Skolnick. *Justice Without Trial* (New York: John Wiley & Sons, 1966), pp. 219–25.

tionment cases was the availability of individuals and groups willing and able to institute litigation to enforce the Court's mandate and also the technical ease with which such litigation was effective. The extent of such enforcement litigation depends upon many factors, among them the status and relative wealth of those affected and the degree to which social, political, or economic sanctions may be invoked against them. Thus in the desegregation cases, at least until 1964, the burden of enforcement litigation fell primarily upon the Negro, whose status was low in the South, where enforcement litigation was most needed, whose resources to finance enforcement litigation were quite limited, and who was likely to have social, economic, and political sanctions invoked against him if he engaged in such litigation.[15] In addition, the enforcement of the desegregation mandate raised technical difficulties: segregation had to be attacked in litigation aimed at individual school districts, which proved costly in both time and resources.

In contrast, there seemed to be an abundance of individuals and groups willing and able to enforce the apportionment mandate, and no social, economic, or political sanctions appear to have been directed against them. In addition, the mandate of the apportionment cases was easily enforced, since only one lawsuit in a federal district court in each state was sufficient to begin the enforcement process.

The availability of individuals and groups willing and able to initiate enforcement litigation, along with the technical ease of enforcement, thus has an important impact upon compliance with the Court's mandates. The lack of individuals and groups willing to initiate enforcement of the Court's decisions relating to religion and the public schools, for example, may explain the widespread lack of compliance with those decisions. Dissenters—particularly in otherwise religiously homogeneous communities—may well be reluctant to initiate enforcement litigation in such cases. Thus, social sanctions were invoked against some of the plaintiffs in *Zorach* v. *Clauson*[16] and against Mrs. Vashti McCollum and her family as a result of *McCollum* v. *Illinois*.[17] One of the families challenging New York's released-

[15] Walter Murphy, "The South Counterattacks: The Anti-NAACP Laws," *Western Political Quarterly*, Vol. 12 (1959), p. 371; George R. Osborne, "The NAACP in Alabama," in C. Herman Pritchett and Alan F. Westin (eds.), *The Third Branch of Government* (New York: Harcourt, Brace & World, 1963).

[16] 343 U.S. 306 (1952).

[17] 333 U.S. 203 (1948).

time plan in the *Zorach* case faced "angry, sullen neighbors; insulting phone calls at all hours; COD orders placed in their names at local stores; anti-Semitic attacks by bigots; and the defection of some of their children's playmates." Mrs. McCollum's son was regularly harassed and occasionally beaten by his schoolmates, and his parents were ultimately forced to withdraw him from the public schools and to enroll him in a private school out of town.[18]

The number of nonjudicial actors in the political system who must acquiesce in or support a given policy of the Court also affects the degree of compliance with that policy. As the circle of such nonjudicial actors expands, it would appear that the *potential* for resistance to the Court's policy increases, particularly if the circle includes nonjudicial actors who possess strongly based positions of power within the system. As Archibald Cox has said, the desegregation, apportionment, and other recent cases expanding the concept of equal protection have required the states "to make changes in the *status quo* —some alteration of a widespread and long accepted practice, some improvement from the standpoint of human rights," and they have imposed "affirmative obligations upon the states," whereas earlier cases were "typically mandates directing the government to refrain from a particular form of regulation."[19] As Cox suggests, the desegregation and apportionment cases were rather unusual uses of judicial power because compliance with their mandates depended greatly upon acquiescence in and, more often, positive action supporting the Court's policies by many nonjudicial actors in the political system.

The apportionment mandate primarily required acquiescence by state legislatures and state election officials, but it did not require positive support by either Congress or the President in order to be enforced effectively. The desegregation mandate, on the other hand, required at least acquiescence on the part of governors, legislatures, and school boards in the South, which was not forthcoming. Ultimately, to secure even minimal compliance, it required the positive support of the President—to enforce federal court orders against strong local resistance—as well as enforcement legislation from Con-

[18] Frank J. Sorauf, "The Released Time Case," in Pritchett and Westin (eds.), *The Third Branch of Government*, pp. 125–26; Vashti Cromwell McCollum, *One Woman's Fight* (Boston: Beacon Press, 1961), chaps. 13 and 19.

[19] Archibald Cox, "Forward: Constitutional Adjudication and the Promotion of Human Rights," 80 *Harvard Law Review* 91, 92 (1966).

gress. Clearly, many more persons outside the courts had to be persuaded of the correctness of the Court's policy in the desegregation cases than in the apportionment cases, and thus the potential for resistance to the Court's desegregation policy was much greater—a potential that has of course been fully realized. As the circle of actors with strong bases of independent power increases, so does the potential for effective resistance to the Court's policy.

A related possibility is that a given policy may not only encounter resistance but may also produce attempts to apply sanctions on the Court. An analysis of the exercise of power by the Court therefore must also discover whose interests are adversely affected by a decision of the Court and their ability to retaliate against the Court. In this respect also there is a clear contrast in the degree to which sanctions were threatened as a result of the decisions in the apportionment and desegregation cases. There was never a realistic threat of a constitutional amendment to overrule the desegregation decisions, or of limitations on the Court's appellate jurisdiction to prevent its review of segregation policies. Yet as a result of the decisions in the apportionment cases, both sanctions seemed—at least for a time—to be within the realm of possibility, even though all other factors affecting compliance were favorable to the apportionment mandate.

The "segregation interest" was not national in scope and possessed political power to act positively at only the state and local levels—and mostly in the South. Although sufficient to prevent positive action supporting desegregation in the Congress until the 1960's, this essentially negative power was insufficient to secure positive congressional action invoking sanctions against the Court. The "segregation interest," therefore, because of its essentially regional scope and its lack of power in the Congress, could not effectively threaten direct sanctions against the Court.

The apportionment decisions, however, adversely affected a nationwide congeries of strategically located interests. First, in almost all the states the political security of incumbent legislators was threatened. Second, a number of interest groups, such as the National Association of Manufacturers, possessing significant national power, thought that their policy interests were adversely affected by the shift of legislative power from rural to urban areas which the apportionment decisions required. As a result, although the Court's apportionment mandate has been decidedly more effectively enforced than its desegregation mandate, the Court also faced a much graver threat of sanctions against it as a result of the apportionment cases.[20]

As we have seen, the Court's power of judicial review allows it to function as a mediator between the dual principles of legitimacy within the American system, and the ambiguity of the great clauses in the Constitution gives the Court a great deal of discretion in its policy-making. Comparison of the desegregation decision and the apportionment cases, however, reveals that the Court's policy-making power is quite situational and is conditioned by a variety of factors. As Martin Shapiro has said, it is "impossible to speak in the abstract of the power or function of the Supreme Court. The Supreme Court, like other agencies, has different powers and different functions depending upon who wants it to do what, when, and in conjunction with or opposition to what other agencies or political forces. If a final answer can even be offered to the question, 'What is the role of the Supreme Court?' it will be in specific areas, rather than by general examination of the nature of the Court."[21]

Charles Evans Hughes' remark that the Constitution means what the Supreme Court says it means has for too long been the supposed mark of sophistication in constitutional politics. But the remark is not truly descriptive because of the factors that condition the effectiveness of the Court's power. When the Court rules that school prayer is unconstitutional, and a local school board continues a policy of prayer in classrooms unchallenged, the Constitution for that school means what the school board says it means, not what the Court says it means. Only when the factors conditioning its powers are favorable will the Constitution mean what the Court says it means, even though the effects of the Court's interpretation are revolutionary. If nothing else, the apportionment cases have taught us this.

The apportionment cases not only afford important insights into

---

[20] A factor difficult to measure but perhaps nonetheless important in this regard is the difference in the moral content in the issues of segregation and apportionment. Certainly it could be argued that the issue of segregation has been perceived more emotionally in terms of the morality involved than has apportionment and that it was perhaps easier for congressmen outside the South, for example, to adopt public positions hostile to the apportionment decisions than to adopt such positions hostile to the desegregation decisions.

[21] Martin Shapiro, "Political Jurisprudence," in Raymond E. Wolfinger (ed.), *Readings in American Political Behavior* (Englewood Cliffs, N.J.: Prentice-Hall, 1966), p. 160.

the nature of judicial power, but also shed light upon the kinds of litigants important in breaking new ground in constitutional interpretation. Although litigating coalitions like those in the apportionment cases are not so common before the Supreme Court as permanently organized interest groups such as the NAACP, they do belong to a class of litigants that contribute a substantial creative element to constitutional development.[22]

These litigants depend upon the judicial process as a means of pursuing their policy interests, usually because they are temporarily, or even permanently, disadvantaged—that is, they cannot attain their goals in the electoral process, within elected political institutions, or in the bureaucracy. To succeed in the pursuit of their goals they are almost compelled to resort to litigation.

Such litigants may be classified as either "defensive" or "aggressive." A defensive litigant does not seek the creation of new constitutional interpretations by the courts; instead, he attempts to convince the courts that prevailing constitutional norms, already favorable to his interests, should be applied. Such a litigant seeks stability, not change, in constitutional policy. The aggressive litigant, on the other hand, is one who finds the prevailing constitutional policy unfavorable and therefore seeks innovative interpretations of the Constitution from the courts.

The strategies pursued by business interests in the judicial process during two periods of our history serve to illustrate this classification. Facing a rising tide of regulatory state legislation during the period following the Civil War, business interests asked the courts to invalidate such legislation as contrary to the due process clause of the Fourteenth Amendment. The prevailing interpretation of due process was that it imposed essentially procedural limitations on the exercise of governmental power. Business interests thus were compelled to seek change in the prevailing constitutional policy and acceptance of the concept of substantive due process. As an aggressive litigant, business succeeded in this cause and contributed to one of the most important changes in constitutional policy in our history.[23]

[22] The analysis that follows is based substantially upon the author's article, "Strategies and Tactics of Litigants in Constitutional Cases," *Journal of Public Law*, Vol. 17 (1968), p. 287.
[23] See the author's *The Wagner Act Cases* (Knoxville: University of Tennes-

During the New Deal period, a spate of regulatory legislation at the national level caused business interests again to engage in extensive litigation. During the New Deal, however, business interests sought, not innovation, but adherence to prevailing constitutional policy which was hostile to the regulation of property and economic rights. For example, the Liberty League, which condemned much of the New Deal as unconstitutional, did not call upon the courts to change constitutional policy but rather to adhere to established policy.[24] During the New Deal, in contrast to the period following the Civil War, business was thus a defensive litigant in the judicial process.

Another, almost classic, example of an aggressive judicial interest group is the Jehovah's Witnesses. The Witnesses may be regarded as a permanently disadvantaged group because their doctrinal conception of the state as a manifestation of evil precludes their participation in the political process (excluding, paradoxically, the judicial process). The Witnesses have relied almost exclusively upon the judicial process to protect their interests, and, beginning in the late 1930's, their relation to the judicial process was that of an aggressive group seeking new interpretations of the Fourteenth Amendment to protect their proselytizing activities and their refusal to salute the flag. The Witnesses' resort to the judicial process as an aggressive group produced a notable series of Supreme Court decisions which significantly expanded the protection of freedom of religion and expression afforded under the First and Fourteenth amendments.[25]

Both the Negro and those seeking change in legislative apportionment also fit the description of disadvantaged, aggressive judicial interest groups. The Negro, disadvantaged in the electoral process because of discrimination in voting, turned to the judicial process as the primary means by which racial discrimination could be attacked. The NAACP in its litigation efforts, at least until the 1950's, was an aggressive judicial interest group since the system of segregation had been legitimated by the Court in *Plessy* v. *Ferguson* in 1896,[26] and the

---

see Press, 1964), chap 1; see also Arnold M. Paul, *Conservative Crisis and the Rule of Law* (Ithaca: Cornell University Press, 1960).

[24] For a history of the Liberty League, see George Wolfskill, *The Revolt of the Conservatives* (Boston: Houghton Mifflin Co., 1962).

[25] Milton R. Konvitz, *Expanding Liberties* (New York: The Viking Press, 1966), pp. 12–13; David Manwaring, *Render Unto Caesar* (Chicago: University of Chicago Press, 1962).

[26] 163 U.S. 537.

thrust of NAACP litigation had to be aimed at overturning the established interpretation of the Constitution and creating new, favorable precedents.[27]

Those who sought change in the apportionment of state legislatures were also disadvantaged in the electoral process because they usually resided in the areas most discriminated against, with the result that they lacked power to work their will on the issue. Since the avenues to change through the electoral process were blocked, except in those states providing for the initiative and referendum, they had to seek relief through the judicial process, just as the Negro had. In addition, the forces litigating the issue of apportionment, such as the Tennessee litigating coalition, were compelled to play the role of aggressive litigants since the precedents (or the received understanding of them) were contrary to their objectives. They had to become creative and innovative in constitutional doctrine, and when the product of their creativity was recognized by the Court, a new and important chapter in American constitutional development was written.

Aggressive litigants, such as those responsible for the apportionment cases, undoubtedly supply a high proportion of the losers in constitutional cases. This is because of the novelty of the demands they make upon the judiciary; as Justice Holmes once said, judges "commonly are elderly men, and are more likely to hate at sight any analysis to which they are not accustomed, and which disturbs repose of mind, than to fall in love with novelties."[28] We of course tend to remember the successes of the aggressive litigant, such as *Baker* v. *Carr* and *Reynolds* v. *Sims*, and forget the failures, such as *Colegrove* v. *Barrett*[29] and the other *per curiam* refusals of the Supreme Court to rule on apportionment cases. Perhaps in losing a substantial portion of their cases, aggressive litigants educate the justices so that their "repose of mind" is not so much disturbed by ideas which, because they have been repeatedly presented, have ceased to be novelties.

The litigants in the apportionment cases had first broken through the doctrine of political questions in *Baker* v. *Carr* and finally succeeded in establishing population as the constitutionally required

[27] For a study of the NAACP's strategy in the restrictive covenant cases, *Shelley* v. *Kraemer*, 334 U.S. 1 (1948); *Hurd* v. *Hodge*, 334 U.S. 24 (1948); and *Barrows* v. *Jackson*, 346 U.S. 249 (1953), which illustrates this point, see Clement E. Vose, *Caucasians Only* (Berkeley: University of California Press, 1959).
[28] Oliver W. Holmes, *Collected Legal Papers* (1920), p. 230.
[29] 330 U.S. 804 (1946).

basis of the apportionment of state legislatures. As a result, there was a massive shift of political power to the urban areas directed by an extraordinary exercise of federal judicial power. By any measure, the victory of the litigants in the apportionment cases was a momentous one—one whose import will best be determined in the decades to come. As the decade of the 1970's dawns, however, it is already clear that legislative power in the hands of the great urban populations of the nation is a minimum requirement if we are to grapple successfully with the awesome problem of making the nation once again livable. The doctrine of the apportionment cases does not insure that this power will be exercised either effectively or wisely. But an open, democratic society is a gamble, and one in which historically we as a nation have bet our lives. The apportionment cases mean that that bet is still on.

TABLE I

Counties Having an Excess of Direct Representatives
According to 1950 Population and Tennessee State
Constitution, Article II, Section 5–1951 Tennessee
General Assembly

County	1950 Voting Population	Ratio	Number of Direct Representatives by Formula	Actual Number of Direct Representatives
Cannon	5,341	.2672	0	1
Chester	6,391	.3198	0	1
Claiborne	12,799	.6404	0	1
Cocke	12,572	.6291	0	1
Crockett	9,676	.4842	0	1
DeKalb	6,984	.3495	0	1
Dickson	11,294	.5651	0	1
Gibson	48,132	1.4927	1	2
Hardin	16,908	.4792	0	1
Hickman	7,598	.3802	0	1
Jackson	6,719	.3362	0	1
Lake	6,252	.3128	0	1
McNairy	11,601	.5805	0	1
Madison	37,245	1.8636	1	2
Marion	10,988	.5503	0	1
Marshall	11,288	.5648	0	1
Monroe	12,884	.6447	0	1
Moore	2,340	.1171	0	1
Overton	9,474	.4740	0	1
Sevier	12,793	.6401	0	1
Smith	8,731	.4369	0	1
Stewart	5,238	.2621	0	1
White	9,244	.4625	0	1
Total			2	25

Ratio—*county voting population* x 99 (total house membership is 99) divided by total Tennessee voting population (1,978,548 in 1950).

TABLE II

Counties Having a Deficiency of Direct Representatives
According to 1950 Voting Population and Tennessee
State Constitution, Article II, Section 5–1951 Tennessee
General Assembly

County	1950 Voting Population	Ratio	Number of Direct Representatives by Formula	Actual Number of Direct Representatives
Anderson	33,990	1.7007	1	0
Bradley	18,273	.9143	1	0
Campbell	17,477	.8745	1	0
Carter	23,303	1.1660	1	0
Davidson	211,930	10.6043	10	6
Hamblen	14,090	.7050	1	0
Hamilton	131,971	6.6034	6	3
Knox	140,559	7.0331	7	3
Shelby	312,345	15.6287	15	7
Sullivan	55,712	2.7876	2	1
Total			45	20

Ratio—*county voting population* x *99* (total house membership is 99) divided
by total Tennessee voting population (1,978,548 in 1950).

TABLE III

Tennessee Senatorial Districts in 1901 and 1951, By Counties and Voting Population in 1900 and 1950

Senatorial District Number	Counties	Total Voting Population 1900	Voting Population per Senator 1900	Total Voting Population 1950	Voting Population per Senator 1950
1	Carter	3,748		23,303	
	Greene	6,967		23,649	
	Johnson	2,211		6,649	
	Unicoi	1,320		8,787	
	Washington	5,408		36,967	
			19,654		99,355
2	Hawkins	5,192		16,900	
	Sullivan	6,059		55,712	
			11,251		72,612
3	Campbell	3,967		17,477	
	Claiborne	4,559		12,799	
	Grainger	3,576		7,125	
	Hancock	2,274		4,710	
	Morgan	*		8,308	
	Scott	2,378		8,417	
	Union	2,841		4,600	
			19,604		63,436
4	Blount	4,359		30,353	
	Cocke	4,072		12,572	
	Hamblen	2,997		14,090	
	Jefferson	4,130		11,359	
	Sevier	4,434		12,793	
			19,992		81,167
5	Knox	10,049		140,559	
			14,130†		102,726†
6	Knox	19,049		140,559	
	Anderson	*		33,990	
	Loudon	2,467		13,264	
	Roane	*		17,639	
	Monroe	4,065		*	
	Polk	2,679		*	
			14,130†		102,726†
7	Anderson	4,130		*	
	Roane	5,470		*	

* County is in another district for the year indicated.

† In cases where a county has both a direct and floterial senator, the sum of the voting population of all the counties in such floterial district is divided by the number of direct and floterial districts involved to determine the average population for each district.

269

TABLE III (continued)

Senatorial District Number	Counties	Total Voting Population 1900	Voting Population per Senator 1900	Total Voting Population 1950	Voting Population per Senator 1950
	Bradley	3,687		18,273	
	McMinn	4,278		18,347	
	James	1,281		*	
	Polk	*		7,330	
	Monroe	*		12,884	
			18,846		56,834
8	Hamilton	16,892		131,971	
			16,892		131,971
9	Bledsoe	1,490		4,198	
	Cumberland	2,237		9,593	
	Meigs	1,604		3,039	
	Rhea	3,405		8,837	
	Sequatchie	766		2,904	
	Van Buren	700		2,039	
	White	3,118		9,244	
			13,320		39,954
10	Clay	1,853		4,528	
	Fentress	1,331		7,057	
	Jackson	3,178		6,719	
	Morgan	2,544		*	
	Overton	2,925		9,474	
	Pickett	1,135		2,565	
	Putnam	3,679		17,071	
			16,645		47,414
11	Franklin	4,686		14,297	
	Grundy	1,737		6,540	
	Marion	4,066		10,998	
	Warren	3,804		13,337	
			14,293		45,172
12	Cannon	2,781		5,341	
	DeKalb	3,656		6,984	
	Rutherford	7,677		23,316	
			14,114		37,641
13	Smith	4,372		8,731	
	Wilson	6,550		16,459	
			10,922		25,190
14	Macon	2,938		7,974	

* County is in another district for the year indicated.

TABLE III (continued)

Senatorial District Number	Counties	Total Voting Population 1900	Voting Population per Senator 1900	Total Voting Population 1950	Voting Population per Senator 1950
	Sumner	6,394		20,143	
	Trousdale	1,482		3,351	
			10,814		31,468
15	Montgomery	8,712		26,284	
	Robertson	6,274		16,456	
			14,986		42,740
16	Davidson	33,311		211,930	
			16,656		105,965
17	Davidson	33,311		211,930	
			16,656		105,965
18	Bedford	5,777		14,732	
	Coffee	3,720		13,406	
	Moore	1,333		2,340	
			10,830		30,478
19	Lincoln	6,239		15,092	
	Marshall	4,591		11,288	
			10,830		26,380
20	Lewis	1,075		3,413	
	Maury	11,286		24,556	
	Perry	1,957		3,711	
			14,318		31,680
21	Cheatham	2,467		5,263	
	Hickman	3,891		7,598	
	Williamson	6,271		14,064	
			12,629		26,925
22	Giles	7,565		15,935	
	Lawrence	3,730		15,847	
	Wayne	2,974		7,176	
			14,269		38,958
23	Dickson	4,402		11,294	
	Humphreys	3,203		6,588	
	Houston	1,545		3,084	
	Stewart	3,512		5,238	
			12,662		26,204
24	Carroll	5,804		16,472	
	Henry	5,873		15,465	
			11,677		31,937

TABLE III (continued)

Senatorial District Number	Counties	Total Voting Population 1900	Voting Population per Senator 1900	Total Voting Population 1950	Voting Population Per Senator 1950
25	Chester	2,372		6,391	
	Henderson	4,050		10,199	
	Madison	8,756		37,245	
			15,178		53,835
26	Benton	2,712		7,023	
	Decatur	2,356		5,563	
	Hardin	4,357		9,577	
	Hardeman	5,119		13,565	
	McNairy	4,060		11,601	
			18,604		47,329
27	Gibson	9,466		29,832	
			9,466		29,832
28	Lake	1,972		6,252	
	Obion	7,173		18,444	
	Weakley	7,862		18,007	
			17,007		42,703
29	Crockett	3,556		9,676	
	Dyer	5,935		20,062	
	Lauderdale	5,075		14,413	
			14,566		44,151
30	Tipton	6,970		15,944	
	Shelby	43,843		312,345	
			16,938†		109,430†
31	Haywood	5,447		13,934	
	Fayette	6,180		13,577	
			11,627		27,511
32	Shelby	43,843		312,345	
			16,938†		109,430†
33	Shelby	43,843		312,345	
			16,938†		109,430†

† In cases where a county has both a direct and floterial senator, the sum of the voting population of all the counties in such floterial district is divided by the number of direct and floterial districts involved to determine the average population for each district.

TABLE I

Senatorial Districts Under the 1901 Alabama Apportionment Act

District	1900 Population	1960 Population	Counties in District
1	48,946	98,135	Lauderdale and Limestone
2	48,944	84,955	Lawrence and Morgan
3	50,522	85,879	Blount, Cullman, and Winston
4	43,702	117,348	Madison
5	53,797	84,699	Jackson and Marshall
6	52,749	122,368	Etowah and St. Clair
7	34,874	95,878	Calhoun
8	35,773	65,495	Talladega
9	54,201	57,305	Chambers and Randolph
10	55,774	65,531	Elmore and Tallapoosa
11	36,147	109,047	Tuscaloosa
12	55,378	84,630	Fayette, Lamar, and Walker
13	140,420	634,864	Jefferson
14	57,112	41,923	Pickens and Sumter
15	57,121	76,564	Autauga, Chilton, and Shelby
16	35,651	15,417	Lowndes
17	58,621	77,953	Butler, Conecuh, and Covington
18	50,281	31,715	Bibb and Perry
19	57,060	59,180	Choctow, Clarke, and Washington
20	38,315	27,098	Marengo
21	48,180	104,971	Baldwin, Escambia, and Monroe
22	35,631	18,736	Wilcox
23	40,285	53,376	Dale and Geneva
24	35,152	24,700	Barbour
25	69,812	70,479	Coffee, Crenshaw, and Pike
26	55,070	40,179	Bullock and Macon
27	58,090	96,105	Lee and Russell
28	72,047	169,210	Montgomery
29	44,654	57,720	Cherokee and DeKalb

Ideal senatorial district under 1901 population (1,828,697) = 52,248
Ideal senatorial district under 1960 population (3,266,740) = 93,335

District	1900 Population	1960 Population	Counties in District
30	54,657	56,667	Dallas
31	52,346	90,331	Colbert, Franklin, and Marion
32	55,193	33,137	Greene and Hale
33	62,740	314,301	Mobile
34	46,449	34,037	Clay, Cleburne, and Coosa
35	36,147	66,037	Henry and Houston

TABLE II

Apportionment of the Alabama House of Representatives
Under the 1901 Act

County	1900 Population	1960 Population	Number of Representatives
Autauga	17,915	18,739	1
Baldwin	13,194	49,088	1
Barbour	35,152	24,700	2
Bibb	18,498	14,357	1
Blount	23,119	25,449	1
Bullock	31,944	13,462	2
Butler	25,761	24,560	2
Calhoun	34,874	95,878	2
Chambers	32,554	37,828	2
Cherokee	21,096	16,303	1
Chilton	16,522	25,693	1
Choctaw	18,136	17,870	1
Clarke	27,790	25,738	2
Clay	17,099	12,400	1
Cleburne	13,206	10,911	1
Coffee	20,972	30,583	1
Colbert	22,341	46,506	1
Conecuh	17,514	17,762	1
Coosa	16,144	10,726	1
Covington	15,346	35,631	1
Crenshaw	19,668	14,909	1
Cullman	17,849	45,572	1
Dale	21,189	31,066	1
Dallas	54,657	56,667	3
DeKalb	23,558	41,417	1
Elmore	26,099	30,524	2
Escambia	11,320	33,511	1
Etowah	27,361	96,980	2
Fayette	14,132	16,148	1
Franklin	16,511	21,988	1
Geneva	19,096	23,310	1
Greene	24,182	13,600	2
Hale	31,011	19,536	2
Henry	36,147	15,286	1
Houston	(created in 1903)	50,718	1
Jackson	30,508	36,681	2
Jefferson	140,420	634,864	7
Lamar	16,084	14,271	1
Lauderdale	26,559	61,622	2

TABLE II (continued)

County	1900 Population	1960 Population	Number of Representatives
Lawrence	20,134	24,501	1
Lee	31,826	49,754	2
Limestone	22,387	36,513	1
Lowndes	35,651	15,417	2
Macon	14,494	21,837	1
Madison	43,702	117,348	2
Marengo	38,315	27,098	2
Marion	14,494	21,837	1
Marshall	23,289	48,018	1
Mobile	62,740	314,301	3
Monroe	23,666	22,372	1
Montgomery	72,047	169,210	4
Morgan	28,820	60,454	2
Perry	31,783	17,358	2
Pickens	24,402	21,882	1
Pike	29,172	25,987	2
Randolph	21,647	19,477	1
Russell	27,083	46,351	2
St. Clair	19,425	25,388	1
Shelby	23,684	32,132	1
Sumter	32,710	20,041	2
Talladega	35,773	65,495	2
Tallapoosa	29,675	35,007	2
Tuscaloosa	36,147	109,047	2
Walker	25,162	54,211	2
Washington	11,132	15,372	1
Wilcox	35,631	18,739	2
Winston	9,554	14,858	1

Abram, Morris B., 146
Active Voters of Atlanta, 146
Advisory Commission on Intergovern-
     mental Relations
     Apportionment of State Legislatures
     report, 206
AFL-CIO, 145, 244
     of Michigan, 71, 130
     Tennessee Labor Council, 154
Allott, Gordon, 237
American Bar Association, 48, 75, 242,
     243
American Civil Liberties Union, 244
     as *amicus* in 1964 apportionment
         cases, 207
     of Detroit, 71
American Farm Bureau Federation,
     243
American Jewish Congress, 244
     as *amicus* in 1964 apportionment
         cases, 207
American League of Cities, 244
American Liberty League, 264
American Municipal Association, 35,
     74, 145
Americans for Democratic Action, 71,
     244
Anderson, William, 52
Anderson v. *Jordan*, 25, 47
Anti-Saloon League, 12
Asbury Park Press, Inc. v. *Woolley*,
     70–71, 82, 83, 91–92
Ashmore, Robert, 224
Atkins, Hobart, 44, 47, 150–51, 247–48
     role in *Baker* v. *Carr*, 54–55, 61, 66,
         78; in *Kidd* v. *McCanless*, 39, 50
Avery v. *Midland County*, 256

Bailey, John M., 236
Baird, William D., 153, 158, 159
Baird-Bomar plans, 153–54
Baker, Charles W., 56
Baker, David, 165
Baker, Howard, 147
Baker v. *Carr*, 27
     district court arguments in, 61–68
     district court decision in, 68–69
     impact in Alabama, 164, 168–69; in
         nation, 158–59; in Tennessee, 147–
         54
     initiation of, 53–57
     reaction to, 144–47
     role of solicitor general in, 76–78, 83,
         89–91, 103–17
     Supreme Court arguments in, 79–83,
         95–103, 117–31
     Supreme Court decision in, 135–42
Barrett, Edward J., 15
Birmingham *Age-Herald*, 161
Birmingham *News*, 165, 191
Black, Hugo, 24–26, 49, 85–86, 101–3,
         113–14, 133, 169, 171, 211–13, 217–
         19
     opinion in *Colegrove* v. *Green*, 21–
         22; in *Wesberry* v. *Sanders*, 227
     position in *Baker* v. *Carr*, 143–44
Boling, Bernard, 127
Bomar, James L., 43, 153
Bond, John A., 52
Borden, Luther, 9
Boswell, E. C., 170
Botter, Theodore I., 213
Bourbon, Robert S., 212–13
Boyd, Marion S., 60
Bralley, Clarence, 37
Brandeis, Louis D., 19

Brennan, William, 49, 111–12, 115, 133, 203, 208, 218, 225
  opinion in *Baker* v. *Carr*, 135–38; 143–44
Brooks, Hubert, 58
Brown v. *Board of Education*, 45, 66, 67, 88, 130, 219–20
  compared to apportionment cases, 256–62
Browning, Gordon, 53
  conflict with E. H. Crump, 30–33
Brownlow, William G., 28
Bryant, Frank, 37, 44
Burnett, Hamilton, 42–43
Burton, Harold H., 20

Cardozo, Benjamin N., 19
Carmichael, James V., 23
Carr, Joe C., 57
Carroll v. *Becker*, 97, 106
Carter, James J., 85–86
Carter, Robert L., 85
Celler, Emanuel, 224, 226, 238–39
Chamales, Peter, 15
Chandler, Walter, 247–48
  role in *Baker* v. *Carr*, 53–55, 57, 61, 63–68, 74–78, 125, 133–35, 150–51, 154–55, 158
Chattanooga *Times*, 31
Child, John T., 9
Church, Frank, 243
Citizens Committee for Representative Government on a Fair Basis, 172
Civil Rights Act of 1964, 226, 240, 244
Clark, Tom C., 20, 133, 150, 171, 175, 212
  opinion in *Baker* v. *Carr*, 138–39, 143–44; in 1964 apportionment cases, 232–34
Clement, Frank G., 30, 40, 43, 247
Colegrove, Kenneth W., 15–16
Colegrove v. *Barrett*, 24–25
Colegrove v. *Green*, 49, 72, 78, 124
  as a bar to apportionment suits, 23–25
  as applied in *Baker* v. *Carr*, 62–63, 65–67, 79–83, 95–96, 100–3, 106–14, 118–20, 135–38, 140; in *Gomillion* v. *Lightfoot*, 85–88; in *Kidd* v. *McCanless*, 46–47
  origin of, 15–16
  Supreme Court decision in, 20–23

Conference of State Supreme Court Chief Justices, 48
Cook v. *Fortson*, 23–25
Cooper, Jerome A., 250
  role in *Reynolds* v. *Sims*, 168–69, 172, 186, 188–90, 199
Cooper, Prentice, 32
Council of State Governments, 222, 242–43
  General Assembly of the States, 222
  National Legislative Conference, 222
Cox, Archibald, 89–91, 133, 260
  arguments in *Baker* v. *Carr*, 103–17; in *Gray* v. *Sanders*, 193; in 1964 apportionment cases, 194–98, 201–6, 215–17
Cox v. *Peters*, 24, 77
Crawford-Webb Act, 177–78, 182, 197, 200, 230
Crump, E. H., 53, 60
  conflict with Gordon Browning, 30–33
Cummings, James, 43, 93, 147–48, 247

David, Paul, 4
Davis, Maclin P., 37, 43
Davis v. *Mann*, 186, 204–5, 214, 232
Dirksen, Everett
  opposition to apportionment cases, 236–40, 243–46
Dixon, Frank M., 162
Doar, John, 250
Dodd, Thomas, 245–46
Dorr, Thomas W., 9
Dorr War, 9
Douglas, Paul, 243–44
Douglas, William O., 24–26, 49, 86, 133, 175, 223
  opinion in *Baker* v. *Carr*, 138, 143–44; in *Gomillion* v. *Lightfoot*, 87–88; in *Gray* v. *Sanders*, 193–94
  position in *Colegrove* v. *Green*, 21–22
Dyer v. *Kazuhisa Abe*, 45–46, 62–63, 65, 79

Edmondson, J. Howard, 125–27
Eisenberg, Ralph, 4
Eisenhower, Dwight D., 48, 58, 86–87, 146, 167
Ellington, Buford, 93, 149–50, 154
Elman, Philip, 85–86

Emerson, Thomas I., 175
Engelhardt, Sam, Jr., 71
English, John F., 128
equal protection clause, 45–46
    as basis of *Baker* v. *Carr*, 57, 66, 68,
        72, 80–82, 95, 99–100, 104–5, 114–18,
        140–44, 155–56, 159; of *Reynolds*
        v. *Sims*, 166, 174–75, 182, 194–97
    as enforced in desegregation cases,
        48–49
    as interpreted in *Gray* v. *Sanders*,
        193–94; in *MacDougall* v. *Green*,
        26; in white primary cases, 16–18;
        in 1964 apportionment cases, 228–
        32
Erickson, John O., 51
Everett, Robert A. (Fats), 147

Faubus, Orval, 48
federal analogy theory, 194, 204–6,
    209–11, 213, 230
Fergus, John B., 13
Flowers, Richmond, 199–200, 250
Folsom, James, 172
Frankfurter, Felix, 81, 85–86, 98, 100–
    2, 115–17, 119, 124, 128–29, 133–34,
    220, 234
    opinion in *Baker* v. *Carr*, 139–42, 143;
        in *Colegrove* v. *Green*, 20–21; in
        Gomillion v. *Lightfoot*, 87
Frink, Bettye, 165

Galt, Irving, 211–12
Gayle, Thomas G., 190
General Assembly of the States, 222;
    see also Council of State Govern-
    ments
Georgia county unit case; *see Gray* v.
    Sanders
Georgia county unit system, 49, 146
    early challenges of, 23–24
    invalidation of, 192–94
Gilbert, Harris, 79, 89
Glasgow, James
    argument in *Baker* v. *Carr*, 120–22
Goldberg, Arthur J., 144, 197–98, 212,
    214, 218–19, 223
    position in *Gray* v. *Sanders*, 194; in
        Wesberry v. *Sanders*, 227
Goldwater, Barry, 145
    opposition to 1964 apportionment
        cases, 240–42

Gomillion v. Lightfoot, 105, 137
    initiation of, 71–72
    relation to *Baker* v. *Carr*, 79, 86, 88,
        96
    Supreme Court arguments in, 84–86
    Supreme Court decision in, 87–88
Gosnell, Cullen G., 24
Gray v. *Sanders*, 192–94, 203
Green, Dwight H., 15
guaranty clause, 13–14, 82, 107, 118, 137
    interpretation in *Luther* v. *Borden*,
        10–11

Hain, Val, 176
Hammonds, Harrell, 170
Hampton, Peter, 37
Harlan, John Marshall, 102, 133, 193,
    201, 203, 208, 218–19, 227
    opinion in *Baker* v. *Carr*, 142–43; in
        1964 apportionment cases, 234–35
Harris, J. P., 127
Hart, Stephen H., 219
Hartsfield v. *Sloan*, 49
Henry, E. William, 90
Herrin, Kent, 37
Holmes, Oliver W., Jr., 17, 44–45, 265
Hooker, John J., Jr., 89
Hooper, Ben W., 30
Horton, Henry, 30
Howell, Kenneth, 165
Hudson, W. D., 57
Hughes, Charles Evans, 19, 256, 262
Humphrey, Richard P., 171
Humphreys, Allison B.
    as counsel for Tennessee in *Baker* v.
        Carr, 61–63, 67
Hunt, Edwin, 151–52
Hutchison (Kansas) *News*, 127

Jackson, Robert, 20, 25, 254
Javits, Jacob, 243
Jefferson County Democratic Cam-
    paign Committee, 171, 189
Jehovah's Witnesses, 264
Johnson, Ernest W., 127
Johnson, Frank M., Jr., 165–68, 179–80
Johnson, Lyndon B., 236, 241–42

Kasper, John, 58
Keating, Kenneth, 145
Kefauver, Estes, 53, 147

Kennedy, John F., 84, 86, 89, 90, 144, 146–47, 223, 226
Kennedy, Robert, 89, 90, 145
Key, V. O., Jr., 8
Kidd, Gates, 38
Kidd v. McCanless, 49–51, 56, 58, 63, 66–68, 97–98, 107–8, 118–19, 121–22, 141–42
  appeal of, 44–47
  chancery court decision in, 40–41
  initiation of, 37–38
  Tennessee Supreme Court decision in, 41–42
  U. S. Supreme Court decision in, 47
Knoxville Journal, 39, 50
Knoxville Journal and Tribune, 29
Koegh, John W., 13–14
Koenig v. Flynn, 106

Langan, Joseph, 171
Leadership Conference on Civil Rights, 244
League of Women Voters, 36, 55–56; see also Tennessee League of Women Voters
Lee, Jack W., 38
Lewis, Anthony, 206–7, 217, 221, 236
Liberty League; see American Liberty League
Loeb, Robert, 165
Long, Huey, 31
Long, Russell, 239
Lucas v. Colorado General Assembly, 186, 214–19, 232, 255
Lueder, Arthur C., 16
Luther v. Borden, 9–11, 25, 82, 107, 118, 122
Luther, Martin, 9
LWV; see League of Women Voters

McCanless, George, 38, 57, 124–25, 149, 155, 157–58
  arguments in Kidd v. McCanless, 46–47
  role in Kidd v. McCanless, 39–40
McCollum, Vashti, 259–60
McCollum v. Illinois, 259–60
McConnell, John W., Jr., 249
  role in Reynolds v. Sims, 171–72, 175, 179, 183–84, 187, 189–91, 199
McCord, Jim, 34
McCord, Roy D., 170

McCormally, John, 127
MacDonald, Peter, 127
MacDougall v. Green, 25–26, 79, 136, 138, 214
McDowell, May Ross, 37
McGraw, Daniel B., 51
McGraw v. Donovan, 62–63, 65, 70, 79
  impact in Tennessee, 51–54, 57, 59
McIllwaine, Robert D., 214
McKellar, Kenneth D., 32
Madison, Gordon, 170, 181
Mansfield, Mike, 239
Marbury v. Madison, 254
Marine and Shipbuilding Workers of America, 172
Marshall, Burke, 243
Marshall, John, 254
Martin, John D., 32–33, 154
  as trial judge in Baker v. Carr, 60, 62–68
Maryland Committee for Fair Representation, 244
Maryland Committee for Fair Representation v. Tawes, 186, 195, 203–4, 208, 212–13, 232
Memphis, City of
  county unit system applied to, 30–33
  role in Baker v. Carr, 53–54, 56, 61, 75
Meyner, Robert, 91
Miller, Haynes, 37–38, 44
Miller, Mayne, 37
Miller, Shackelford, Jr., 60
Miller, William E. (Judge)
  as trial judge in Baker v. Carr, 58–60, 66, 151–53, 248
Miller, William E., 236
Morgan, Charles, Jr.
  role in Reynolds v. Sims, 163–65, 169–70, 172–73, 178–80, 183, 188–90, 199
Murphy, Frank, 21–22, 26

NAACP; see National Association for the Advancement of Colored People
Nashville, City of
  role in Baker v. Carr, 56, 61, 74–75
Nashville, C. & St. L. Ry. Co. v. Browning, 81
Nashville Metropolitan Planning Commission, 56, 69, 75, 78
Nashville Tennessean, 40, 50

National Association for the Advancement of Colored People, 207, 219, 244, 264–65
National Association of Manufacturers, 243, 261
National Association of Real Estate Boards, 243
National Cattlemen's Association, 243
National Committee for Fair Representation, 244
National Farmers Union, 243
National Grange, 243
National Institute of Municipal Law Officers, 75, 82, 88, 125–26
National Legislative Conference, 222; *see also* Council of State Governments
Newberry v. *United States*, 18
New York Times, 186, 206–7, 217, 236
NIMLO; *see* National Institute of Municipal Law Officers
Nixon, Richard M., 75, 84
Nixon v. *Condon*, 16
Nixon v. *Herndon*, 16

O'Dell, Ruth H., 51
one man, one vote theory, 206–9, 228–32
Osborn, Z. T., Jr.
role in *Baker* v. *Carr*, 56, 61, 66–67, 77–78, 83–84, 86–87, 89–90, 124–25, 133–34, 158; in *Kidd* v. *McCanless*, 37–38, 43–44, 50

Patterson, John, 175–77
Pearce, Frank, 189, 200
Perlman, Philip, 76
Perry, Walter, 177
Peters, Robert, 93
Pitts, McLean, 189, 200–1, 250
Plessy v. *Ferguson*, 264
political questions, doctrine of
in *Baker* v. *Carr*, 59, 61–63, 65–69, 72, 78–83, 95–96, 100–3, 106–14, 118–20, 135–38, 140–42
in *Colegrove* v. *Green*, 20–21
in *Gomillion* v. *Lightfoot*, 85–88
in *Kidd* v. *McCanless*, 47
in *Luther* v. *Borden*, 8–11

Radford v. *Gary*, 49, 65, 67

Rankin, J. Lee, 77, 90, 243
rationality theory, 211–12, 232–34
Reece, B. Carroll, 78
Reed, Stanley, 20
Regent's prayer case, 223–24
Remmy v. *Smith*, 25
Reynolds, B. A., 189, 200
Reynolds v. *Sims*
compared to desegregation cases, 256–62
impact in Alabama, 248–52; in nation, 253; in Tennessee, 246–48
in district court, 169–71, 177–83
in Supreme Court, 194–201, 207–13, 227–32
initiation of, 164–66
Rhyne, Charles S.
role in *Baker* v. *Carr*, 74–78, 83–88, 91, 98–103
Rives, Richard T., 168, 177–78, 180–81
Roberts, Owen J., 19
Rogers, William G., 78
Roman v. *Sincock*, 186, 205–6, 210–11, 213, 232
Ross, Ella V., 44
Russell, Richard, 145–46
Rutledge, Wiley, 21, 24–26

Sand, Leonard B., 208
Sanders, James O'Hear, 146
Sands, C. D., 180, 181
Scanlan, Alfred L., 208
Scholle, August, 71, 125, 130
Scholle v. *Hare*, 185, 188, 190; *see also Scholle* v. *Secretary of State*
Scholle v. *Secretary of State*, 71, 83, 130; *see also Scholle* v. *Hare*
School prayer and Bible-reading cases, 224
Sears, Kenneth C., 15
Shapiro, Martin, 262
Shelby County (Tennessee)
county unit system applied to, 30–33
role in *Baker* v. *Carr*, 53–54, 61, 75
Sims, M. O., 164
Sixty-seven Senator Amendment, 177, 178, 182, 197, 200, 230
Skinner v. *Oklahoma*, 174–75
Smiley v. *Holm*, 19, 21–22, 63, 66, 97, 106, 135
Smith, Guy L., 147

Smith, Guy L. (*cont.*)
role in *Baker* v. *Carr*, 54, 78; in *Kidd* v. *McCanless*, 39, 50
Smith, Howard, 238
Smith, Jay W., 51–52
Smith v. *Allwright*, 17
solicitor general, U. S. Office of
role in *Baker* v. *Carr*, 76–78, 83, 89–91, 103–17; in *Gray* v. *Sanders*, 193; in *Wesberry* v. *Sanders*, 227; in 1964 apportionment cases, 192, 194–98, 201–6, 215–17
South v. *Peters*, 24, 72, 79, 88, 95, 136, 143
Speiser, Lawrence, 244
Steele, Thomas Wardlaw, 40–41
Stewart, Potter, 109–14, 133–34, 208, 212, 218–19
opinion in *Baker* v. *Carr*, 139, 143–44; in 1964 apportionment cases, 232–34
Stone, Harlan F., 19, 20, 196, 220
Swan, Arthur R., 51
Swepston, John E., 41–42

Talmadge, Eugene, 23
Taney, Roger B., 10–11
Taylor, George Peach, 165, 183, 188, 199
Taylor, Robert L., 58
Tennessee Committee for Constitutional Reapportionment, 37, 40, 44
Tennessee Farm Bureau Federation, 151–52
Tennessee Labor Council, 154; *see also* AFL-CIO
Tennessee League of Women Voters, 36, 55, 56; *see also* League of Women Voters
Tennessee Municipal League, 35–36
Thomas, Daniel H., 168
Thurmond, Strom, 239
Todd, Mrs. James M., 38
Tuck, William, 238
Tuck bill, 238–39
Turman, Mrs. Robert Lee, 24
Turman v. *Duckworth*, 23–25
Tuttle, Elbert, 167
Twentieth Century Fund
One Man, One Vote report of, 206

Tydings, Joseph, 245
Unitarian Fellowship for Social Justice, 145
United States Chamber of Commerce, 243
United States Conference of Mayors, 49, 145, 244
United States v. *Carolene Products Co.*, 105–6, 196
United States v. *Classic*, 17
United Steel Workers (of Alabama), 168–69, 186

Vance, Robert S.
role in *Reynolds* v. *Sims*, 171–72, 177–79, 181, 183–84, 188–91, 198
Vann, David J., 250
role in *Reynolds* v. *Sims*, 171–74, 177, 181, 183–84, 188–91, 198–99
Vinson, Fred M., 25, 89
Von Antwerp, Garet, 172
Voting Rights Act of 1965, 251

Wallace, George C., 167, 190, 248–49
Warren, Earl, 49, 86, 110, 133, 201, 211, 213, 218–19, 223–24, 236, 241–42
opinion in 1964 apportionment cases, 228–32
position in *Baker* v. *Carr*, 135, 143–44
Webb, Douglas S., 179–81
Weick, Paul, 154
Wesberry v. *Sanders*, 226–27
West, Ben, 37, 58, 123
role in *Baker* v. *Carr*, 56, 61, 69, 74–75; in Tennessee reapportionment conflict, 35–36
White, Byron R., 89, 144, 212, 214, 216–17
position in *Gray* v. *Sanders*, 194; in *Wesberry* v. *Sanders*, 227
White, Robert, 61
white primary cases, 16–18, 32
Whittaker, Charles E., 85, 88, 101–3, 109–10, 112–14, 116, 120–23, 134, 143
Whittaker & Baxter, 246
Wiener, Frederick Bernays, 213
Wilkinson, Joseph, Jr., 189
Williams, William M., 171
Williamson v. *Lee Optical Co.*, 174–75
Wilson, Jack, 122–24

W.M.C.A. v. *Lomenzo*, 201–3, 207–8, 211–12, 232; *see also W.M.C.A.* v. *Simon*

W.M.C.A. v. *Simon*, 185–86; *see also W.M.C.A.* v. *Lomenzo*

Wood v. *Broom*, 19, 20, 135

Young Men's Business Club, 164, 168

YMBC; *see* Young Men's Business Club

Zarlengo, Anthony F., 217–19

Zorach v. *Clauson*, 259–60

The Apportionment Cases has been set on the Linotype in ten point Janson with two points line spacing. Eighteen point Goudy Old Style was selected for display. The book was designed by Jim Billingsley, composed and printed by Heritage Printers, Inc., Charlotte, North Carolina, and bound by the Becktold Company, St. Louis, Missouri. The paper on which the book is printed is designed for an effective life of at least three hundred years.

THE UNIVERSITY OF TENNESSEE PRESS
KNOXVILLE